Boating Secrets:

127 Top Tips To Help You Buy and Enjoy Your Boat

Revealed by Eleven Marine Industry Experts

Robin G. Coles

www.TheNauticalLifestyle.com

Boating Secrets: 127 Top Tips To Help You buy and Enjoy Your Boat.
Copyright © 2011 Robin G. Coles

All rights reserved. No part of this publication may be reproduced or transmitted in any form or by any means, electronic or mechanical, including photocopying, recording, or by any information storage and retrieval system, without permission in writing from the publisher, except by a reviewer who wishes to quote brief passages in connection with a review written for inclusion in a magazine, newspaper, or broadcast.

For further information:

The Nautical Lifestyle

P O Box 520461

Winthrop, MA 02152

www.TheNauticalLifestyle.com

First Edition

June 2011

Printed in USA

ISBN-13 978-09836381-4-8

ISBN-10 09836381-4-8

Cover design by: Janja Baćac

Cover photograph by: Robin G. Coles

CopyEditor: Fifine Ball

Dedication

For my aunt, Ruth Shoer, who passed away before this book was finished.

I miss you!

TheNauticalLifestyle Order Form

Telephone Orders   Call 339-532-8334
                        and have your credit card ready

Postal Orders
TheNauticalLifestyle
C/o Robin G. Coles
P O Box 520461 ~ Winthrop, MA 02152
orders@TheNauticalLifestyle.com

Please send the following:

☐ Boating Secrets: 127 Top Tips To Help You Buy and Enjoy Your Boat, by Robin G. Coles $29.97

☐ TheNauticalLifestyle Expert Speaker Series Complete live interview series of 11 Marine Industry experts on CDs, by Robin G. Coles $97.00

Please send more FREE information on:

☐ Other books   ☐ Other Audios   ☐ Speaking/Seminars

Or visit www.TheNauticalLifestyle.com

Name_____
Address_____
City_____ State_____ Zip_____
Telephone_____ Email_____

Payment:
☐ Check   ☐ Mastercard   ☐ American Express   ☐ Visa   ☐ Discover

Account Number_____ Expiration Date_____
Cardholder's Name_____ Cardholder's Signature_____

Table of Contents

Title page i
Copyright page ii
Dedication iii
Table of Contents v
Introduction 1

Chapters

1. *Buying a Boat*, Captain Chris Kourtakis 5
2. *Marine Surveys*, Rob Scanlan 21
3. *Insuring a Boat*, Mike Smith 35
4. *Financing a Boat Purchase*, Jim Coburn 53
5. *Rent Your Boat*, Brian Stefka 67
6. *Bad Storms/Heavy Weather*, Timothy Wyand 83
7. *Search and Rescue*, Alan Sorum 103
8. *Digital Selective Calling, the Automatic Identification System, and Automated Radio Checks*, Captain Chris Kourtakis 115
9. *Multihulls*, Jim Brown 129
10. *Custom Electrical Panels and Wiring Harnesses*, Mark Rogers 155
11. *Making a Living as a Professional Sailor*, Brian Hancock 173

Bonus chapter: *Seven Tips for a Successful Sale of Your Used Boat*, Robin G. Coles 193

Appendices

I. Glossary 197
II. Resources 205
III. Contacts 209

Acknowledgements 211
About the Interviewer: Robin G. Coles and TheNauticalLifestyle.com 213
Index 215

Introduction

So why am I writing or, more to the point, why did I make this interview series into a book?

Not everyone likes to listen or learns by listening. Some of us still like holding a book in our hands, feeling the weight of it on our laps, and even going through it page by page with a highlighter and marking what's important to us as we read. I'm one of those rare birds who still likes to hold a book and feel its weight in the crook of my arm while I have a good cup of tea. Others nowadays are reading books on their computers or even on Amazon's Kindle or Barnes and Noble's NOOK. Who knows? There might even be something new by the time you read this. I also find that a reference book, which this certainly could be, is great when it's accessible on your book shelf—you can quickly thumb through it to find the information you're looking for. You could add a different colored sticky note to the first page of each chapter for quick reference.

Others learn by listening, and that's great too! But I wanted to make sure I had this book in different media for everybody. That's how important I believe this project is. It's important because for years now, as I've learned more and more about boating, I've found there isn't a lot of basic information out there; and the information that I *can* find is scattered all over the place. Also, I'm not always sure of the credentials of the people writing articles about boating.

But, let's back up a few years and start at the beginning.

Growing up, I always had a fascination for the ocean and the skies—the moon and the stars. At night I would watch the moon follow me around and search the sky for the big dipper, little dipper, Hercules, and other constellations. When I was a little girl, my aunt Dee would take me to Revere Beach and we would walk the beach. She never let me go into the water without shoes on my feet for fear of seaweed wrapping around my legs and pulling me under. (What wearing shoes had to do with that, I'm not sure.) So I never went into the water, but always dreamed about it. When I got my own car I would head to Storrow and Memorial Drives on my lunch breaks and watch the sailboats on the Charles River, wishing it was me on one of them. (I also had a fascination for airplanes—watching them take off and land at airports—but that's another story for another time. Maybe I've just wanted to escape from day-to-day life. I guess that's why I now live near both an airport and the ocean.)

Fast forward to April 5, 2001. I was told over the phone that I had cancer. A couple of days later, in the doctor's office, I was told that I had less than ten years to live. The year before I'd been misdiagnosed with multiple sclerosis and told that I'd be confined to a wheel chair within a year. Doctors can be so cruel in what they tell you and, more importantly, how they tell you.

After I came to terms with this news, and after I grieved for the person I once knew and had been, I set out to make some changes in my life. It was time to conquer my fear of being on the ocean. I called a friend of mine and asked him to take me kayaking. He did, and that experience really changed my outlook. Kayaking was so peaceful and fun. If I hadn't almost been hit by a tanker, I probably would have gone again. Of course, I'd also been afraid of tipping over (I'm not a very good swimmer), an odd fear to have surfaced in me since my sons and I had done a lot of canoeing and rowing during our many camping trips when they were young and I hadn't been afraid then.

Next, I took up sailing. I had looked into sailing on the Charles River, but at that school one first had to pass a swim test, which I didn't believe I could do, and I really wanted to learn on the ocean. Ocean sailing was an experience that I found to be the epitome of relaxation. I absolutely fell in love with sailing and couldn't get out into Boston Harbor enough. Mark, my primary sailing instructor, had so much passion both for the sport and for teaching that he made learning to sail really enjoyable. As with everything, some of my instructors were better than others. But Mark was awesome and whenever I went sailing on the 23-foot Sonar, I felt the boat and I were one. I could hop into the cockpit, grab the tiller, and feel her every move as we'd glide through the waves.

One day I went to the Sailing Center with a sailing buddy and we took out a boat with which neither of us was familiar. The boat was six feet longer than what we were used to and it had a steering wheel. I had never sailed a boat with a wheel before, but off we went. This was something new to learn—great! Wrong. Neither of us was experienced with this size or type of boat and we had no business taking it out by ourselves. What happened to us that afternoon would never have happened if we had taken out the 23-foot Sonar instead. We got caught in a couple of wind and rain storms. We tried taking the sails down, but the furlings came off. The wind kept pushing us sideways. I was trying to hold the wheel *and* watch the skipper on deck to make sure he didn't fall overboard. The wind and rain squall picked up and pushed us right onto the beach—we ended up going aground. Then the engine wouldn't start and we had to call Sea Tow. One of the topics we discuss in this book is heavy weather. A big part of that is *knowing your boat*, which neither of us did. It was scary.

In 2006, I went to a National Geographic Travel Writing workshop in New York. There I met a woman who also loved sailing and we hung out together for the day. When the workshop was over, she told me that she knew someone who was looking for a reviewer, writer, and photographer for a cruising guide book. She suggested I take a look at the website and then call her if I was interested. I did. A few days later, the publisher called me. That year, after they'd trained me, the project was cancelled. In 2007, the project was on again, so off I went.

My assignment was to review, write about, and photograph over 200 marinas from Block Island, Rhode Island, to St. John's River in New Brunswick, Canada. I spent three months on the road, staying in hotels, motels, and bed and breakfasts, keeping a ridiculous schedule in order to get that project done. One thing I learned along the way is that boaters are a very friendly group. There's a different mindset when you're on the water versus being in the corporate grind every day. I liked it. For a number of other reasons, this project turned sour and never came to fruition.

But it was during this project that I met Chuck, the local harbormaster, and got to know and work alongside him. It was also during this time that Winthrop, Massachusetts, the town I'd just moved back to, was putting in a new marina. There were lots of questions being asked, and speculations being made, by the townspeople about the new marina. I approached Chuck the following spring and we did an interview which I recorded and put up on the web. This interview answered a lot of questions for the residents and the project continued with fewer objections. For a while after that I wrote a weekly column for the local newspaper reporting on activities at the local marinas and yacht clubs.

Around that time I started studying marketing on the internet with Mark Hendricks. I needed something to work on and decided to take everything I'd learned during the project from hell and turn it into something positive. This new project became TheNauticalLifestyle.com and it is always evolving. I'm not afraid to try something new and if it sticks, great. If not, why not?

One thing I learned during both projects is that I love interviewing people—I guess it goes with that curious mind of mine. You know how some children are always asking why, why, why? That's me, still to this day—always asking why; always seeking, searching for answers. But it can't be just any answer—it has to make sense.

Content, content, content is what Google looks for and what Mark stresses in his internet marketing lessons. So I posted a request on LinkedIn indicating that I was looking for speakers for an interview series that I was putting together. The rest, as they say, is history.

In this book I have tried to cover all of the basics as well as some more advanced boating topics for the old salts. It's filled with lots of answers that should enhance your boating experiences. Interviewing these knowledgeable gentlemen has taught me a lot and it's truly been a pleasure working with them. My wish is for you to get just as much out of reading this book as I have in putting it together.

The final reason for creating this book is that as I have ventured out on my journey to become a better boater, I've had many questions. What better way to get them answered than to interview the experts? So that's what I did.

Buying a Boat
An Interview with Chris Kourtakis

Introduction

Robin: Hello everyone. This is Robin Coles and it's my pleasure to welcome you to the 2010 Nautical Lifestyle Expert Series brought to you by TheNauticalLifestyle.com. During the next hour, you're going to learn the ins and outs of buying the right boat for you and your family. With me today, I am honored to have Captain Christopher Kourtakis as my special guest. Hello, Chris.

Chris: 'Morning Robin. I really appreciate you having me on and talking about this great topic today.

Robin: Thank you so much for joining me today. Chris Kourtakis has been boating for over 20 years and has been working in the marine industry for over 15 years. Chris is a licensed United States Coast Guard captain. He owns and operates H2O Limos, which offers yacht rentals and on-water boating courses. H2O Limos has been nationally recognized for its boating education. You can find articles written by Chris in numerous marine trade magazines around the world. Chris holds a bachelor's degree in business and an MBA. When Chris is not working, he can be found somewhere on the water with his family.

Buying a Boat

Robin: **What are the steps someone should take when considering buying a boat?**

Chris: When my customers come to me and say they're looking to buy a boat and don't know what they're going to do with it, I ask them some simple questions. Have you sat down and gone through your finances to make sure you can afford a boat? A lot of people don't realize what is involved in actually owning a boat. The annual maintenance and other costs can be 10-15% of your actual purchase price, and that doesn't include your fuel. For example, if you buy a $200,000 boat, you've got to expect that your costs-per-year will be around $20,000 for maintenance and storage. This would include winterization if you're in the northern states, dockage, and other amenities. That doesn't include fuel. I always say, you've got to sit down as a family and make sure you've gone through your finances and can afford the boat.

Another thing I recommend to people when they tell me they're buying a boat is to make this decision as a family. Sit down with the kids and ask them what they want to do with the boat, why they want a boat, and what they envision the family doing with it. In too many families I see the parents get the boat, but they don't involve the kids. Later, the kids may start to dislike using the boat because they weren't involved in choosing it and feel they're being told what to do, versus, "We get to go on the boat for the weekend," or, "We're going to trailer the boat to the lake today and go water skiing." If you involve them in the decision, let them pick colors, style, and things like that, they get more involved and enjoy the boat much more. It's got to be a family decision. As a husband, you just can't go out and buy a boat and come home and say,

"Honey, look what I bought." It doesn't work that way. The family structure has really changed from the 1950s 'til 2000 and the present. I always say, "The family that boats together, stays together." Boating does draw families together.

Robin: Wouldn't you also say that as the family dynamics change during boat ownership, you should have another family meeting to discuss maybe getting a different boat?

Chris: Absolutely—I see that all the time. Every two to three years people get what I call two- to three-foot-itis, where they want a different boat, a little bit larger boat. Their family may have had an addition. As the kids get older, they want to bring friends out. When you bought your original boat, potentially a runabout, you bought an 18-foot, which was perfect for the four people in your family at the time. But now you've had the boat five years, and your eight- and nine-year-old son and daughter are now teenagers, and they can't go anywhere without a friend. You've just added two extra people and two extra bags, so you may want to get into an extra three feet just to get a little more room in the bow or a little seating configuration change. Or you buy the boat when the kids are in high school and now they're off to college and they're no longer skiing or on the boat doing water sports. You may want to switch from a runabout, but you still want to go out, park on a sandbar, and enjoy it. So you switch to a pontoon boat so you can go, relax, lay out, and have much more room.

I'm working with a couple right now that has had a 38-foot aft-style cabin cruiser for the last 10 years. Now that their daughters are in college and post-college and working, they don't come out as much, so they have me looking for a larger express style cruiser, that, instead of having two or three staterooms or bedrooms, just has one large bedroom and a small guest bedroom in case the girls or another family does come out. The upstairs, or the cockpit area, gives them a lot more space to enjoy the sun, versus more cabin space that they needed when people would come out and stay the weekend with them.

Here are a few other steps to take when considering buying a boat. Check into a pre-approval loan process. Know what you can afford, what you can get a good interest rate for, and how much you can get a loan for. It makes the shopping process a lot easier, so you don't get your heart set on a boat and find out you can't afford it. Plan ahead—where are you going to shop for the boat and when are you going to the store? If you're going to a boat show, what are you going to look for and how much time are you going to spend? If you've got all day there, it's perfect. If you've only got a certain amount of time, then make sure you spend that time looking at the specific boats that you would potentially want. Another thing customers run into all the time is where they are going to store a boat. If you're looking to buy a runabout for your family and you know you're going to trailer the boat to the lake, then when you come back from the lake, where are you going to store it? If you are going to store it on the side of the house, make sure your subdivision doesn't have rules against that. If you are going to store it in a garage, make sure the boat, motor, and trailer will fit. Too many times I see people buy a boat, get it home, and, when they go to put it in the garage, find out the trailer is too long; or with the motor up or down, it just doesn't fit. Even though you're buying an 18-foot boat, there are many other extensions that make that boat a lot longer when you actually start trailering it.

If you're buying a larger cruiser, it may have to come out of the water in the winter and you're not going to be able to store it at your house. Make sure you know the costs. Some of the local marinas can haul it out for you, clean the sides, and store it properly in a fenced yard so it's safe and you know that nothing's going to happen to it throughout the winter.

Another thing I ask families is, "do you have the time to use the boat or is it just going to sit?" For example, you may have soccer every Saturday, baseball on Sundays, and during the week not be able to use it because you've got other events with school or work. I hate to see somebody purchase a boat and just let it sit there—that doesn't benefit anybody. You'll see it and you'll really want to use it. Make sure it's a good idea and fits the schedule of the family. Shop around; don't buy the first boat you see. It's a real exciting and fun time for a family, but don't say this is the only boat I'm going to buy. Make sure you compare it with other boats out there and other dealerships that will offer you services.

The next thing I ask people, which I also help them out with, is where they are going to get their boating education? A lot of people are buying their first boats and don't know the rules—they don't actually know how to use or drive a boat. The United States Coast Guard Auxiliary (USCGA) and the local US Power Squadrons do a phenomenal job with boating education—teaching people the rules of the road. They start at age 13 and go up to 90 years old. Then somebody like me, or a local dealer, will take over and actually teach you how to drive your boat—trimming, driving off, using trim tabs, if you have them, and other amenities. If you get into a larger cruiser, we'll teach you how to use your air conditioning and your generator, how to fill up your gas tank on water versus off water, and little things like that that a lot of people don't know.

Finally, I ask people, "What do you want to do with a boat?" and, "Why do you want one?" "What is your main reason for wanting to get into boating?" If that love, passion, and drive is there, you will use the boat much more. But, if you just want one because you think it's going to help bring the family together—and if you don't include them in the decision—it really could create a lot of problems in the end.

Robin: That is so true. I know a few boaters who actually bought a boat just because they liked the first one they saw or they thought they could convince their partner or someone else they were trying to impress to go out on the boat with them. Then, as soon as they bought it, they realized that the boat wasn't really what they wanted, and now they're stuck.

Chris: Unfortunately, I see that all the time.

Robin: **Can you give me a few examples of boating activities that match different types of boats—both power and sail?**

Chris: There are so many variations out there. The overall boat is a runabout, which gives you the option to lay out. More runabouts than anything today have bow riders, which give you extra seating in front of the driver. This allows you to take a few more people. It allows the kids to maybe be separate, if there is such a thing on a boat, from the parents. But, with a runabout, you can do water sports, anchor out, tube, wakeboard, and then cruise the lake or inner coastal waters.

Another kind of runabout is more like a ski boat, with the engine more times than not in the middle of the boat. This style is great for shallow water applications—if you have a shallow lake or sandbars to go over. The engine actually acts as an inboard. Instead of a stern drive, which a runabout would have, or an outboard, where the engine's in the back or hanging off, a ski boat will have a prop shaft and a small propeller underneath the boat. This is really good when you have a lot of people on the boat and/or you want to pull skiers. It's what I call the torque aspect, where it can pull people out of the water—it's designed and developed for skiing and doing those specific types of things. A runabout will have a little bit faster top-end speed than a ski boat because a runabout is, again, your most versatile boat. A ski boat is more designed for skiing or wake boarding. However, you can do either one with either boat.

Today's pontoons are not like when we were growing up when our fathers and grandfathers had pontoons. Today's pontoons are very plush. As it sounds, they sit on two pontoons. They can be a little rocky at times, but for the most part they're great. They're putting larger engines on them now, so you can actually do skiing—they're becoming a versatile boat. In the past, somebody had a runabout, and they also had a pontoon boat if they just wanted to go slow and cruise. Today you can get a pontoon with a larger motor on it and actually do some skiing, tubing, and other water sports behind the boat, and still put 10 or 12 people on the boat—that's a great boat.

There are the fishing boats set up with fly and bait wells, trolling motors, and casting platforms. These boats are not necessarily good for putting a family on for a day—the seating is going to be limited because it really is designed for fishing; it's giving you a lot of flat areas to walk around on for fishing and things like that.

Cruisers give you a small cabin up front. When I say small, your cruisers start at 23 feet long and go up to endless from that point. The cruiser style gives you sleeping amenities, cooking amenities, and bathroom facilities. There are several styles of cruisers. When you start getting into the cruiser market, there's the express cruiser, aft-cabin, bridge boat—a lot of great styles to fit a person's needs.

Trawlers are in the powerboat market, but they're slower. Sometimes they have one engine instead of two for larger boats. They're kind of a home away from home. They give you the large amenities—like a floating cottage. You're not going to go very fast, but you're going to get there eventually and you're going to enjoy the time taken to get there.

Buying a Boat   Chris Kourtakis

There are many different kinds of sailboats—small catamarans, J12s, and larger performance sailboats that will give you the amenities downstairs to stay for the weekend. If you're a recreational sailor, then you don't mind having the air conditioner and refrigerator—home-away-from-home amenities—on the boat. If you're more of a racing sailor, your boat's going to be a little stripped down and not have as many creature comforts.

Robin: **Is there anything a boater needs to know about buying a used boat versus a new boat, or about buying a boat from a private seller versus from a yacht broker?**

Chris: It's no different from when you're buying a car. Today, there are a lot more used boats than there have been in the past. New boats give you a warranty, peace of mind. You're buying a new boat from a dealer who hopefully has a good reputation; where you know you're going to be able to get service after the sale; education, if needed; and they'll really be able to help you along. That boat is new; you'll have factory support—if anything goes wrong they should be able to help you. There are a lot of great companies out there.

When you buy from a private seller it is 'as is.' There's no help—if something goes wrong, you're on your own. With a private seller you've got to do all the homework—find your own financing, find your own insurance, and also maybe get the boat surveyed. If it's a larger boat, a lot of banks will ask for surveys now, so you'll have to arrange all that. If you buy a new boat you don't need a survey. The bank sometimes likes working with dealers over private sellers.

A broker is kind of the combination of both a dealer and a private seller. He or she works to make sure you get everything you need. He'll work on getting you financing. He'll work on taking care of storage for your boat. He'll take you out to teach you how to use the boat. If you need a survey, he can help arrange that. He works as a go-between. Some banks like working with brokers. It's really a fine line between the three—a comfort level of what you want. If you want a new boat, you're going to go to a dealer. There are a lot of great deals out there with private sellers right now and you can work with them, but you're on your own. A broker will help you work through the process and the steps and make sure you've got everything covered so there are no last-minute unexpected surprises.

Robin: **I've seen the terminology 'used' boats and 'pre-owned' boats. What's the difference?**

Chris: The biggest difference is coming from the dealership. In a used boat, probably a dealer has not gone through the boat and corrected any hidden engine issues that may have been there, any major flaws on the boat—you're buying it as is. Let's just say on a larger boat that the trim tabs didn't work—when you buy that used boat, the trim tabs more than likely do not still work. Whereas with a pre-owned, pre-logged, pre-enjoyed boat, more than likely a dealer has gone through that boat and fixed the trim tabs, and fixed the speedometer if it didn't work, and if it's a larger cabin boat that they might have gone through and made sure the air conditioner works. If they didn't, then it's more likely a used boat.

Dealers today really take care of a trade-in boat that they bring in, which is a pre-logged, pre-enjoyed, pre-used boat. They take it in, they go through it. You'll hear it's no different than buying from a GM certified dealer—you know they've gone through a 120-point inspection and made sure this car is good for when you drive it off the lot; whereas buying from a used car lot, you don't know what to expect because they're just selling a used car. They don't know the history of the boat. Those are the two biggest differences between a pre-owned or pre-enjoyed versus buying a used boat.

Robin: What about buying a boat that's been repossessed?

Chris: A repossessed boat can be a double-edged sword. I've worked with people that have purchased repossessed boats and they've gotten great deals. And I've worked with people that have had some problems doing that. Unfortunately, in this current market, somebody out there that had a stable job, they bought this boat, it's a year old or two years old; then they lost their job or changed their priorities, and, unfortunately, the boat got repossessed by the bank and it goes to a repossession place. Somebody goes in to pick up a two-year-old boat that a lot of times will have the plastic still on the seats and no engine hours on it. The boat's been meticulously maintained and they get a great deal on the boat. The flip side is that somebody loved their boat; they know it's getting repossessed, so they'll strip it clean—they'll take all the electronics out, they'll take anything and everything off of it. The seats will be ripped and when somebody goes to buy this boat, they know they're going to have to put a significant amount of money and work into the boat. However, if you're a handy man, it's a good buy because you can go out and potentially get a boat that's a lot cheaper and then do a lot of the work yourself. If you have to put in all these electronics and new seats and fix some stuff, you can do it yourself for a fraction of the cost and you're still getting a good savings. That's why a lot of people are looking for repossessed boats right now. The down side is that the guy or the bank selling it—nobody knows the history of the boat. If you're buying it from a used boat seller, a private owner, or something like that, you can ask questions. If you're buying it from a dealer, they might know the history because they originally sold the boat new or they've already taken it in and made sure the bottom is safe and everything else. With a lot of repossessed boats, you don't know if it was in a hurricane, if the boat ended up being grounded—you just don't know the extent of it. I caution people on it, but there are some very good deals out there for somebody willing to take that chance.

Robin: Does that mean there's no longer a warranty or anything on a repossessed boat for sale?

Chris: Many companies, even with a boat being only a year or two old, will not honor the warranty, because they don't know the history or what happened to the boat, it being repossessed. They may or may not honor warranties. I can't speak specifically for certain manufacturers, but some will honor the warranty just because it's a three-year-old boat that shouldn't have any issues. Whereas some will say, this is a repossessed boat, you bought it 'as is,' you know there are no warranties on it, so please don't come asking for little things to be fixed, because we know it was a repossessed boat.

Robin: **A buyer of a repossessed boat should assume there is no warranty and if they find out afterwards with some research that there is one, all the better.**

Chris: Don't assume that it has one just because the boat is only a year or two old. Always think worse case scenario, then if you get lucky, you can go from there.

Robin: **What are some mistakes people make when buying a boat?**

Chris: The biggest mistake I see people make is not test driving the boat in the conditions in which they're going to use the boat. A mom and dad go out shopping for a boat and they take the boat out with a salesman—so there are three people on the boat and barely any gas in it. The lake is calm as can be and they zip around and come back and everybody loves the boat. The reality is they're going to have eight people on the boat on a Saturday. The water is going to be two- to three-foot waves, and it will be a lot busier out there. If that's how you're going to be boating on a consistent basis, I recommend that on the test drive, you put eight people on the boat, take a cooler, and load the boat up like you're going to use it.

Ask the dealer if he can put a little extra fuel in it, so it's not an empty fuel tank. If they've got a problem with it, for your own peace of mind, pay to put the gas in. Pay for $100 worth of fuel, put it in there, load the boat up, and take it out. The weather conditions may or may not be good. For example, on the Lake of the Ozark—and I've seen this a couple times—new boaters don't understand that down there you can get three-, four-, or five-foot choppy waves. They test drive a boat on a Tuesday afternoon when no one's there, and then they go to use it on a Saturday and they're just not happy with the way the boat handles. I always tell people, load it up the way you want it, put some fuel in it, go out, and hopefully the water conditions will match something like you know you're going to be using the boat in on a consistent basis. That's a true test drive.

That'll give people an idea. A lot of times it's just one person in the boat. They go out with no gear in the boat, no water in the holding tanks, or anything else like that. They run out and they run back. They say, "This boat runs great, I've got to have it." When they finally go out and use it on their maiden voyage, it's a whole different feel—trolling speeds change, planing speeds change, handling changes, and people don't understand. They say, it ran great during the test drive, I don't understand what happened. Then you start looking at why; that's the unfortunate part.

Look at where you're going to go out boating most of the time. If you're going to be boating in the Boston Harbor, look at the size and style of boats people are using out there. I've seen people try to buy a certain style of boat, get it, then all of a sudden realize they're constrained by bridges and can't actually use their boat because it's too tall and can't get under some of the bridges. Then you look around and see that everybody else has another style of boat and you're the oddball out there. If you're in Boston Harbor, you don't want to get a 22-foot boat; you want to get a little larger boat. You're going to be the only 22-foot boat out there, and there's a reason for that—the waves, the wind, what have you. Take a look at where you're going to boat and see what other people are using out there.

The other thing I always tell people is check into the cost of insurance and the availability of dockage. As water access is becoming limited, make sure there is a place that you can keep a boat. I would hate to see somebody go out and spend a couple hundred thousand dollars on a boat and find out there are no wells available in your area at this time. The other thing is to make sure you can insure the boat—the style of boat that you want, for the body of water that you are going to be boating on. That's a small issue and it may never come up, but I have seen it come up, so I just want to make people aware of that. I've seen people that can get insurance, but it's got to be special insurance and they're paying more than they thought they would—just always check in on your insurance.

Robin: A good example of that is buying a wooden boat—a lot of marinas don't want them.

Chris: No. Most marinas don't want wood boats—they don't want to store them, maintain them, pick them up, or haul them out of the water. That's a great example.

Some people make mistakes because they don't understand the up-front and maintenance costs of boating. Like I said before, with boating, the maintenance and other costs could be 10-15% a year for the boat—make sure you understand them. I've seen some people say, "I can afford the boat," and then realize that the slip is $5,000 a year for a larger boat. Now they've got haul-out fees and winterization fees, and all of a sudden they realize they bought more boat than they could really afford, because they didn't know all the other associated or up-front fees. When you're purchasing a larger boat, you're going to have documentation fees, boat registration fees, titling fees, and, of course, you're going to have some bank fees and potentially some dealership fees. Just know when you are buying a boat that there are going to be other associated fees. If you have $10,000 to spend on a boat, take a look at all the up-front costs that you're going to have; you're going to have to get an $8,000 boat because you have to spend $2,000 on the other things, including tax. Florida did a great thing recently where they passed a cap on the tax. I can't remember exactly what it was, I think it was $15,000 or something like that, but now people can buy a boat and know exactly what the taxes are. I see a lot of people sometimes forget to count taxes into it. The next thing you know, they're putting 20% down on the boat and the bank comes back and says, "How are you going to pay the taxes?" It's like, "Wow, I forgot all about those—that's another $12,000 I've got to come up with." Know your up-front costs, your maintenance costs; so that when you're buying the boat, you know exactly what you're getting into.

Robin: Speaking of Florida, is it truth or fiction that a boat from Florida, or anywhere down south for that matter, is a better deal than buying a boat up here in the north?

Chris: That's a great question. Recently, I'm actually seeing the opposite. What I mean by that is I see a lot of people in Florida and the Gulf states purchasing boats from the north. This is happening for two reasons: when they go to buy a used boat, they don't know if it was damaged in one of the recent hurricanes that have come through in the last couple years; they don't know if the boat's been under water or had any issues from the unfortunate storms that have come through. Also, people like to buy boats from up north that are down south because the boats have never seen salt water. They also know the boat's only been used half of the year, so they could potentially be getting a pretty good boat with low hours on it—it's been maintained and is in really good shape. The other thing is with recent, unfortunate oil spills and things like that going on down there, people know they're getting a boat that hasn't weathered the storms per se—it hasn't had any main issues on it. People like to buy boats up here from down south for the pure fact that they think they're getting a better deal because of the economic situations. People need to get rid of their boats; they're getting rid of them because they're not using them, and so they think they're getting a good buy.

Buying a boat from Florida and down there, do you get a better deal? Not necessarily. When you do buy a boat from Florida and bring it up, just be prepared it has been in salt water and if it hasn't been properly maintained you're going to have some corrosion issues and other things you're going to have to deal with that you may not have dealt with in a northern boat.

Robin: **I would think that buying a boat that's in the water all the time, or even sitting on the hard in Florida or down south, between the hurricanes/storms they're getting, but also the sun beating down on the boat and all those other things, I would think, possibly because the boat is in use all the time, that it would get beaten up more than what we have up here.**

Chris: You're absolutely right on that. Everybody used to think that you could get a great deal down in Florida, but you're also getting what you pay for, as I always tell people. Nowadays, people are looking in the Great Lakes, Missouri, the Ozarks, and maybe Virginia—with the fresh water rivers that are up there—for some larger boats and runabouts. They know they're stored half of the year and they've been run in fresh water. Those are the kinds of boats that are being shipped down south now. They know they weren't prone to hurricanes. I would hate to see anybody buy a boat who didn't know its history and see a picture a couple years later of your own boat sitting in a tree.

Robin: **Should a boater be concerned with the number of hours on any given boat they're considering buying?**

Chris: Everybody asks that question. It's a really good question, in the sense of looking at a boat with 200 hours. It really seems high to me—is it? I don't look at the hours as much as I look at the maintenance. If I'm buying a used boat from someone and it's got 500 hours on it and the boat's five years old, I know he used it an average of 100 hours per year. But, if he didn't maintain it—didn't change the oil in that engine every year, didn't flush it if it has a stern drive, or, if it has inboards, he didn't check the staff packing and change transmission oils and things like that, that makes me more leery and afraid of that boat than if somebody came to me and said, "I've got 500 hours, I've changed the oil every 50 hours and have the maintenance logs and all the records and everything from a dealership that serviced it." The receipts show they've done all this work—that to me shows somebody who took care of their boat. Yeah, they used it. It's not a big issue to me. It's kind of like buying a car—one engine hour is comparable to 36 to 40 miles on the road in a car, so two hours on an engine is roughly 80 miles on a car. When you start looking in those terms, 200 hours, 300, 400, or 500 hours really isn't that much, especially if somebody maintained it. It's like if you're going to buy a used car, you want low miles, but you'll settle for something with 50,000 miles if you know it's had oil changes, tires rotated, and all the maintenance has really been kept up on the thing and you look at it and you go, "Wow, I can't believe this thing's got 50,000 miles on it." The same thing goes for boats. I look at boats all the time and somebody says, "This thing's got 500 hours on it." That doesn't scare me as much as if they say, "This has 500 hours on it and it hasn't been run in three years." That kind of makes me nervous. How has it been stored? Does it have oil in it? What's been done to the fuel system? Those kinds of things are what I look at—I look at the lack of maintenance over the guy that keeps a meticulous boat even though it has high hours, like me. I put a couple of hours on my boats every day, but they're professionally cleaned and maintained and I do a lot of work myself, so my neighbors enjoy buying boats from me and other people do, because even if it has high hours, they know that the boat has been treated with white gloves.

Robin: **Should you be asking to see their maintenance records?**

Chris: I always recommend that people ask for maintenance records if possible, especially when buying from a private seller. One of the first questions I always ask is, "Who did the maintenance?" If they say a dealership did it, I say, "Great. Can I see the maintenance records?" If they say they don't have them, go talk to the dealership. The service manager, if they've been maintaining the boat properly, should know the boat. The service manager should know that the guy comes in each year and be able to say, "Yup, I've got it right here. I can't tell you what was done, but I can tell you that the guy came in and maintained it regularly."

If you're buying a pre-enjoyed or pre-owned boat, they can't tell you by law the exact things that have been done on the boat, but the dealership can say, "We sold this boat new, maintained it, took care of it; all the work has been done here." That gives you that comfort level and that comfort feeling.

Robin: **What if they didn't take it to a dealer, but they did the work themselves and don't have a record?**

Chris: Then you want to check what their knowledge is of maintaining the boat—if it's been engine oil changes or little things like that, that's not a problem. If they start telling you, "We tore the engines apart, we put new carburetors on it, we rebuilt the heads and cylinders, and did a lot of major fiberglass work on the boat," then you need to look and see what their qualifications are. Unfortunately, there are many people out there who think they can do things that they just can't. Or they thought they did something right and they didn't. Whereas, if you have a receipt and some work was done on an engine or some fiberglass work was done, at least you know that there's some kind of guarantee, warranty, or recourse to go back to that person on. If the private seller did the work himself, you don't know his level of competency in pulling drives or fixing major things. If someone tells me they fixed the minor stuff that may or may not break, that I know I can fix again, I'm not worried about that. If the guy tells me, "I hit something last year and had to re-spray some gel coat and some sidings—fiberglass work—and I did it myself," that makes me a little bit nervous. Whereas, if he said, "I had it professionally maintained at Glass X store fiberglass repair, here's the bill," or "I don't have a receipt, but if you go talk to him and tell him it's this boat, he'll remember the state and the side repair,"—it's going back to the level of confidence and knowing that the work was done right versus questioning whether the work was done right.

Robin: **Isn't that also where having a really good marine survey comes in?**

Chris: Absolutely. A great marine surveyor, for people that don't know what they are—they're kind of like a home inspection company where they actually go through all the systems on the boat, they look at the bottom of the boat, and if they realize that there are some things that need to be changed, they'll let you know about it; if there are some things that are questionable, they'll let you know about it. A surveyor should be a third person who has no ties to either the buyer or the seller. You can find a great surveyor through SAMS® (the Society of Accredited Marine Surveyors®—www.MarineSurvey.org/index2.html) or NAMS® (the National Association of Marine Surveyors®—www.NAMSGlobal.org). Those are the two sites that I always check. I always tell people to get a third party who neither of us knows.

Robin: We're actually also interviewing Rob Scanlon who's a master marine surveyor, as well.

Chris: He'll probably tell you the same thing. Somebody like that that's been in the industry for a lot of years, their knowledge is hands down, and they can spot things on a boat—repairs that were done poorly, engine leaks that were done wrong, and different things.

Robin: **What's an HIN and is there anything about this HIN that buyers should be looking at?**

Chris: Yeah. By law every boat must have an HIN (hull identification number) on it—if it doesn't have an HIN on it, then it's very suspicious. There's also a location mandated by the United States Coast Guard that that boat HIN must be—in the back right corner of a boat. It's either going to be on the stern or the aft of the boat on the right corner, or it's going to be just around the corner on the right side of the boat in that right corner. The hull identification number is like the serial number for the boat. That serial number tells you a couple of things—the manufacturer of the boat, and, if you're buying a brand boat, you can go to the US Coast Guard's Boating Safety Division (www.USCGBoating.org) and actually look up a given number or given three letters that the Coast Guard gives to every boat builder. For example, Sea Ray might have SRY and then a serial number—that tells you every Sea Ray's going to have SRY. So if you're buying a Sea Ray and you see the first three letters of the serial number don't start with SRY, then you know that something is wrong and I would walk from that deal right away. The middle numbers—the manufacturer's code—always tell you the model; it might tell you the number of builds within that model. As you get towards the end, there's a letter and three digits. That letter might be A, B, C, or D all the way through. Those letters will also tell you in what month that boat was built—A equals January, B equals February, C equals March, and so on. The next number will be, let's say, 596—the 96 tells you it was a 1996 model, however, it was built in 1995. So if you see D696, you know that that boat was built in April of 1996 and it's a 1996 model. The HIN kind of tells you as a buyer if the guy tells you it's a 2001 boat then that serial number should either be 101 at the very end of the ten digits or it's going to be 001. If he tells you it's either 2000 or 2001, and it's stamped 898 or 999, then you know that boat was a 1999 model and he's trying to pass if off as a 2000 or 2001. I'd start questioning and if the documentation says that, then you know there's a problem.

Robin: What exactly is a boat broker?

Chris: A boat broker is very similar to a real estate agent. They don't own the inventory that they're selling, but they will work to show the inventory to prospective buyers. They advertise and put the listing out there—they do all the work for the seller. They show the boat if there is a buyer that wants to buy that boat, they will then accept the contract, negotiate for you, and ultimately put the deal together. A lot of times, like when you buy a house, the buyer of the boat works with the broker and never meets the owner of that boat. A broker works as an independent third person party in between the buyer and the seller. What's nice, if you're a buyer, is you can go to that broker and say, "This is the style of boat I'm looking for. What do you have available?" A lot of times that broker will have numerous listings and he can say, "I've got three boats that fit within your size," or "I've got four boats that fit within what you want to do," so if you're looking at tubing and everything else, great, "I've got four runabouts for you that'll work perfect." Or, if you're looking for a cruising style, he might say he's got five boats that describe exactly what you're looking to do and let's go look at them; then he'll take you around and show you the five different boats. Again, this is like a real estate agent who'll take you around and show you five different houses. If you do boating and don't necessarily have the time to sell your boat yourself, a broker works out great. The commission can be 2-15%, depending on the dealer and the broker and things like that. I tell people those are their costs for advertising, those are their costs for working. Just make sure you get the best deal. Some of the better brokers are going to charge more, but it doesn't mean that somebody that charges less doesn't do a great job. There's a local dealer here that only charges 5%. The reason they can do that is because they move boats on a continuous basis; they charge less and move boats a lot faster.

Robin: So there's really no difference between boat broker and yacht broker?

Chris: In certain states there is. The difference is going to be their license and certifications. A boat broker might only be able to go up to, in some states, I think 50 feet. Then you've got to have your yacht broker's license to go over 50 feet—working with mega-yachts and things like that are boats over 50 feet. It's really no difference per se in the sense of they still do the same thing. They still show the boat, work with the customer, broker the deal, and put everything together—a lot of it comes down to the licensing and experience.

Robin: **What are some of the dos and don'ts at a boat show when you're looking to buy a boat?**

Chris: Shop around and compare the boats. Sit in the boats; get a feel for the boats. A boat show is the best place to see all the boats you can ever want to see in one location. I always tell people, "If you're truly shopping for a boat, plan on spending the day there, two days there. Walk the show; get a feel for what you like; start sitting in the boats, climbing in the boats, and really enjoy what's there." I always tell people, "Compare the dealerships that you're considering buying from. Make sure the dealership you choose has a good reputation. If you're buying a new boat, make sure the dealership has a service department that can help you with service and take care of your warranty needs. You're buying the company that you're going to buy the boat from just as much as you're buying the boat itself. You want to make sure that they can meet the needs you have." Some people don't need the service department because they're going to have all the maintenance and everything done at their local marina. That's fine and great; then they can buy from anywhere. Make sure that you know the dealership you're buying it from. One thing is, do go home and think about what you're going to do. Don't rush into anything. You can put a small deposit on a boat, but don't allow that guy to pressure you to say you've got to buy today or somebody else is going to buy it. You can always order another boat. They can always get another boat. Things are a little different in this day and age where some manufacturers aren't producing as many boats, but during the boat show season there's plenty of time to put your order in and get a boat before spring season. Go home, think about what you want to do, think about whether the boat is right for you; make sure you look at the brochures, go online, take a look at the manufacturer, take a look at the dealer, and do your homework. Then come back the next day to the show, and if it's still something you want to do, then absolutely go for it and do it. If you're the household guy, as we talked about earlier, and you walk into the show by yourself after work with a couple buddies, don't put that money down. Bring the family back on Saturday, the dealer should be able to get you some passes to get in and bring the family down. Let the family see the boat, let them sit in it, show them two other options that you might have been looking at, then ultimately tell them why you want to get this boat; and then get in it and go with it. But, don't get pressured into buying the boat at the show unless you have made up your mind and your intentions are to buy that boat at the show. However, if you are going to order a boat, the boat show is the best place to order it, because that gives the manufacturer enough time to insure that you're going to get that delivery. If your show's in November, December, January, or February, there should be no issues of getting you a boat and having it in the water, behind your house, or at the marina by May.

Robin: **If you go to a boat show and you find *the* boat that you want, you've taken your family and they love it, the whole nine yards, should you wait until the last day to buy this boat or does it really matter?**

Chris: It really doesn't matter at that point. You're going to get the best boat show deal at the boat show whether it's the first day or the last day. The interest rates, if they're special for the boat show, are going to be about the same. You might be able to save a few hundred bucks or a few thousand bucks if you wait till the end of the show because the dealer knows that he wants to get rid of it, where he thought he might have been able to sell it. You know, it's a 10-day show and you come in day one and want to buy it, if you hold off a couple days then you might be able to save a few thousand bucks, but the flip side of it is that during that 10 days a lot of other people are going to be looking at that boat and it may not be there at the end of the 10 days. Then you're ordering one and potentially you could have to wait longer than you may or may not have wanted to. So, if you go to the boat show and you have the mindset that you want to buy the boat, go down and just take care of business, don't necessarily play the games to try and save a couple extra bucks. It may not benefit you in the end. It's good to just take care of it, but get it done. Like I said, if somebody waits until the last day of the show, the boat will more than likely be available, you'll be able to order one, you'll be able to get the boat show financing whether it's day one of the show or the end of the show. The other thing I always tell customers is, don't settle for less. If the boat's not exactly what you want, or it doesn't fit your needs, don't buy it and don't get it; don't get caught up in the show. Wait. Tell the dealer that the color isn't what you like or you want to order a different one or the seating configuration doesn't meet your family's needs, but don't settle for that. If there's time to get it, then get it. If there isn't time, wait now, wait a couple months. If you're buying the boat in March, April, or May, and the seating configuration doesn't fit what you need, and you're not going to get the boat 'til the end of June, waiting one extra month now is going to save you a lot of time and hassle in years to come. Finally, customers just need to enjoy the show and it's a fun event. It shouldn't be stressful. Go out, enjoy it, walk around, let the kids enjoy some of the events there for the kids and make it a fun time when you're buying the boat for everybody, because it really is truly an exciting time for everybody.

Robin: Can you give me an example of someone you've helped buy a boat that came to you with one boat in mind and ended up being extremely happy buying something totally different?

Chris: A recent customer of mine came to me and said he had to have a trawler style boat because he wanted to spend a lot of time on it. A couple months out of the year, he had to have certain aspects—style, spacing, things like that. By the time we were all said and done, he actually got into a cruiser style with two engines, two bedrooms, and a large kitchen. He got into an aft-style cabin boat and was ecstatic, once I found the style that met his needs. When a customer comes to me, we sit down and say, "What do you want to do with it?" and "Why do you want to do it?" Then we start going through this checklist—it really helps narrow down the boats. When he came to me and said, "I have to have a trawler, but this is what I want to do," I came back to him and said, "Here are three boats that meet your needs." When he got on the boats, he absolutely fell in love with them. He bought a different style than he was originally looking for. I had a customer last fall that came to me and said, "I've got to have a ski boat. My neighbors have a ski boat. I was told to get a ski boat. I have to get an inboard. That's it." When we sat down, I started asking him, "What are you going to do with it? Why are you going to do this?" At the end of the day, he really wasn't going to be doing a lot of skiing. We ended up getting him into a pontoon with a larger motor. When his grandkids come over, he can take them tubing and do some other things. But that wasn't the main focus of what he was going to do with the boat. He was going to have people over; he wanted to entertain; he needed a bathroom facility that his wife could get into and out of; he needed a comfort to get up and anchor, an easy accessibility. At the end of the day, he needed something easy for him to drive and put the cover on. We put him in a pontoon over the ski boat and to this day he absolutely loves the pontoon. His wife is ecstatic with it, and the grandkids love it because they go, they anchor, and the grandkids can run around the boat because it has more of an open feel and space to it. On a runabout they wouldn't have had that freedom out of the water that they do on the pontoon.

Robin: **What are some of the other services you provide?**

Chris: Besides the Captainzine services, the yacht rental, and fractional ownership, I work with customers and try to match boat buyers with boat sellers. I'm not a broker by any means, I don't list boats, I don't go out hustling to try and do that. But I do monitor dealer inventories and work with a lot of dealers. When a customer comes to me and says he's looking for a specific boat, I will work with them and look at my dealer list and I will say, alright, today we're going to go look at five different boats, here's where they're at and then they'll tell me which ones they like or dislike. Then I'll actually work in their favor and do the test drive with them, work with the surveyor for them. I'll make sure the technician's looking at their engines and things like that. I basically do what we discussed today and make sure the steps are not missed when they are buying the boat. I also make sure that the customers get into the style of boat that meets their needs. I walk with people around boat shows every year around the country. We'll spend time at the show. I'll say, "Sit in this boat. What do you like about this boat? What don't you like about this boat?" We'll actually develop a sheet of likes and dislikes, and then we'll compare them to the sheet we did before we went to the boat show that says what we're looking for. Ultimately, we'll get into the boat that people want, meets their needs, and has enough power to do what they want it to do. I make sure they're doing their test drive with 10 people in the boat, a full cooler, and half a tank of gas. Dealers enjoy working with me as well, because they know I'm looking to push their inventory. It's a win-win for everybody. We offer on-water boating education, which is a little bit different from the classroom style. We actually teach people how to run their boats and use their boats safely and effectively.

Closing

Robin: Thank you for being so generous with your time today. You've given me and probably most of us on the call a lot of insight regarding not being so quick to buy just any old boat, but the right boat with your activities and family in mind.

Chris: I really appreciate you having me on. This is something I'm passionate about—any person I can get into a boat or see a family grow with boating. A family that boats together stays together. Alleviating all the stress about boating and going out and having fun is in all these steps we discussed today. It's making sure you get the right boat—the right size—and using it in the right places.

Robin: **How does someone find you if they have further questions?**

Chris: Check out my website at www.H2OLimos.com or email me at Chris@H2OLimos.com. My mobile number is 248-890-1116.

Key Points

1. Go through your finances and make sure you can afford to buy a boat. Annual maintenance and other costs can be 10-15% of your purchase price.
2. Before you buy, sit down with your kids and ask them why they want a boat and what they want to do with it.
3. New boats give you a warranty and peace of mind. When you buy a boat from a private seller it comes 'as is.'
4. Repossessed boats can be a double-edged sword. You get a boat that's a bargain, and if you can do a lot of the necessary repair work yourself, you're still getting a good savings. The down side is that the bank that's selling it doesn't know the history of the boat.
5. Test drive the boat in the same waters in which you'll use the boat.
6. Before purchasing, check the cost of insurance and the availability of dockage.
7. Most marinas don't want wooden boats—they don't want to haul them out of the water, maintain them, or store them.
8. When you buy a boat from Florida or further south and bring it up north, be prepared—it has been constantly in salt water and if it hasn't been maintained properly, you'll have some corrosion and other issues that you may not have in a northern boat.
9. Obtain maintenance records if possible, especially if you're buying from a private seller.
10. A boat show is the best place to see all the boats you ever want to see in one location. Make sure you shop around, sit in and get a feel for the boats, and compare them.

Notes

Marine Surveys
An Interview with Rob Scanlan

Introduction

Robin: Hello everyone. This is Robin Coles and it's my pleasure to welcome you to the 2010 Nautical Lifestyle Expert Series brought to you by TheNauticalLifestyle.com. During the next hour you'll be learning all about marine surveys from my special guest Rob Scanlan of MasterMarineSurveyor.com. Hello Rob!

Rob: Good evening, Robin.

Robin: Thank you so much for joining me today. Rob Scanlan is a certified and credited marine surveyor. He was the first marine surveyor in the United States to be accepted by the National Marine Bankers Association and the Yacht Brokers Association of America. Rob's been in business since 1986 and knows his way around just about every type of vessel. He's also got an extensive background in pre-purchase and financial surveys, insurance appraisals, adjusting, and bank, estate, and tax donation appraisals. Rob is also called in as a key witness in various lawsuits.

Marine Surveys

Robin: **What is a marine survey and how does it differ from a home inspection?**

Rob: First of all, homes do not float. A marine survey is a little more detailed than a home inspection. When I do a survey on a boat, yacht, or commercial vessel, I am actually structurally inspecting and percussion-sounding the hull. I'm doing mechanical engine diagnostics and pressure testing—plugging my computers into the engines. I'm also testing all the A/C and D/C wiring systems—air conditioning, heat, electronics, and generator—and making safety recommendations to U.S. Coast Guard Title 46[1] standards. A boat, yacht, or ship survey involves much more detailed testing than is done in a typical home inspection. Let's face it, windows leak on a home and the basement floods. On a yacht, the bilge floods and pumps have to keep up with it. If portholes or hatches are leaking, you've got water coming into the yacht. That's pretty much how you can define the difference between a marine survey and a cursory checklist for a home inspection.

Robin: **What is a condition and valuation survey?**

Rob: Condition and valuation surveys are mostly pre-purchase surveys. When somebody is buying a boat, yacht, commercial vessel, or ship, it is a thorough testing of the hull, wiring systems, and engines, determining the condition of the vessel and the value placed on it. A boat's evaluation is derived from the overall condition of the boat and comparable boats or yachts that are out there in a particular region of the United States. It is a very detailed survey

---

[1] Coast Guard Title 46 pertains to shipping. For more information, see http://ecfr.gpoaccess.gov/cgi/t/text/text-idx?sid=b5bb8938f3917718e4359600df690da1&c=ecfr&tpl=/ecfrbrowse/Title46/46tab_02.tpl

and the condition and valuation survey report should be a document that you can hand to an insurance underwriter for coverage and another copy to a bank for financing.

Robin: **Does this need to be done if someone is going to finance a boat purchase?**

Rob: When purchasing a boat or yacht, some insurance companies will require a condition and valuation survey because of the age of the boat. They want a more detailed survey done rather than what's called an insurance survey. The condition and valuation survey involves more testing of the hull, wiring systems, and engines.

Robin: **What if somebody's just buying a boat for short money, say under $10,000. Do they still need a condition and valuation survey?**

Rob: Not really—for any boat that someone is buying for under $10,000, they can put a rider for it on their homeowner's insurance policy.

Robin: **What if they don't own a home?**

Rob: If a boat buyer doesn't own a home, but they have apartment renter's insurance, he or she can put it on the tenant's insurance policy as a rider. Banks and insurance companies require a condition and valuation survey on a boat that is being purchased in order to bind coverage and get financing if the boat is going to be financed for over $20,000 to $25,000.

Robin: **Who's responsible for the costs of this pre-purchase survey?**

Rob: The person purchasing the boat is responsible for the cost of the survey as well as for the additional expenses of launching the boat for a sea trial and for short-hauling the boat for an out-of-water inspection.

Robin: **Let's talk about an engine survey for a minute. What's involved in that?**

Rob: A critical part of a pre-purchase survey is a full computer diagnostic, compression testing, and analysis of the engines. You can have engines that look beautiful, that just had tune-ups and fluid and filter changes. And I can plug my computers into the engines and do a full engine diagnostic, analysis, and compression check with the boat or yacht just at the dock or out of the water with all operational readings coming back fine. But you still want to do a sea trial, because a lot of problems can develop at half, three-quarters, or full throttle—things we wouldn't know about just doing an in-neutral and idle engine analysis. Compression testing on a gas or diesel engine should be done after the engine has been brought up to operating temperature.

Robin: **What other types of surveys are there?**

Rob: Most underwriters will want an updated insurance survey every five to seven years to keep the boat insured and keep the insurance underwriter abreast of the condition of the boat—structurally, mechanically, and electrically—but they don't require the detailed testing that would be done in a pre-purchase survey.

Marine Surveys — Rob Scanlan

So, we have the pre-purchase survey, the insurance survey, and what we call an appraisal. An appraisal could be used if the boat is being donated. An appraisal can also be used for a boat that's in an estate in probate where the owner has passed away, or in a divorce where the boat or yacht must be appraised in order to divide the marital assets.

Other surveys are damage surveys. If a yacht has sustained damage or loss, usually the underwriter will send their assigned marine surveyor out to assess the damage. This is done in order to protect the insurance company. If the owner sustained a loss, it's best for the owner to retain his own marine surveyor working on his behalf to make sure the insurance company surveyor isn't taking advantage of the insured.

The types of surveys are 1) a pre-purchase (condition and valuation) survey if you're buying a boat, 2) an insurance survey to keep insurance current and ongoing for another five to seven years, 3) the appraisal of a boat involved in a divorce or estate settlement, and 4) a damage survey if the boat or yacht sustains damage through a storm or an accident.

Robin: **That's a lot of different surveys to keep track of. When a surveyor is hired, who exactly are they working for and what kinds of expectations can the hirer have?**

Rob: A surveyor is hired by the person paying him, period. They're working for that person; that person has retained the surveyor. The surveyor has allegiances to the person paying him. The person hiring the surveyor should expect the surveyor's total allegiance to him. The person hiring the surveyor is the only person entitled to receive the results of the survey. Opinions, photographs, any other documentation, and the survey report itself all go directly to the person hiring the surveyor. The hirer makes the decision about who else he might want to send that information to.

Robin: **If someone's buying a boat and they're hiring you to do a survey, you're working for them. What if the buyer was told by the insurance company that he or she had to have a specific type of survey? Are you still working for the buyer?**

Rob: Correct. You're still working for the person who's paying you.

Robin: **How long is an average written report? And does a typical report contain photographs?**

Rob: Typical written reports, my written reports, which also encompass an engine analysis, computer diagnostics, and compression testing, vary in length depending on the boat. The report contains digital photos—port, starboard, bow, stern. I also like to get photos of the interior, electronics, engine compartments, and machinery. A 30-foot power boat with twin inboard engines would be 18-25 pages. A 30-foot sailboat with a single diesel engine would be 16-18 pages with the photographs. For up to a 40-foot yacht with much bigger engines, more tests to be done if they are diesel, and all the onboard systems—that report could be 30-35 pages with digital photos.

Robin: **That's how *you* do it, but is that the norm?**

Rob: I don't follow the norm. I conduct my surveys and do my reports the way I designed my survey reports. These formats are used by many, many surveyors, not only throughout the United States, but in Europe, Canada, and Australia. A lot of marine surveyors don't do engines. They'll just read the helm instrumentation. One engine—gas or diesel—represents four pages of my survey report devoted to testing, analysis, computer printouts, diagnostics, and compression on that particular engine, on usually a 30- to 40-foot yacht.

Robin: **What kind of guarantees do marine surveyors give for their work?**

Rob: The only guarantee you'll get is from a new yacht that the manufacturer warranties. No marine surveyor that I know of, and I've been doing it since 1986, will guarantee that there aren't any unforeseen or internal problems with the engines, hull laminate, or wiring that you can't see because, for example, the wire is all in a loom. There are no guarantees. The comfort that any client should have with a marine surveyor is the liability insurance that the surveyor may carry in the event that he damages a yacht or boat structurally, mechanically, or electrically during the course of conducting a survey. For instance, when I plug my computers into the engines, I key in different things that I want the injectors to do. If I damage the injectors or the engines, I'm responsible for that. If I run the air conditioning system, forgetting to open up the sea cock, and burn out the raw water pump, I'm responsible for that. As far as a guarantee or warranty by a surveyor on his work, you can have all the 'hold harmless' clauses and signoffs from a potential buyer, seller, broker, or other concerns, but the surveyor is still pretty much responsible for anything he or she missed because of out-and-out neglect or just didn't get in far enough to inspect, such as a delaminated stringer. If you didn't get behind the A/C or D/C electrical panel to see that the back of certain breakers were burned by overload, you would be responsible for not picking that up.

Robin: **When should oil testing be done, and what's involved in that?**

Rob: Oil analysis, testing oil, is like testing blood. You have to draw the oil samples when the engine's warm. You need a separate extraction hose and bottle, with everything ultra clean when you're extracting the oil. You usually get an ounce or an ounce and a half into the plastic bottle and then make all your markings—the make and model number of the engine, number of hours, and hours since last oil change. In the lab that I use, they do 27 tests on my oil samples. These tell us if the oil is getting contaminated with raw saltwater or antifreeze. The labs are pretty good. The one I use here in Boston will come back and tell me if there is any critical bearing or cylinder wear, and where it's coming from. Oil tests are recommended when you're buying a boat. It's best to draw the oil after the sea trial so you get at least an hour or an hour and a half of run time on the oil sample being drawn. The oil goes out to the lab; the lab does all the tests on it and comes back with the report. If you own a boat, I recommend that you have the oil tested maybe every 200 hours.

Robin: **Are there any differences between fiberglass and wooden boat surveys?**

Rob: A lot—wood boat surveys are a lot harder to conduct. There are very few marine surveyors that are well versed in surveying wood boats. With wood boats, you have the strakes below the waterline and the planks above the waterline fastened to the ribs of the frames. For wood boat surveys, as well as for any survey on a boat or hull, the vessel's got to be up out of the water. Wood boat surveys require a real close inspection of the fasteners. You need to do a random pulling of the screws or fasteners that are below the water line, usually every four square feet, to test the integrity of the fasteners. You also do percussion-sounding of the strakes and planks below the waterline and above.

Fiberglass boat surveying is percussion-sounding the hull with, let's say, a phenolic hammer, to detect if there are any voids or delamination in the fiberglass layup. When I do a survey on a fiberglass boat, I have some different hammers that I use. I use a phenolic plastic head hammer for outside the boat: percussion-sounding the hull, decks, superstructure, and cockpit sole; and inside the boat: stringers around the engine compartment. I use modified ball-peen hammers with extended handles so I can percussion-sound or tap the longitudinal stringers and transverse frames from under the engines. You can look at stringers and they'll look fine. You can percussion-sound or tap out the stringers with a ball-peen hammer and detect a lot of delamination of the coring material or the laminated plywood that the fiberglass is actually encapsulating.

Wood boat surveys take longer and cost more because there's a lot more time involved.

Robin: **How would you determine dry rot in a wooden boat?**

Rob: Dry rot is decay. It's also delignified wood. In other words, the lignin in the wood has just, if you will, dried up or drained off. To test for dry rot on a wood boat, I usually take a pick and just pick at the wood ever so gently, easily. You can almost just look at a wooden boat's frame, the stringers—that's where you're going to find your delignified wood, where the wood looks almost like hair or straw. The decay or delamination is usually in the bulkheads or the superstructure—the cabin sides, interior, and transverse members that run port to starboard like partitions.

Robin: **How would you determine the strength of a fiberglass hull?**

Rob: To test the strength of a fiberglass hull during a survey requires percussion-sounding the entire bottom/keel on your hands and knees, every square foot. It's done with a phenolic hammer that helps to detect if there is any void or de-lamination and whether there have been any grounding repairs. Tapping out the bottom detects any structural problems below the water line. You can use that same method for the waterline up to the rub rail just by tapping out the hull. Most decks are cored with Divinycell® (polymer foam), laminated plywood, or balsa. You tap out the hulls and superstructure looking for any delamination of the fiberglass lay-up and the coring. You can look at the sides and bottom of a hull; you can look at the superstructure—cabin, trunk, and decks—and everything looks cleaned and waxed. You're not going to know whether there's any delamination unless you do a percussion-sounding or tapping out of those areas.

Another way you can tell the strength of a fiberglass hull is at the rub rail or hull-to-deck joint, underneath where the top of the hull is connected to the hull itself. If you see under the rub rail that you've got some serious cracks, then you know the hull-to-deck joint might be fractured inside. There might be a kind of fabric covering that area. Checking it might require removing the fabric to see if, in fact, the hull-to-deck clamp has been fractured.

Robin: **Is that something that would be done during the survey, if need be?**

Rob: Only if you see that the perimeter hull-to-deck joint at the rub rail has significant cracks. This would suggest that the hull might be flexing, that the hull-to-deck joint might be coming apart. Hull-to-deck joints, where the top of the boat and the hull are connected, are usually attached with a chemical bond and a mechanical fastening program.

Robin: **Can engine batteries be charged off of an outboard motor?**

Rob: I've found that outboards above ten horsepower have engine-driven alternators that actually keep the batteries charged up and topped off while the engine's running. So, yes, batteries can be charged off of an outboard motor. On the more powerful outboard motors and the wiring systems on newer boats, the alternators and wiring systems have diodes that detect that a particular battery is low on charge. They will leave fully charged batteries in their state of full charge, but go after a poorly charged battery and send a quick charge to it. Then the alternator shuts off and remains in stand-by waiting to keep the batteries topped off.

Robin: **If a boat has been sitting for a couple of years since its last survey on the hard, should you get a full survey again before purchasing it? Is there such a thing as a partial survey, like everything except a sea trial?**

Rob: There is no such thing as a partial survey. I haven't done them. I will not do a partial survey, especially on a boat that's been sitting for a couple of years that my client is actually purchasing. It would have to be a full condition and valuation survey addressing structural, mechanical, electrical, and Coast Guard safety standards. Sea trials are very, very important. You can have great operational readings from your engines—good compression—with a boat that's been out of the water and laid up for two years, but get the boat into a sea trial where it's half, three-quarter, and full throttle, and there are a bunch of problems that can develop that you'd never know about by just looking at the engines, or just starting them and shifting them in and out of gear. I've done a lot of boats and yachts that have been in extended lay-ups of two to three years. Before you start any engine, you always want to check your crankcase, oil, transmission fluid, and coolant. On a boat that's been in lay-up for a couple of years you don't want the engines to fire right up—you want them to turn over, work the oil up into the engines, and then fire up. You've got the get the water circulating through the cooling system.

Robin: This is the same thing you would do if your car had been sitting in the driveway or parked in a garage for a long time. **If a boat has been on land for over a year, is there any real expectation that water would or should be found, especially in the bilge?**

Marine Surveys — Rob Scanlan

Rob: If you find water in the bilge, it's coming from leaking or blocked cockpit scupper drains and coming in through the deck or cockpit hatches. If it's a sailboat, it could be coming into the mast boot—the mast goes through the cabin roof and water could be following the mast right down into the bilge. Water in a boat that's been in lay-up could also come from poor gaskets or seals around the hatches or portholes.

Robin: **Hence the reason for shrink wrapping it while it's sitting there.**

Rob: Shrink wrapping or a frame and canvas is a good idea, to keep not only water out, but also any leaves or debris; to keep your boat clean and protected. It's amazing to me how many people don't cover their boats.

Robin: I've been seen a lot of them lately that are just not covered. **On a sailboat, is it necessary for a surveyor to climb the mast to inspect it?**

Rob: It all depends on when the mast was last taken down. In nine out of ten sailboat surveys, the masts are already down. It's kind of neat to be able to inspect the masthead, fittings, spreaders, and mast hardware. Is it necessary for a surveyor to get up the mast? It all depends on how much the client wants to pay to do that and when the mast was last unstepped and inspected; when it was last surveyed and whether the mast was up or down then. On a sailboat, it's best to remove your mast for inspection every three years.

Robin: **What credentials should someone look for before hiring a surveyor? Should you ask for written qualifications and/or a resume, or are there specific "trick" questions you can ask a surveyor to see how knowledgeable they are?**

Rob: There's no licensing for marine surveyors in the United States. The Coast Guard doesn't do it and there's no one body or marine surveyors group that licenses marine surveyors. Currently, we've got the US Surveyors Association, which I've been a member and a board member of and active in since 1988, which is based in Fort Myers, Florida. We train marine surveyors. They go on to become members of NAMS® (National Association of Marine Surveyors®), SAMS® (Society of Accredited Marine Surveyors®), two other organizations that certify or accredit marine surveyors. A surveyor that you choose should be one that has extensive background, hands-on education, and credentials in a marine surveying profession. Yes, you should ask for a copy of qualifications and a resume, but for most surveyors, it's on their websites (that can be found on my website now). You should check references—many, many of my clients do check references.

Trick questions you should ask to see how knowledgeable they are might include how long have they been in business and a list of banks or insurance companies that they have had surveys accepted by. Another thing you can ask a surveyor about is their work in the past. For instance, were they a bar tender, were they a construction worker and five years ago they started their practice. Clients will ask me to send a sample survey from this year and one from five, ten, 15 years ago to see the difference in survey format.

Robin: Can an insurance agency tell you who to hire for a surveyor?

Rob: No, they can't. What's important to understand about an insurance agency is they are not the underwriter. An insurance agency gets a commission for sending the business to the underwriter. It's really the underwriter that will say whether they've heard of a particular surveyor and if the surveyor has a great reputation, or "We've never heard of this guy. How long has he been in business?" The insurance agent cannot tell you who to hire for a surveyor. If an insurance agency tells you that there's only one list to draw from or there are one or two particular surveyors you can use, then you know those surveyors have a situation with that insurance agency that's not comfortable for you, the insured. It's like a bank financing company telling you which person to choose to do the survey on the boat in order for them to finance the boat. Insurance underwriters know who the reputable, certified, and accredited marine surveyors are and the ones that are only doing it part-time, based on the number of surveys they see come over their desks year in and year out.

Robin: What would happen if an insurance agent or a bank financing person did recommend somebody? What can happen if they suggest one and you act upon it?

Rob: You could go with that, but bear in mind, that's putting them in a situation where if that surveyor misses something, then after the yacht or boat is purchased and the buyer is now shelling out a lot of money because of a structural, mechanical or electrical problem, he can go back to the insurance agent and say this is the guy you recommended. You're going to be next to him in court—the attorney will be calling you. No insurance agency, bank, or financing person wants to recommend one or two particular surveyors. If they have a list, you can draw from the list, but you've got to make the final decision yourself based on the surveyor's references, credentials, and continuing education, and the scope of the survey.

Robin: Who is the best person to go to, to get a recommendation?

Rob: The internet is very good. You go to the internet, you type in marine surveyors, and you can see by who comes up in the first two pages who has been at it the longest. A lot of people at your own marina would be able to refer you to a good surveyor. But, if you've been doing business with a particular insurance agent—he or she is writing your home, your business, your automobiles—and he also writes boats; he could make a good recommendation, protecting you and your family as he has with your other insurance needs.

Robin: I would think they could go out on the different forums and put a question out there or even ask their fellow boaters who they're using.

Rob: You also want to find out whether the surveyor is a member of the National Marine Bankers Association (NMBA). The NMBA are the people that finance boats, yachts, and commercial vessels. The American Institute of Marine Underwriters (AIMU) is a governing body of marine insurance underwriters. You want to make sure your surveyor is not only certified and accredited, but also well recognized by the NMBA and the AIMU.

Robin: **Can you explain compliance with boating safety standards set by National Fire Protection Association, American Boat and Yacht Council, and the good old US Coast Guard?**

Rob: Coast Guard standards were around long before the National Fire Protection Association (NFPA) and the American Boat and Yacht Council (ABYC). You've got to understand that the NFPA and the ABYC standards for boating safety, for both pleasure and commercial, are *recommended* standards. They are not gospel, not the final answer. They have their own 'hold harmless,' disclaimers, standards, and practices, but they are not mandatory. Insurance underwriters and banks like to see that during a pre-purchase or insurance survey, their guidelines were somewhat followed. That's good practice.

I use US Coast Guard standards more for commercial boats—fishing draggers, trawlers, commercial charter boats, and schooners—whereas a commercial boat doesn't really follow the American Boat and Yacht Council standards. Although I do refer to ABYC standards when I'm doing commercial boats, I stick with US Coast Guard standards.

Robin: **Is there a book that lists a boat's age, condition, etc., that surveyors use?**

Rob: Yes, there is. I have several of these reference materials. One of them is the annual *Powerboat Guide*—both in hard copy and on CD. I also use YachtWorld.com[2] for the age and condition of a boat being sold. But with Yacht World—or any yacht broker's listing sheet where they show the digital photos, equipment, and asking price—all that info comes from the selling party; it doesn't come from the broker doing anything more than a walk through of the boat and photographing. I do not use the National Automobile Dealers Association (NADA)[3] for here in New England. NADA is not accurate for our New England area because here our average boating season is five months (and the NADA guide lists boats by year manufactured). I stick with the *Powerboat Guide*, Yacht World, and Boat Wizard. In Boat Wizard, not only are you looking for a particular boat and what comparable boats are selling for, but what they sold for last year and the year before.

I pride myself on my library. A lot of clients will call to talk to me about a boat they're looking at. I will look it up, do the comps, and tell them what comparable boats are listing for in that area of the country and what that boat sold for last year and the year before. After talking with me, they understand what they should reasonably offer for the boat, pending a satisfactory survey.

Robin: **Is there someplace to find information about the construction of a particular boat for any known problems?**

---

[2] YachtWorld.com – a website and brokerage firm for yacht brokers

[3] National Automobile Dealers Association – also lists boats; NADAGuides.com is an online guide for selling and pricing boats, etc.

Rob: One of the things I do, as part of my pre-purchase survey, is access the national crime bureau boat history report to see if that boat has had a particular problem in the past. For instance, I'm just finishing up a survey on a beautiful 1997 Tiara 31. The engine's beautiful, it's a beautiful boat. When I ran the hull number this afternoon in my office through the national crime bureau for a history report, I found out that the boat had a previous run-aground back in 2001 with $5,000 worth of damage. The report also went on to say that the owner at the time filed an insurance claim. That information was with the national crime bureau boat history report for that particular boat. In percussion-sounding it, the hull was beautiful. The bottom, frames, decks, the entire boat was just a showpiece. If the boat had run aground and the shafts or struts were bent, that repair would cost $5,000 to $8,000. Could the props have just kissed the boulders or the sand and maybe got little nicks and dings? To recondition the props is upward of $800 each. The report doesn't really say what damages were, but how much the claim was. After I complete the survey report, I'll go into the national crime bureau boat history report and say I did a survey last week on the boat—hull, wiring, compression, engines, sea trial—and found no delamination in the hull. I'll update their listing to say that the boat had a pre-purchase survey and the results of that survey. Any buyer down the road will see that it had this accident in 2001, sustained $5,000 worth of damage, but that in June 2010 it had a full pre-purchase condition and valuation survey and it was fine structurally, mechanically, and electrically.

Robin: **What a great find and great piece of information to know.**

Rob: For the boats that are Coast Guard documented, I'll take the number or name of the boat, run it through a Coast Guard search query, and find out if there are any liens on the boat, who the current owner is, and who the previous owners were. That's all part of my pre-purchase survey—I don't charge extra for that.

Robin: That's awesome, especially now with so many boats being repossessed, you don't know what you're getting.

Rob: Correct—the listing won't even say, in most cases, whether the boat was repossessed. It'll just say who the previous owner was, but on the abstract title from the Coast Guard, I'll learn not only who the previous owner was, but who the bank was. Nine out of 10 times, the bank is a member of the National Marine Bankers Association. I'll contact the bank to see if there are any liens, whether the boat's been paid off, then they'll disclose that the boat was repossessed.

Robin: **If the bank repossesses a boat, they will not note that on the listing?**

Rob: The abstracted title that the Coast Guard has will tell you the history of the boat as far as whether the boat was repossessed.

Robin: **If someone's buying a boat and they live miles away, either miles away as in the other end of the state or, you know, we're up here in New England, so if they live in Florida or somewhere, is it crazy for them to entrust the inspection of the boat to the surveyor without being there themselves?**

Marine Surveys — Rob Scanlan

Rob: I cover Maine to Long Island, New York; upstate New York; and New Jersey. It surprises me that many clients don't want to be present during the survey. That's ok, I just tell the client that I want the option to call them periodically during the survey and keep them posted on the process. I wouldn't want to charge a client for a survey, have a client pay me in full, and go do the survey, then learn an hour or an hour and a half after I started that this client isn't going to buy the boat because of structural, mechanical, or electrical problems, and then continue with the survey and prepare the report knowing I've already been paid. I would rather call the client and say this is what we've got structurally, mechanically, or electrically—this is not the boat for us, so let's stop right here and withdraw our offer to purchase. Any client who retains a marine surveyor should be real comfortable with the surveyor's background, education, certification, and experience. To be able to trust a surveyor to step up and say, this is what we've got, let's stop here instead of taking advantage of the client, knowing you've already been paid and knowing the client's not going to buy the boat or the yacht. That's been my practice since I've started. I'm adamant about a client having either a cell phone on his hip for the day I do a survey or access to a phone from his office or home. My clients like that. They like the fact that I'll step up and do that. Just be paid for my time and then refund the balance—a client has to be very comfortable with that surveyor.

Robin: What are some things surveyors should look for?

Rob: When I'm first retained to do a survey, I email the broker or selling party, with a copy to my client, asking to see maintenance logs and receipts for all work that's been done on the boat and its engines and a copy of the last survey. If there are no maintenance logs or receipts, and no copy of the last survey—I've been doing this since 1986—I know I'm stepping onto a boat with problems.

Robin: They're hiding something.

Rob: Yup. Anybody that's taken good care of their boat or yacht has a great maintenance log with all their receipts and a copy of the last survey. I'll get the history of the boat using the hull identification number (HIN) before I even go to the survey to make sure there isn't a previous problem—maybe the boat was declared a total loss in another part of the country, brought up here, and spruced up to be flipped and sold. And doing a Coast Guard documentation query—there are a lot of things surveyors should look for before they even start a survey to protect the client who is paying them.

Robin: How long does a survey normally take to complete?

Rob: A survey on a 30-foot powerboat takes four to four and a half hours. That includes structural testing, testing of the engines (diagnostic and compression), electrical tests, and the sea trial. For the official written report, it all depends. Sometimes you have to go back a second time because there were problems during the initial sea trial. Or maybe you did the survey during the lay-up period—late fall, winter, early spring—when you couldn't do a sea trial. You can go ahead and generate a report, but kind of hold it open pending a satisfactory sea trial in the spring. If you can get to a particular boat or yacht and get the whole thing done—structural, mechanical, electrical, sea trial, everything—the average time to prepare a written report for a 30-foot power boat with twin engines is about two hours. For a 40- to 80-foot boat, it would take me three or three and a half hours to prepare the written report.

Robin: Should they expect it a day or a couple of hours later?

Rob: A survey hirer should expect their written report 48 to 72 hours after the completion of the survey. Don't forget, oil samples have to be brought to the lab and analyzed. Fortunately, I use a lab in Boston. In most cases I drop the oil off at the lab on the way home or send it out priority mail. They'll get it within two days.

Robin: You mentioned that if you can't do a sea trial right away, then you're going to write up a partial report. Would you give a copy of that partial report to the potential buyer in the meantime?

Rob: Yes, emphasizing that you've agreed to return to conduct the sea trial. My service truck is set up to run the engines and generator with the boat or yacht out of the water. I get access to a water source to get a hose into the sea strainer or, if it's an outdrive, to get water to the outdrive fitting muffs, to be able to run the engines up to operating temperature, shift in and out of gear, get all the operational readings, and do the compression testing; then, if I'm doing a survey during the late fall/winter/early spring, I will re-winterize the engines and generator when I'm done that day.

You schedule a time for a sea trial. If things go well—the boat's relatively new, the hull was percussion-sounded and is fine, the wiring systems tested fine, engines fine, compression good, the computer diagnostics fine—you can proceed with the purchase of the boat, but hold out an amount of money in escrow for sea trials in the spring or when the boat is launched. All parties are curious as to how much money should be held out in escrow. I make that determination, not the broker, the selling party, or my client purchasing the boat. Because, for example, on a 40-foot yacht with diesel engines, all your operation and independent readings were good, the wiring systems were fine, the hull's intact, you lubed the cutlass bearings and the shaft struts so you could shift the engines in and out of gear, and then you said, "Things are looking good. Let's hold out $5,000 in escrow." Now comes spring time and you launch the boat. The buyer already owns the boat thinking he's comfortable with $5,000 held out in escrow. Halfway through the sea trial you realize you've got some serious mechanical problems you couldn't detect with the yacht out of the water, but these problems make themselves known at half, three-quarter, or full throttle. Now there's $15,000 to $17,000 worth of work that has to be done to the engine. You can't go back to the selling party or the broker and say, "We held out $5,000—we didn't hold out enough." You already own the boat. On my website, I go into escrow and make the determination of how much should be held out, number one covering my client's investment.

Robin: Is there a difference between doing a sea trial on a lake versus on the ocean?

Marine Surveys   Rob Scanlan

Rob: Most lakes now have speed limits. Some of your boats now are doing 45, 50, 60 miles an hour. You can't do that on lakes any more. The speed limits on lakes now are 45 miles per hour during the day and 25 miles per hour at night. If you're going to use a boat on a lake, that's fine if it's going to *stay* on the lake. But if you're buying a boat on a lake and you're intending to bring it out on the open ocean where there are three-, four-, five-, six-foot swells, and you're buying a 32- to 36-foot boat, you're going to want to know how this boat feels in sea conditions. You can't test that on a lake.

What are you using the boat for? If you're going to use it on a lake for water skiing, great. If you're going to take that boat that's on a lake and take your family around coastal New England, down on the Cape, over to Gloucester, you're going to want to make sure that's the boat you want and that it was trialed at sea in at least two- to three-foot chops or waves.

An important thing here is to qualify the boat for the potential buyer, asking where they are going to use it. If it's going to stay on a lake, there is a whole different kind of sea trial expectation. If they're going to use it on the ocean, they'll want the feel of the boat in two- to three-foot seas.

Robin: **Do you have any tips for boaters on working with a surveyor to ensure a successful survey?**

Rob: Boat buyers have to understand that the day of the boat survey, if you're going to be there, including the sea trial, is a very serious day. It's a day that the in-laws, the out-laws, and the brother-in-law who works on cars under a shade tree should stay home.

The person buying the boat, and if he or she's got a spouse or partner that's going to be involved in the boat, they're the only people that should be at the survey and on the boat for the sea trial. The people buying the boat should be able to stop the surveyor at any point and ask questions. I welcome that. I tape all my surveys. I don't bring a clipboard and make field notes. I speak into a tape player. I've learned over the years that it's a lot more thorough to speak into a tape than to stop and make field notes.

A successful survey comes from the comfort that client has with his surveyor—the surveyor's references and credentials, and the way the boater is treated over the phone when he first calls. Many surveyors will treat a client calling with, let's say, a 21-foot Boston whaler with a single outboard, a lot less well than they would if it was a high ticket survey like a 35- to 40-foot yacht.

It's very important to ask questions of the surveyor to determine the scope of what he is going to do. What I like to do is email my clients after that phone call and put everything in black and white—the scope of what I'm going to do structurally, mechanically, electrically, and with regards to Coast Guard safety.

Closing

Robin: Thank you for being so generous with your time today. You've given both boat owners and buyers a lot to think about with regards to having a survey done and, more importantly, what to look for in a surveyor before they hire one. Rob, how can someone get in touch with you for more information?

Rob: My website is www.MasterMarineSurveyor.com. People can also call me at 781-595-6225 or email me at Rob@MasterMarineSurveyor.com.

Key Points

1. Choose a surveyor that has an extensive background, hands-on education, and credentials in the marine surveying profession. Your surveyor should be a member of NAMS® (National Association of Marine Surveyors®) or SAMS® (Society of Accredited Marine Surveyors®).
2. Most insurance underwriters want an updated insurance survey—structural, mechanical, and electrical—every five to seven years, but not the detailed testing done during a pre-purchase survey.
3. Oil samples should be drawn when the engine's warm, using a separate extraction hose and bottle—everything ultra clean.
4. Wooden boat surveys include a close inspection of the boat's fasteners—random pulling of the screws every four square feet below the water line.
5. A fiberglass boat survey involves percussion-sounding the hull with a phenolic hammer to detect if there are any voids in the lamination of the fiberglass layup.
6. Dry rot on a wooden boat is detected by picking gently at the wood in the boat's frame and stringers. De-lignified wood looks like hair or straw.
7. After sitting on the hard for a couple of years, a boat needs a full condition and valuation survey. This is more detailed than an insurance survey—it includes hull testing, a wiring systems review, a full computer diagnostic, compression testing, and engine analysis.
8. Access the national crime bureau's boat history report to see if a boat has had a problem in the past.
9. If you're buying a boat on a lake and you intend to take it out on open ocean, you can't sea trial it on the lake—you'll want the feel of the boat in two- to three-foot seas.
10. The only people that should be at the survey, and on the boat for the sea trial, are the people actually buying the boat. The buyer should be able to stop the surveyor at any point and to ask questions.

Notes

Insuring a Boat
An Interview with Mike Smith

Introduction

Robin: Hello everyone. This is Robin Coles and it's my pleasure to welcome you to the 2010 Nautical Lifestyle Expert Series brought to you by TheNauticalLifestyle.com. One of the biggest necessities when buying a boat is having insurance. During the next hour we'll be talking with Mike Smith and learning how to determine the right type of insurance for your boat and, just as important, who's mandating which coverage. Hello Mike!

Mike: Hi. I'm sitting here looking out my window at a marina full of boats in a very calm Grand Traverse Bay in Northwest Lower Michigan.

Robin: That sounds heavenly. I'm going to just picture myself right there with you now.

Mike: Come on over. We've got a beautiful day going, it's going to be about 85° with a little breeze—we can go sailing.

Robin: Thank you so much for joining me today. Mike Smith grew up in a boating family, raced sail boats, has boated extensively in the Great Lakes, and has chartered in the Caribbean. Mike began his insurance career in 1975 as a general commercial agent and began specializing in marine insurance in 1984. Michael J. Smith is co-founder, former president, and current senior vice-president of Global Marine Insurance Agency, headquartered in Traverse City, Michigan. Global Marine is an independent marine insurance specialty agency with offices in Florida, California, and Delaware; and with 40 marine insurance professionals insuring boats throughout the US.

Michael is a board member of the National Marine Bankers Association (NMBA) and the Traverse Area Community Sailing non-profit organization. He is a certified instructor in yacht insurance for the Michigan Independent Insurance Agents Association and speaks regularly to groups around the country.

Mike specializes in all forms of marine insurance coverage including charter boats, excursion vessels, marinas, boat dealers, boat rentals, etc. He designed a special endorsement for bare boat charter fleets many years ago, which many companies adopted and still use in their policies today.

Insuring a Boat

Robin: **What are the different types of boat insurance?**

Mike: There are many types of boat insurance, but basically, in our world, there are two main types—one is called a boat policy and one is called a yacht policy. Generally in the industry, the division is between boats that are 26 feet long and below and those 26 feet long and above. Boats 26 feet long and below are usually covered by boat policies, 26 feet long and above are covered by what are called a "true yacht policies." There are differences in coverage, particularly in those two different policies—we can get into more detail on that later in the conference call—but those are the primary types of boat insurance out there. I guess I should add one more—some companies write boats under their homeowner's policies, which we don't do. We don't believe that's the best way for a boat owner to cover their boat unless it's very small—say a 14-15-foot aluminum fishing boat or something like that. Anything of any size, say 18 feet and up, should have either a boat or a yacht policy on it.

Robin: **What's the difference between ACV (actual cash value) and an agreed value?**

Mike: There's a big difference. Your auto policy has an actual cash value (ACV) loss adjustment form in it. This means that when a loss occurs, the value of what is paid to the insured is depreciated. It is adjusted to the current actual cash value of the covered item. For instance, if you own a $100,000 boat and you have an ACV policy, maybe that boat is only worth $80,000 when it sinks or burns or whatever might happen in a total loss. The insurance company has the right to adjust what they pay you based on the boat's current market value (before the loss, of course). They would do studies in the marketplace, look at the *BUC® Used Boat Price Guide*, look at YachtWorld.com, and say, "We think this boat is currently worth $80,000; here's our check." You get a chance to negotiate that, but, at the end of the day, the policy allows them to depreciate the value of the boat.

All that is versus an agreed value policy which is what we prefer and sell probably 99% of the time. An agreed value policy is unique in that when you insure your boat, the insurance company agrees with a certain value as stated on the policy declarations page, and that value is what is paid in the case of a total loss. For instance, with the $100,000 boat, if it's a total loss and there's no salvage or anything, and you've agreed on $100,000 as the value of the boat, you get a check for $100,000, no questions asked, other than how the loss occurred, obviously. When there's a total loss on a true yacht policy, they don't even charge the deductible.

There's a huge difference between the two coverages. The price difference, which you might expect to be substantial, is really quite minimal between agreed value and actual cash value policies. That's why most owners prefer the agreed value policy—it gives them a sense of confidence knowing exactly what they will get in the case of a total loss.

Robin: **What about watercraft versus indemnity liability and pollution coverage.**

Mike: That's the difference between a boat policy and a yacht policy. A boat insurance policy will typically have what is termed watercraft liability, which includes liability for bodily injury and property damage, but may or may not include other coverages that are typically included in a protection and indemnity policy (we shorten that up and call it P&I). P&I insurance is a form of liability coverage designed for maritime exposures and maritime law. It has come down over the years from Lloyds of London traditions of liability coverage. P&I on a true yacht policy—typically, if it's a true yacht policy, and many boat policies are—used to be called watercraft liabilities. There are exceptions; some insurance companies include P&I in their boat policies, but generally not.

Insuring a Boat

There are some major differences between P&I and watercraft liabilities. One of them is the way wreck removal coverage is treated. If you sink your boat in a federally navigable waterway, federal law says you must mark that boat 24 hours a day and/or remove it as quickly as possible. Wreck removal can be a very expensive and onerous process. If it's in the middle of the channel, there's a lot of traffic, you may have to get a barge coming from 100 miles away to try and raise it. Many times when they try to raise a wreck, it's unsuccessful the first or second time, so there's even coverage for attempted wreck removal. What happens is the wreck removal is covered by the P&I or liability portion of the policy—you might have limits of $500,000 of coverage there. If it costs $100,000 to remove the wreck, you've got $100,000 of coverage on the liability side. But then you've still got, let's say, $100,000 of physical damage coverage on that side of the policy whereby we pay for the boat. So, there's no shortage of funds to pay for both of those exposures.

Many boat policies include wreck removal coverage on the hull side. Using the same example, you have a $100,000 boat sink in a federally navigable waterway and it cost $50,000 to raise the wreck. That comes off of the hull value amount, so there's only $50,000 left for coverage of the boat itself—there's a huge difference.

There are other differences. Most P&I policies include pollution coverage. Some boat policies do, but that's a federally mandated responsibility these days. The federal government has said you will be responsible for up to $854,000 of pollution and fuel spill liability. Most yacht policies include it; some boat policies do. It's a very important coverage if you sink your boat and you pollute a bay or a river or a lake. The federal government says, "You get to pay for that." Even if you don't have insurance, you have a financial responsibility per the federal law to clean that spill up. There are huge differences between the two coverages and the pricing difference between P&I and watercraft liability is minimal—it's well worth the extra few dollars you might spend on it.

Robin: **What is covered under boat insurance, or actually, might it be easier to say what *isn't* covered?**

Mike: It *is* easier to say what isn't covered. There are a couple of critical policy exclusions and warranties that really tell you what is *not* covered by your policy. Fortunately, the yacht insurance industry has simplified the language in our policies—it is very easy to read, even if you're not a lawyer. Everyone that buys a policy should read and understand their exclusions and their warranties.

We'll start with the warranty side. Those are promises you make to the company insuring your vessel that you will do certain things. You promise to use the boat only for private pleasure—that's called the private pleasure warranty. You promise to only navigate the waters that are stated on your policy declarations pages. For instance, here in the Great Lakes, the navigation warranty says you may navigate this vessel in the Great Lakes or inland waters, rivers, or tributaries. If you leave those waters without informing the company and getting permission, the policy is voided. There is no coverage if you sink halfway down the Mississippi

River after leaving the Great Lakes. You can get coverage for the Mississippi River—you just have to call your agent and inform them; usually they charge a trip premium for that—but if you don't tell us, there may not be any coverage.

There is a lay-up warranty, usually, on any boats that are kept in the northern part of the country. For instance, you might agree to lay your boat up beginning November 1st and you agree not to put it back in the water and use it until April 1st. If you do put it in the water and use it after November 1st or before April 15th or 1st, whatever date they choose, there may not be coverage for a loss. We've had instances where people have taken their boats out of lay-up five days early because there's a beautiful spring day and they just forget to call and say, "Hey, I'm going to put the boat in the water." If they do call there's coverage; if they don't and have a loss, there isn't any coverage.

You've got your private pleasure warranty, your navigation warranty, and then you've got the exclusions. There is a list of exclusions in all yacht policies and it's a list of maybe 20 things that are not covered. If something happens to your boat in the way of physical damage, and it's not excluded, it's deemed covered. Things that are excluded are wear and tear, depreciation, normal scratches and dents, small stuff like that, osmosis, blistering, electrolysis, maintenance items that you should be doing the maintenance on anyway, marine life not covered, you know, the barnacles and stuff that might do damage. In the Great Lakes, zebra mussels *are* covered—they came out with that coverage some time ago, though we really haven't had any trouble with losses from zebra mussels, but they did decide to cover that. You need to read the list, understand it, and, if you have questions, ask your insurance agent—he should be able to explain those to you.

One interesting exclusion or coverage, if you will, you could look at it both ways, is called 'latent defect.' A yacht policy is very unique in that regard because latent defect covers the engine and machinery for the ensuing damage from a latent defective part. For example, you have a three-year-old boat. Somewhere inside that engine a part is latently defective—you don't know it, the manufacturer didn't know it, he put it in there, but it was cracked when he put it in. At the end of three years, it breaks, and that little, let's say, $2 part causes $5,000 worth of damage. If you can prove that that part was defective that caused this damage on the inside of your engine, the insurance company will pay for the ensuing damage. They won't pay for the $2 part but they'll pay for the parts and labor to repair that engine. Now, there is a duty to prove that that happened and sometimes that's very difficult. Sometimes people have to call in metallurgists to prove this spring was weak and broke. Another thing you have to prove is that you did the maintenance on the boat; that it is in seaworthy condition and was maintained. If you can prove all those things, we buy people new engines sometimes. And that is a very unique coverage in the yacht insurance world. It's not highly publicized, but it is there. It is there for them to use if they need it.

Robin: **If they had to hire a specialist to come in and help prove this, would that expense be reimbursed?**

Insuring a Boat   Mike Smith

Mike: If the loss is covered, yes it would; if the loss is denied, no. But the companies are pretty good. They have their own metallurgists and those metallurgists are objective third parties, typically. But, if the client doesn't believe their report, then they have the right to go out and pay for their own. If the loss ends up being covered, then the insurance company would pay for that. Otherwise, it's the owner's risk.

We don't have very many of those claims. But when they happen, such as a fellow with a big Hatteras and a couple big MTU diesels in there, those are very expensive engines; they're very finely tuned and highly maintained. If they're maintained right and something happens, it can be covered. Unfortunately, to repair a big engine like that or get it out, sometimes you have to cut a hole in the side of the boat and that's covered too.

You need to look at your warranties and your exclusions—that really pertains to the physical damage side of the policy. There are also exclusions on the liability side. They are very standard in the industry and include things like intentional acts—if you intentionally run your boat into somebody and they can prove it, if you intentionally hurt someone aboard your boat and they can prove it, then there is no liability coverage in place. But, there are very few exclusions on the liability side, and it's a very broad coverage.

There are two coverages included in the P&I liability on a yacht policy that are federal laws—one is called the US Long Shore Harbor Worker's Compensation Act (USL&H we call it) and the other is the Jones Act. Those deal with people that are hired to work on the boat on a temporary basis. For instance, a land-based person who is temporarily aboard your boat doing some work on it, that's USL&H coverage. And then there's the Jones Act which is really more for the captain or crew that is paid by the vessel. Both of these coverages are like workers' compensation coverage for these "employees of the boat." They could both be temporary employees, but a Jones Act seaman is in the duty of the ship—there are clear definitions of what makes a Jones Act seaman—if they're deemed a Jones Act seaman, then there is coverage for that exposure and it is very extensive coverage, well beyond the limits and the coverages of a standard state workers' compensation coverage. I'm getting a little technical here, excuse me. Those are two important coverages that are not used much at all in the recreational boating insurance industry, but are important to have if, for instance, I own a 46-foot something and I hire a captain to take it up to the marina 20 miles away. If something seriously happens to the captain, he's injured or killed or whatever, g-d forbid. The Jones Act coverage in that policy responds and takes care of that man's medical bills, his rehabilitation, lost wages, etc.—it's important coverage to have.

Morally speaking, all employers in this country are supposed to be carrying workers' comp on their employees and this is an extension of that.

Robin: **How much boat insurance does a boater need?**

Mike: That's a moving target. We all know boat values have been decreasing right along with our wonderful home values. Typically an insurance company underwrites the boat based on its current sale price adding in any additional extras that are added and adding the sales tax. For example, you pay $100,000 for a new boat and you say, "Put on $15,000 of electronics and I'm going to pay sales tax of $10,000." Add those numbers up and that's what you would want in the way of agreed value coverage on that boat and its equipment. Then you'd probably want to have $500,000 of liability coverage or more. You can buy all the way up to $100 million of liability coverage, but typical recreational boater we see today has probably somewhere between $300,000 and $500,000 of liability coverage.

When you buy a used boat, though, that's more of a moving target. You do have a purchase price on it. Maybe there's a trade-in at the dealer, even on a new boat there could be. You have to kind of figure out these values. If it's a used boat, and you bought it from your neighbor in the boat yard, and maybe you needed a survey to get the boat insured, and the surveyor says it's worth $100,000, and you paid $80,000, and you'd like to insure it for $100,000, the insurance company may say, "We don't know about that—we've looked in the BUC book (*BUC® Used Boat Price Guide*) and even though the surveyor thinks it's worth $100,000, the BUC book or YachtWorld.com says it's worth $90,000." There are some negotiations that take place and the insurance industry has some flexibility.

The key issue here is that the insurance companies do not want to over-insure anything to create an increased moral hazard. By moral hazard I mean that when you know that you have an agreed value policy, it becomes almost a guarantee of what you would get if the boat sinks or is a total loss. We have had instances over the years where boat owners who get in (financial) trouble for whatever reason—divorce, bankruptcy, whatever—decide that they don't want the boat anymore and they can't sell it; they owe more than it's worth; so they go out and they find a deep hole and they scuttle it. That hurts us all because we all end up paying for that loss in our premiums. That's insurance fraud, clearly. What happens is if the insurance company over-insures something, they just increase that moral hazard potential. Now, very few boat owners do that, but big picture-wise that is something that the industry looks at and tracks very closely, because they don't want to pay for some intentional insurance fraud loss.

The value is somewhat negotiable when you insure it. If you clearly have a bill of sale for $100,000 and you add these things it's pretty straightforward. If you get into a trade, and the value of the trade is nebulous, and the price is way too low, you know there's some discussion that has to take place. At the end of the day, when you buy an agreed value policy, the insurance company says this is what it's insured for, you know what it's insured for and as I said earlier, if she sinks that's what you get.

Robin: **What are the steps to follow before buying boat insurance?**

Mike: Find an insurance company or agent that knows what they're doing, that knows something about boats. There are a lot of good marine specialty agents in this country; you can find them on the web very easily. These agencies are typically owned or managed or run by boaters who have the water gene, who love boating, who understands the industry. They typically represent many different insurance companies like us, an independent agency, we represent 20 different marine insurance companies. We get to shop around, like in the ads for

Insuring a Boat — Mike Smith

Progressive Insurance where the dog pushes the button and shops around—that's us, not to steal Progressive's thunder here, and we actually sell for Progressive. Basically, find somebody that knows what they're doing, has access to the best products in the marketplace, and also has access to and can quickly shop around. The industry is changing all the time. On any given day, one company says we will write coverage in Florida, and this company over here, Company B, says, "We don't want any business in Florida; we're full up. Our capacity is over burdened with hurricane exposure right now. We need to write more business in the Great Lakes or on the east coast or whatever." It's a very fluctuating industry. It's hard for us to keep track of, but it's what we're paid to do. For example, we might say, "This company is very competitive in the Great Lakes; it's not competitive in California. Here's a company that's got some really neat new coverages that are unique and they are still competitive, so you should take a hard look at that product." There are a lot of coverage differences to make comparisons on; an independent agent that can make those choices available to the boat owner is the best possible scenario.

If a perspective boat owner goes out to the web and shops just one company, I think they are doing themselves a disservice, because we know for sure that one company can't be all things to all people. If you're lucky in that in your circumstances—your boat, your use, and everything—fit exactly that company's underwriting box and they're pricing is good, then ok, you got a good deal and a good policy. But we all know that it pays to shop around. If you go to a website that automatically shops for you, you can get some options to look at and maybe custom design your own policy—there are some websites out there like that. If you type in yacht insurance or boat insurance and Google™ brings up a list, that's probably going to be a pretty good list of independent agents and some direct-writing insurance companies. When I say direct writing, that means that the boat owner goes directly to the insurance company. In the case of Progressive, for instance, you can buy online directly from Progressive, or you can buy from a company like ours through Progressive and the prices are the same. The difference is that we have underwriters that know and shop the marketplace, and Progressive uses a computerized rating system. We get the same rate that Progressive does given the same information, but we might shop two or three other companies and compare that with Progressive and say, "Here are some coverage differences that really make a difference."

If you just shop price, the old adage still holds true—you get what you pay for. There are yacht policies out there that are very low… I can't think of a good term to describe it, but compare it to a cheap car with very few bells and whistles versus a Lexus or a Cadillac or a Mercedes. A lot of times, the better policies are priced competitive even with the fewer bells and whistles policies, because they are designed by companies that know the industry, know where the losses come from, and can throw in a lot of bells and whistles. They write enough volume that they can afford to do that. My advice would be to go on the web and shop around; find somebody that maybe your boat mate in the marina referred you to, or you heard the name or the branding—many of these agencies have been around. We've been around for 25 years and that's all we do is marine boat insurance. There are lots of agencies out there like us, that do the same thing. There are some direct writing companies like State Farm and Allstate and Progressive and some others that have boat products and yacht products, but when they quote you a price it's just one company's price. If you take that and compare it with the rest of the world, then let the chips fall where they may, as they say.

Robin: **What exactly *does* affect the cost of boat insurance?**

Mike: Certainly the value of the hull has a huge affect. There are two sections to a yacht or boat policy—the physical damage and the liability side. The physical damage side is probably where 80% of the premium comes from. We'll use the $100,000 boat value again—the premium is, let's say, $1,000—the boat's down in Florida, on the east coast, or something like that; $800 of that $1,000 premium would be for the hull and $200 would be for the liability, and we'll use $500,000 limits of P&I liability for that—those two factors really bear on the premium directly.

Many other factors bear on the premium amount. In today's world, many yacht marine insurance companies have gone to insurance scoring, which includes a credit score, whether you're married or not, how old you are, and how much experience you have in both operating and owning a boat—that's real important in the scheme of things as to the quality of boater you are. If you've had experience in ownership and use—you know the local waters—then the insurance industry competes aggressively for that business. If you have a good credit score or if you score well in all these other areas, the rates are as low as I have seen them in 40 years for a good quality boater. Even though the boating industry is in a steep decline from a sales perspective, the insurance industry wants to attract and keep good boaters that don't have losses; the rates have reflected that, maybe not so much in Florida because of the hurricane thing, but, even there, capacity has increased and rates have begun to decrease because people are now utilizing hurricane plans. But in the Great Lakes and California, the rates are as low as I've ever seen them. Companies want good business. If you can tell the story about how good you are—experienced and with no losses—a lot of things factor into how they rate you. More and more, computer systems are doing the ratings—they're taking all these factors into account; they have these great big formulas with logarithms and everything. They can factor in these 32 different metrics and come up with a rate that fits just you, for instance, for a really good policy. Some companies have not gone to insurance scoring yet. They still do it kind of by the seat of their pants; not so much, but it's a little less structured. If you shop around, you'll get to view all these various different rates and companies. You'd be surprised how much difference there can be between companies on a given risk and a given navigation territory—it's amazing to us. There can be $200, $300, $400 difference between companies—it certainly pays to shop around. The value of the boat, the liability coverage, and the extra coverages that you get—these all have a bearing on the cost of the insurance. Some companies have what is called a disappearing deductible, which is a very nice feature. If you buy a policy, every year that you don't have a loss, your deductible decreases by 25%. At the end of four years, you have a zero deductible on your hull insurance coverage. Now, if you have a loss, the loss is paid with whatever deductible applies at that time. If it's maybe 50% of the original deductible or now maybe you're lucky and it's down to zero, but then the deductible resets back to the original amount. And we can talk about deductibles a little bit here too, because that affects the premium. Typically on the yacht policy, the standard deductible is one percent of the insured value. Using our $100,000 hull value, one percent would be $1,000 hull deductible. Some companies, very few, have a stated deductible like $500. But most yacht policies are one percent of the value. If you want to go to a two percent hull deductible, you save a little premium by doing that. You can go to a three percent deductible. Down in Florida and the Gulf Coast States there is a different deductible for a named storm. If your boat is damaged by a hurricane that has a name, it is usually ten percent of the hull value that is deductible. That really gives a boat owner an incentive to get that boat out of harms way before a storm hits. The insurance industry is highly exposed down there; when Andrew and those other storms in '04 and '05 came through, the insurance industry paid the most they've ever paid out in boat losses. They sat up and took notice and said we better do some risk management here and figure out how to reduce this exposure, which they did. And the boat owners have responded—they have built hurricane proof buildings down there, they've got hurricane holes, they are better prepared—there are ways that you can protect your boat and get it through a hurricane with minimum or no losses. The deductible affects the premium; the values that you purchased affect it, the coverages, like the disappearing deductible. There's personal affects coverage that's included, you can maybe get $5,000 personal affects coverage and you have more than that on your big yacht, so you buy $50,000 personal affects coverage for your furniture, TVs, and stuff like that—you can spend more premium there. There are lots of optional coverages that you can add on and some of them add premium. There are many factors—that's again why dealing with a marine insurance specialist that knows all these things and can say, "Yeah, that's a good value," "No, you don't need that," or "Oh, you're going to take a trip some place. Are you going to make the great circle tour?" If you are, we need to know that, we need to extend the navigation, and usually there's a trip charge. If you're going to take your boat to Florida, but you keep it in the Great Lakes in the summer time, there's a different premium for the Great Lakes versus Florida. There are a myriad of factors that enter into what your final premium's going to be. And if you change your mind in the middle of the policy period and you tell us, maybe we reduce the premium, maybe we increase it, based on what you're doing. Talk to a good marine specialist and you'll find out all those different factors.

Robin: **Let's just talk about the credit score for a minute, because you mentioned that. I know when you're trying to get financing for a boat, you need to have a stellar score of at least 720 or better. Is that the same with boat insurance?**

Mike: No, it is not. There is no hard and fast rule as to whether you qualify or not. What the insurance companies do is base their rates on where your credit score is, but they also factor in many other measurements. These might include age, boating experience, and all those other things. Based on just your credit score, you don't qualify or not qualify. The price changes based on all those factors going through a big computer system and saying this is the level of risk based on all these factors. Here's the premium based on what we think this risk is; versus this other person with a different set of risk criteria.

The insurance industry has proven to a very real degree that if you have a book of business, you have many boats insured, and they all have good credit score—and I won't define that, it's kind of a moving target—your loss ratio will be reduced by 15%. This is a huge number when you're talking hundreds of millions of dollars in premiums. What that has done, I think (this is my personal opinion), is helped reduce the premium for boaters country wide because many boaters have good credit scores. If you insure a lot of boaters with bad credit scores then you have a 15% worse loss ratio, the rates for that company have got to go up to cover their losses. In many ways, the emphasis on good credit scores has had a positive effect on our insurance industry—people understand they need a good credit score or that affects their auto insurance, their homeowner's insurance, and now their boat insurance.

Robin: **If they've had some issue with their credit, they need to talk to the agent about it before they continue, right?**

Mike: We don't really talk to our clients about their credit scores. We present them a premium. We don't know what the credit score is. The insurance companies do not share that with us. We know that if one company that is using an insurance score comes up with a premium of, let's say, $1,000, and we've put it through our automated rating system and quoted it to 12 companies or five companies or whatever it fits, and we see that another company that does not use insurance scoring comes up with a premium of $800 and it's the same coverage, then we would say, here's an $800 premium, here are the coverages and this is what we would suggest you take a hard look at. Some companies don't believe in insurance scoring or don't want to use it or haven't invested in it yet because it's a very costly system to implement. There are companies out there that may never use insurance scoring. That's good, because then somebody that's a boater that maybe had a situation where it wasn't really their fault...

Robin: Like in the case of identity theft or something...

Mike: Or a divorce that really decimates somebody's economic situation...

Robin: Or job losses, as we have today...

Mike: ...exactly—things happen. We don't know what your credit score is; we don't want to know, but when we get a quote back from a company that uses credit scores, we say here's an option. Now what we need to know is, is this really a good boater? Can he or she convince us that they're worthy of this good policy at $800 without a credit score? There are a lot of them out there—a lot of old salts or good boaters that know what they're doing that are worthy of that lower price even though their credit score might not be stellar.

Robin: It just seems that since the country's gone to this credit score thing, a lot of people are losing out on things because of it.

Mike: I wouldn't disagree with that, but in our industry there are options available to take care of that. I feel good about that because even though they have had some bad luck they can still get a very competitive, quality yacht policy. As big supporters of the marine industry—we make our living here—that's a good thing.

Robin: **What kinds of insurance are marinas, boat yards, and yacht clubs requiring? And, why the difference?**

Mike: Maritime law is a lot different than normal tort law; marinas and boat dealers have different coverage needs than normal businesses. They have an open lot with about $3 million of boats sitting there. They operate on the water so they need P&I; they need Jones Act coverage; they might need USL&H; they need workers' comp which is designed for the maritime exposures. Within the insurance industry, there are a few marine specialists that know what they're doing, but it's not a huge industry compared to the rest of the insurance world. These unique coverages need to be insured by a company that knows and understands the risks and by an agent that really knows and understands the risks. As I think you mentioned earlier, I've been doing charter fleets for 30 years. There are very unique coverages that they need which cover everybody very well, but most insurance companies say, "Oh no, we don't want the risk, we don't understand the risk, and no, thank you," which is fine. That's a business decision they make. But these marine people need these coverages. It's a very competitive market right now. The boating industry is in a decline, so everybody is fighting for market share in a declining market. We put ourselves out as experts in that area, travel all over the country, and help commercial marine businesses risk manage so they don't have losses. Companies that don't have losses have lower insurance costs at the end of the day, which increases their profits. That's what we like to help them do.

Robin: **When a boater shows up at a marina, or calls a marina or boat yard to say they're coming in, maybe as a transient or to get a slip for the season, some marinas are requiring $100,000 to $300,000 in liability coverage. Some of the boaters get upset because the marinas are asking to see that much coverage.**

Mike: The marinas are coming from a perspective of risk management. If you pull into a marina and you cause a liability loss or you start a fire on your boat and you burn up boats all around you—you may or may not be negligent. The marina carries insurance, obviously, and that insurance company is saying, "Look, all these boats cause exposure for us and we want to be an additional named insured and get a certificate of insurance from the boat owners." Most responsible boat owners have insurance. If they don't want to insure the boats for physical damage—maybe it's all paid for at the bank and they don't care about that—they can buy just liability coverage all by itself at a very low premium, which they should have, because if somebody is injured or drowns or something on their boat, they should have that protection if they get sued. We think it's reasonable in the industry for marinas to say, "Hey, you're using our marina. If something happens, we're additional insured. Yes, we have insurance, but you will be named in the law suit, we'll be named in the law suit, and we probably are a deeper pocket than you are. We want to be protected by your coverage and we're protected by our coverage." It's kind of a doubling up.

It doesn't cost anything for the boat owner to add them as additional insured and get a certificate of insurance. None of the companies I know charge for that. Yes, it's a bit of a hassle. You have to call your agent and say here's the name and address of the marina where I'm keeping my boat, please send them a certificate of insurance. We do it all day long—it's just part of the service of an insurance agency.

Robin: **Is that when the boater is using a particular marina or boat yard for the season? What if they're a transient?**

Mike: We don't see it in the transient world—maybe you have information that I don't have—typically this is for a seasonal slip renter. They know they're going to be there for a while and it's worth a few minutes to get the certificate. It's a bit of a hassle for the marina to manage all this—who did they get it from, who didn't they get it from—they've got to follow up. It's kind of a pain for them. If their insurance company didn't demand it, they probably wouldn't do it—it costs them money.

Robin: **Are there different types of surveys required by insurance companies? If so, what are they?**

Mike: There are two basic kinds of surveys that we deal with—in the water or hauled surveys. Different insurance companies have different rules for when they demand or require surveys. In fresh water, the companies don't usually require a survey on a boat looking for insurance unless it's 15 years old or older. In salt water, most of them are required right around 10 years. Most of the insurance companies we represent require a NAMS® (National Association of Marine Surveyors®) or SAMS® (Society of Accredited Marine Surveyors®) surveyor do the survey. Now, there are other qualified groups that they will accept as well, but those are the two most well known groups of professional surveyors. And, both of those groups have done a pretty good job of building their brand and building their professionalism and I know one of them actually has a professional liability policy in place for their members, which is good. We like to do business with people who are substantial, professional, and have insurance.

There's a huge difference between any two surveyors. Some are really careful, really get into the minutia, write up a good report, really are objective, and you can see that in their work. Others may be sloppy, not so careful, they just use check-off forms, you see a survey come in that's three pages and it's nothing but a list of what's on the boat, with a couple of recommendations on the back just to prove that he looked at the boat. Versus, you get a 20-page report with pictures and a substantial written report at the back that says, "These recommendations are critical; these recommendations are not so critical; these recommendations could be done at leisure,"—it gives you a real photograph in time of what this boat is like. If it's a hauled survey, they'll do the hull soundings and check for water intrusion, hull rigidity, and all those things. If it's in the water, they look at everything above the water line, obviously.

We get a lot of surveys. One factor that affects boat insurance cost is the age of the boat. As the age gets older, the premiums go up, typically. Because, older boats, it is proven, have more losses—it's just as simple as that. When we get an older boat in here, we look at the survey real good, we look at the owner's experience, we underwrite both, and we say, "Yup, this is worthy of this rate," or, "It's an old boat and in less than good condition; we've got a good owner; it's worth this rate." It pays for the owner to shop around and find the best rate and coverage and educate themselves on what the differences might be.

Insuring a Boat   Mike Smith

***Robin:* Why is it so difficult to get insurance for wooden boats?**

Mike: If the boat has been restored or partially restored, it isn't. We used to insure wooden boats, the classic old wood runabouts, cruisers, and things like that—the old Krisses, MasterCrafts, all those old Centuries, and everything. Certainly Hagerty Insurance is one of the nation's leading old wood boat insurers. We no longer even compete or write for that business, because they do such a good job. I think they've got over 50% market share. If it's a runabout and it's been restored, there's no problem getting insurance—very competitive, good coverages. If it's a cruiser, been restored or partially restored, good survey—no problem getting it. Where you run into a problem is an old wood boat that hasn't been maintained, hasn't been restored, and is just sitting there slowly rotting away. Nobody wants that risk because it is a proven risk that it will sink or burn at the dock or something will happen and they'll just pay out a lot of money on it. Or, somebody's hurt aboard and the housekeeping's not good. There are, forgive the term, bad risks out there, and nobody wants to write those because if one insurance company insures a whole bunch of old wood boats and they have a lot of losses, their rates have got to go up to cover that and the rest of us that are insured by that company pay a higher rate. Now, we can go someplace else, obviously, but maybe we've been insured with the company for five years, their rates go up, we go shopping, but we can't move unless we get a new survey—that costs us $500-800 to move to a different company—we're kind of stuck then. It helps keep the industry fleet in a better condition. Insurance is a bit of a social mechanism that helps reduce the risks for everybody—everybody who owns a boat and buys insurance shares the risk of everybody else. You couldn't afford to buy insurance if you were just one person covering the whole risk for your boat and your liability, obviously. Just like all other insurance, you could probably afford to pay off the $100,000 note at the bank, but if somebody sues you for a half a million dollars, that gets a little tougher.

***Robin:* How can boaters find Hagerty Insurance?**

Mike: They're online—www.Hagerty.com.

***Robin:* How do you make a claim?**

Mike: It's real easy. Most of the time, even though there's a loss involved, if no one is injured, the physical damage loss claims really go pretty smoothly. That's one thing I like about our industry—we have about 99.5% customer satisfaction after a claim. Part of this is because it's a unique policy that's run and managed by marine specialists, and the tradition in the marine insurance industry is you find a way in the policy to cover a claim. It is an unwritten tradition in our industry to say, "This client is worthy of our diligent efforts to find a way to pay this claim." Now, if it's clearly excluded or if they breached a warranty, then there's not going to be any coverage.

Basically there's an 800 number that you can call 24/7. Typically that puts you right into the insurance company's claims department. You can call your agent. We take claims reports all the time, we transfer that information to the insurance company's claims department and from that point on you deal directly with the insurance company's claims adjustment department. These people are well versed in marine claims—some of them are surveyors, current or former—and they know the policy coverages backwards and forwards; their job is to quickly adjust a claim; and they do an excellent job of it, they really do. A lot of times they won't even send anybody to look at it. If you get an estimate from your local marina and they look at the estimate and they say, "These prices are in line," even though they may be a little bit high compared to the rest of the world or the rest of the region—they do check to make sure that the marinas aren't overcharging—but if they're not and if they're in line, they say, "Go ahead." You don't have to shop around and get three estimates; they just say, "Go ahead."

All policies say that they have a right to see the old parts if they want to. Someone should save those parts until they've been released by the insurance company. Even on big claims, even if it's a total loss, they say, "Yup, looks good," and boom, "Here's your check." If there are issues, problems, slow service; that's where the agent jumps back in. We want to hear from our customers if there's an issue or there's a problem. We represent every major marine insurance company; we're one of the largest in the country, so we have some clout. We start making some phone calls and find out what the problem is. Usually there are three sides to every two-sided story—you have to try and sort it out and find the middle ground. If there are some negotiations that need to take place, we can have some input on that—that's part of what we get paid for, to help clients get through a difficult claim situation, because not everything is black and white; there are gray areas.

Many boat owners don't understand their coverages. They don't know that there's a warranty in there. We have a lot of people say, "I didn't know that." You know what? In today's world, who sits around reading their yacht policy or auto policy or homeowner's policy? I read it for fun! My passion is to understand the yacht insurance world. But I'm unique in that regard, probably. There can be some difficulties in a claims situation, but there are very few. In the end, most yacht insurance policy claimants are very satisfied with the speed and adjustment. They know there's a deductible and they've got to pay that unless it's a total loss, unless they've got a disappearing deductible, which is a nice feature.

There are types of losses that can get difficult just from the type of loss it is—one would be salvage. Salvage has been an issue in our industry for a long time. If you're on a boat and your cruising along and for some reason you lose an engine and your boat goes on the rocks, but it's a calm day and Grandma and the kids are on board and you call a tow company and say, "Get me off the rocks," and they say, "We'll be there in a while," and all of a sudden the wind picks up, and the boat starts to crunch into these rocks, and it looks like its going to be holed, it becomes the difference between a tow just pulling you off this rocky sandbar or, all of a sudden, your life and your family's life is in jeopardy, and the boat is in jeopardy of being holed, and sinking, and polluting, and all those other things that can happen. Now, it's a salvage. The minute it turns into a salvage, the maritime laws allow that salver to charge a whole lot more money.

He can literally claim the entire value of the boat, depending on the risk that he puts out to save that boat. The courts have gotten very good at negotiating these salvage issues. But, from the boater's concern, if you're standing there and start to see these waves crashing in and you're in trouble, all you care about is getting the heck off that boat and saving the boat. The first priority is always to get the people in a safe situation and then take care of the boat. The salver is risking his life, limb, and equipment to save that boat and save you, so he is due a lot more payment than it would be for just a normal tow. Sometimes a tower might be less than honest and straightforward—there are a few, but not very many—and he talks to you on the radio and says, "This is a salvage job; it's going to be a salvage charge," and you say "Ok, just come get me." You're not in a very strong position to negotiate, which is ok—we don't want you to negotiate at that time. We want you to save your life and your family and your boat, and let us, the insurance company, negotiate with that salver. We're very good at it. We know what the charges should be—let us step in and take care of that for you. But, the emotional situation can be trying sometimes in those situations is all I was trying to say.

Robin: Can you talk about SeaTow, BoatUS, and what to watch for?

Mike: BoatUS (also known as TowBoatUS) has an agreement with SeaTow that they will work together. They have an arrangement whereby if you call for a tow—you run out of gas or something like that—it's part of a BoatUS membership that you have some towing coverage. All yacht policies today, whether you buy it from BoatUS or from us through another company, have towing coverage—it's in everybody's policy. You can buy high limits; you get automatic limits—that coverage is there; so is the salvage coverage in all good yacht policies. What BoatUS has done is negotiated with the towing companies to have a set salvage fee arrangement based on certain factors that they run into. I think that probably saves them some money in the end for salvage claims. There aren't a huge number of salvage claims that happen in this country because typically boaters are pretty safe and rarely do they get into trouble. When they do, you go through that whole salvage situation I just said. They've done a good job of helping the boater get towed off the sandbars, but still do it in a cost effective way.

Robin: If you already have this on your insurance, SeaTow and BoatUS are additional?

Mike: Yeah—I've been a member of BoatUS for many years and I have towing coverage on my membership. On my yacht policy, I have towing as well. I have double coverage, but the cost is minimal. The towing coverage on a yacht policy is basically a throw-in and I think I pay $25 a year for my BoatUS membership. The reason I belong to BoatUS is not necessarily for the towing, but for all the good they do. You know, they help us politically with lobbying, they have a nice foundation. They have an EPIRB rental program and a lifejacket give away program, so even though they're a competitor, they do a lot of good for the boating industry, and I'm very supportive of that.

Robin: Mike, I want to thank you for being so generous with your time today. You've given both boat owners and buyers a lot to think about with regards to insuring their boats. But, more important, they need to shop around and also when they do get that policy, they need to read it, and I think you've actually helped them understand what they're looking at on their policy.

Mike: I hope so, Robin, I really do. We care about this industry, obviously. We insure many boaters all over the country and the world, for that matter, from jet skis to mega-yachts to casino boats to excursion charter boats; whatever. We really do care about our customer, because we want to keep them as a customer and protect their recreational boats and commercial boats. It's an industry that we love. We belong to many associations and are very supportive. It's a fun business, that's what I really like about it. I used to sell auto and homeowner's insurance many years ago—that's just pretty much a generic, same old/same old product. But, you talk to somebody about their brand new boat and, man, there's excitement in the air. They love learning about how to insure their boat, many of them do, and just want to get out on that water and enjoy the boating lifestyle. That's what it's all about. I love the boating lifestyle; many of my employees are boaters, so they love the boating lifestyle. We have this passion in common and that really makes it a lot more fun.

Robin: You can hear it when you talk about this subject.

Mike: I certainly am passionate about it.

Closing

Robin: **How can somebody find you if they want more information?**

Mike: The phone number at my desk is 800-748-0224. Our website is www.GlobalMarineInsurance.com. They can actually put their information in there and we will shop it via the computer for them and give them three different quotes.

I highly recommend that once they get their quotes, they pick up the phone and call one of our underwriters and ask any questions they have; get some education. We like to have educated clients, because they know what they're getting, there's a value attached to that, and then there aren't any bad surprises down the road.

Key Points

1. Boats that are 26 feet long and under are covered by "boat" insurance policies; longer boats are covered by "true yacht" insurance policies.
2. An agreed value policy is unique in that when you insure your boat, the insurance company agrees to a certain value—stated on the policy declarations page—and that value is what is paid in the case of a total loss.
3. Make sure you read and understand the exclusions and warranties on your marine insurance policy.
4. Before buying boat insurance, find an insurance company or agent that knows what they're doing and knows about boats.
5. The value of the hull (physical damage) and liability are the two main sections of a boat insurance policy.
6. Wooden boat insurance is available through Hagerty Insurance at www.hagerty.com.
7. The two basic types of boat surveys are 'in the water' and 'hauled' surveys.

Insuring a Boat   Mike Smith

8. Your marina may be added to your policy as an "additional insured" at no extra cost.
9. To file a claim, call the insurance company's 800 telephone number—that puts you right into the claims adjustment department.
10. Once you get a quote, call the underwriter and ask questions—education can prevent unpleasant surprises later on.

Notes

Notes

Financing a Boat Purchase
An Interview with Jim Coburn

Introduction

Robin: Hello everyone. This is Robin Coles and it's my pleasure to welcome you to the 2010 Nautical Lifestyle Expert Series brought to you by TheNauticalLifestyle.com. One of the biggest obstacles to buying a boat is getting, or more to the point, qualifying for financing. During the next hour we'll be talking with Jim Coburn of Coburn and Associates and learning how to determine the financial side of purchasing your boat. Hello Jim!

Jim: Hi Robin. Thanks for having me today.

Robin: Thank *you* so much for joining me. Jim Coburn is a managing partner of Coburn and Associates LLC, a financial and advisory firm located in Macomb, MI. Jim works with banks, finance companies, dealerships, associations, and other businesses. He most recently worked for Flagstar Bank and First of America/National City Bank (now PNC) as a senior vice president and manager of consumer lending divisions in southeast Michigan.

He has 30 years of commercial banking experience, managing most areas of consumer finance.

Jim has been a member of the National Marine Bankers Association (NMBA) since 1983. He was first elected to the NMBA's board of directors in 1995, after serving as an appointed regional advisor for seven years. He also was elected the Association's secretary and treasurer for four and five years respectively. Jim served as NMBA's president twice—from 2000 to 2002 and 2006 to 2010. He is currently an NMBA director and immediate past president.

Jim is very active in the recreation finance and marine industries. He is a founding director of the Recreational Boating Industries Educational Foundation (RBIEF), a Michigan scholarship foundation. He was also elected a director of the Michigan Boating Industries Association, a group serving dealerships, marinas, and other related businesses in the state of Michigan. He is serving, or was serving, as a member of the Soundings Trade-Only Editorial Advisory Board, Grow Boating Advisory Council, Grow Boating Task Force Statistics Steering Committee (TASS), Marine Industries Association of South Florida (MIASF), and several other marine, recreational vehicle, and automotive industry associations related to consumer financing.

Wow, Jim, that's quite an impressive background!

Jim: As you get to be as old as I am, I guess those accomplishments are pretty easy to come by. I really hope I can help some boat buyers with their finance information today.

Financing a Boat Purchase

Robin: **When it comes to financing a boat today, it seems to be more involved than in years past. What's the first step a boater should take in figuring out what they can afford?**

Jim: Financing a boat purchase might *appear* to be more involved than in years past, but really it's not. What happened was that the mortgage meltdown and financial crisis, which kind of started around the summer of 2007, caused some consumer boat lenders to change their loan approval processes back to more conservative procedures or even exit those business lines altogether. Less overall boat sales in the U.S. has also added to that perception.

The first step a boater should take when thinking of financing is do your financial homework and run a budget before you buy your new or pre-owned boat. In the budget, be sure to allow for boating-related expenses, such as general maintenance, the storage of your boat, insurance, and other important add-on products you may want, such as extended warranties.

Simply measure those expenses next to your income. This will give you a great idea of how much payment you can afford and how much debt you can take on. The first step is really a self-prescreening of your financial picture so that you're confident and prepared to enjoy the process of buying your boat. It's the smart thing to do and it will save you some time.

Robin: I talk to a lot of different boaters and every now and then I actually show a sail boat to someone. The first thing they say is, "I can afford this, sort of, but I don't know how much I should be putting aside for maintenance." A lot of them don't actually budget for ancillary costs. **Is that one of the things, in your experience, that boaters *don't* do is put a budget together or forget to include some of these things?**

Jim: That's right, Robin. You mentioned maintenance. Another one is something as simple as gasoline or fuel for the boat. A lot of people have changed their behavior over the years, particularly in recent years with the cost of fuel going up so much. That's something else that you definitely want to budget into your process to make sure the boating experience is a good one for you. Some of these things are the fixed and variable costs in your boat budget. Budgeting is always a wise thing to do. It's going to save you a lot of time and money and get you your boat loan.

Robin: **How does a boat loan compare to a car loan or even a home mortgage?**

Jim: The terms are the big differential when you compare these three types of loans—boats, cars, or residential mortgages. The loan term (the length of the loan in months), your monthly payment, and the cost of your loan are all related.

Typical boat loans can be financed for up to 240 months (that's 20 years, if you're keeping track). A loan amount of $100,000 or greater is where you're going to get your 20-year term. In comparison, typical car loans finance for 60-84 months (5-7 years). The term of a car loan also depends on the amount borrowed, but the amount is usually a lot less than a boat loan. Mortgage loans are a little different. They're typically available for 360 months (30 years). Residential mortgages often require payment of "points," where boat loans generally do not.

Remember, it is always wiser to finance your boat for the shortest term possible. Remember this formula: *Shorter term = higher payments = lower total interest charges to you.* A shorter term can save you money in the amount of interest you pay your lender and it reduces your loan balance faster.

Financing a Boat Purchase — Jim Coburn

There are other general terms for a boat loan. Here are two of the most popular.
- 15 years is a finance term for a minimum finance amount of $25,000
- 12 years for a $15,000 finance amount

As you can see, boat loan terms are much more generous than those of car loans and help make boating more affordable. Mortgage loans have higher monthly terms available for a fixed asset and that asset has a better chance to appreciate over time, where boats and cars generally depreciate over time.

Robin: **What are the required documents for getting a boat loan?**

Jim: Documents to complete a boat loan with a bank or finance company are fairly easy to deal with, particularly when you start comparing them to a residential mortgage. Typical loan documents will include:

- A *credit application* to be completed and signed by all borrowers

- A *personal financial statement of your assets and liabilities.* This would include proof of your income, which would mean you'd have to submit pay vouchers or tax returns to the bank. They may request them for larger boat loans or in certain situations. Submission of these forms occurs *before* a loan decision is made by the bank, so keep that in mind.

- A completed and signed bank or finance company *contract*. This is also known as a note and security agreement for the boat loan.

- *Proof of insurance*. Your boat must be insured to mitigate your and the bank's risk of loss. The bank will want to be a loss payee on your boat, so proof of insurance is a must.

- Appropriate *title* work or documentation that shows that you are the correct owner and borrower and that the bank or finance company is the first secured party or first lien holder.

- A *bill of sale* describes the entire boat transaction, including financial, which would show a down payment as well.

- A *delivery receipt* has popped up as a loan requirement in the last five or six years. This shows that you actually took physical possession of the boat when you signed the loan contract.

- The last thing to talk about is proper legal *identification*. This most often might be a state driver's license supplemented by two other forms of identification. Name, spelling, and addresses must match on all forms of identification and match the information on all the other documents you provide. Signatures are verified during this process in order to maintain proper identification.

That's it.

Robin: That's it? That's a lot!

Jim: Compared to a mortgage though, it really isn't—it's pretty simple. Again, the larger your boat loan, the more documents you'll need. Here I tried to cover all the possible documents to give the boat buyers out there a chance to see what maximally they might need.

Robin: **Does the bank or finance company look at the boater's credit report itself or is the decision based on a credit score? And what's the difference?**

Jim: Yes, the banks and finance companies purchase credit reports from the major credit agencies in the U.S. and they do review them. The big three credit agencies are Trans Union, Experian, and Equifax. Your lender wants to know what your willingness to pay back the boat loan will be. The credit report provides that data by recording your payment history with all your other creditors.

Many boat loan interest rates are based on perceived risk or your past history in paying loans to banks or financial institutions. This is measured by your credit score. The higher your credit score, the more favorable your interest rate may be with a particular bank. If you are doing your financing business with a dealer or a boat service company, be sure your credit history and lender options are discussed *before* your loan application is submitted by them to the bank. Most lenders in our country have excellent availability for prime boat loans with credit scores of 720 and higher. The maximum credit score is 850.

In summary, remember, your credit score is *your* payment story. It determines the loan approval and often what your interest rate will be. Good or bad, you've earned it!

Robin: **The required credit scores are now 720 and higher?**

Jim: 720 is a measure and for "A" credit, that's what it is. It's interesting that you bring that up because before the finance crisis happened, credit was maybe a little too free wheeling and easy for some. A lot of banks and financial institutions did get burned, the boat guys not as much as the mortgage guys, as you've probably been reading. Consequently, the credit score financing threshold is 25 or 30 points above what it used to be.

Robin: Wow—that's unbelievable—you have to have almost perfect credit now!

Jim: Look at it this way. You don't have to have almost perfect credit; you have to have a high score—720 is an indicator that I'm giving you. What this has done is it has taken credit 'back to the future.' We're looking at credit underwriting guidelines that were in place 20 years ago. It's no different from then. What happened in the past 20 years is that lenders got away from good underwriting criteria. A minimum score of 720 is not a new thing, it's just what it is today.

Robin: It's pretty scary. People were buying homes for 100 percent financing and I'm sure there were plenty of boaters back then that were doing the same thing. That can be very scary, especially if you lose your job and stuff in the meantime. **What happens if you have a bankruptcy on your credit report?**

Jim: In these cases, your chances, obviously, of obtaining a boat loan decrease substantially. Most lenders will not be willing to take the risk on a borrower that has payment problems or a poor credit history. Bankruptcies and even charge-offs (loans that have been "charged off" by a bank as bad debts) are the worst enemies a bank or finance company can see and the worst enemies to paying a boat loan for the borrower, of course. Some banks might be willing to review the reasons for this activity with you. However, those circumstances are rare. Loans following a bankruptcy are performed from time-to time by sub-prime risk lenders who are in the business of pricing certain loans based on poor risk. This comes at a steep cost in interest rate to the borrower, if he or she is approved—so, a warning on that. It's tough to get a boat loan when there is an active bankruptcy and there is no show of reaffirmation or reconfirmation of the debt.

Robin: **What's a non-conforming yacht loan program?**

Jim: Those types of loans are also referred to as non-prime or sub-prime loans. These loans are riskier to a lender because lower credit scores relate to poor credit histories and consumer payment habits.

There are some specialty lenders who will approve credit scores that are less than 720. In these cases, the interest rate is always adjusted upward and other restrictions might apply. Some of those restrictions might be:

- a term may be shorter
- down payment amount requirement may be larger to the borrower
- other collateral might be required for the loan
- other signers might be added to the account

There has been a fundamental change in credit underwriting by all banks and finance companies as a result of the financial crisis. Credit score minimums and underwriting guidelines have increased from what they were 10 years ago. It is more difficult to obtain a boat loan if you don't have a good payment record.

Robin: **What's the best type of loan to get—a fixed rate or a variable rate?**

Jim: I suggest that you look for a fixed-rate, simple interest loan. That's the short answer. Fixed rates allow you to lock in the interest rate for the full term of the boat loan. A fixed-rate loan makes it easier for you to budget your monthly payment and eliminates the possibility of surprises, particularly when we're living in a rising rate environment. Variable rates are often offered at low introductory rates, but have payment-adjust features that could raise your payment and interest expense significantly in these rising rate environments.

Fixed-rate boat loans, right now, are very reasonably priced and there is not enough difference between a fixed-rate and a variable-rate loan to make it worth the gamble for you. Be sure to take a very close look if you are considering a variable-rate loan.

There are other types of loans to steer clear of in today's economic environment that might be offered out there. Those are *balloon-type payment* loans, *interest-only* loans, or *convertible-rate* loans (loans that change on you after an initial introductory period). Beware of those—I would suggest you steer clear of those right now.

Robin: That's sounds like great advice. **Are there any differences in financing a recreational boat versus one for commercial use or even as a live-aboard?**

Jim: That's a good question. Yes, most recreational boat loan functions are performed by a consumer loan department or unit within a bank or finance company. Loans for commercial boats or vessels are generally performed by a commercial loan department with very different guidelines and terms related to businesses and their cash flows, net worth, and business credit ratings. Some consumer banks do, however, review recreational boats used for the business of chartering—both for fishing and recreational chartering. You must shop around as there are a limited amount of consumer lender banks who actually write these types of loans. A commercial loan for a commercial vessel is one way; or you can obtain a charter type of loan in the consumer loan department at some of the banks.

The same goes for live-aboard styles. Many banks do not offer financing for live-aboards, but a limited amount of them do. These loans often have more restrictive terms and guidelines than conventional recreation boat financing. Banks generally have issues with live-aboard styles and feel that they are just a little bit higher risk than a recreation boat loan.

Robin: **Do you need to let the bank know ahead of time that this is going to be a live-aboard situation? Or can you just buy the boat? Then what happens if you change over to become a live aboard?**

Jim: You have to be accurate on your application. Obviously, it causes problems with fraud and other things if you don't. You need to disclose if it's a commercial vessel or a consumer recreational vessel, if the boat is going to be lived on 100 percent of the time (i.e., it's your home), or if it's a charter. These things have to be disclosed up front. If something changes—for example, you move your boat into a charter—don't get caught by a bank with that. Call the bank ahead of time and let them know and see what their policy would be on that. The same goes for a live-aboard—give the bank a call and let them know what's going on.

Robin: With the economy the way it is, a lot of boat owners are now looking into renting their boats out. This is sort of, but not necessarily, a charter situation. An owner may rent a boat out to somebody who's going to become a live-aboard for a while.

Jim: You need to let the bank know that, because there's increased risk involved. You're insurance is going to need to change. The right thing to do is to let them know.

Robin: **I've seen websites where boaters can apply for boat loans online. Are these considered safe?**

Jim: Yes, they're safe, but it's like anything else in life, you have to do your homework and know who you are communicating with. I'm not an expert in websites, encryption, and security, but use common sense—make sure you have a good anti-virus program, be sure to look for a site that has HTTPS (Hypertext Transfer Protocol Secure). That can be found at the address line in the top left on the website. Also look for a lock icon (picture of a lock) usually found at the bottom right of the page on which you're preparing to send your information. Look for those two things before transmitting your boat loan application data to anyone. Again, these are found on the application page of a bank or finance company's website. If you don't see those there, don't submit your information.

Another thing you can do is visit a website called www.marinebankers.org. That's the National Marine Bankers Association (NMBA) site. They provide some great consumer boat loan advice and they list all of their member banks and service companies that specialize in boat loans. You are much more likely to get favorable interest rates, terms, and that sort of thing, from these sources than from a local bank that doesn't specialize in marine lending. Most of these NMBA member banks and finance companies have direct boat loan, dealer, and service company programs; and their sites are secure.

Robin: What a great resource—thanks. **If you're at a boat show and you find the boat you want, should you apply for financing right then and there with the dealer, yacht broker, or one of the financing companies?**

Jim: It's ok to do this, simply use common sense. Ask yourself these questions to find out:

- Does the dealer have a finance department or a financing specialist in their employ?
- Is the dealer known to you or your community — have you ever heard of the dealer?
- Have they been in business more than a year or two?
- Do you know any others that might have purchased from them with some success?

These are simple, easy questions.

When applying for a boat loan with a dealer or service company, always follow up to see that they send your credit application to one, *and only one*, bank source. When your application is submitted to more than one bank, or to several banks at the same time, this will actually lower your credit score due the recording of what the credit bureaus call "multiple or excessive inquiries." This method is called "shotgunning" in the dealer business. Be sure you control it and make sure you ask about it.

Robin: What a great tip!

Jim: That's something many folks don't know about.

If you apply at a boat show with a service company, practice that same common sense. Don't allow shotgunning. Be sure the business has a track history and make sure that they have solid lenders in their fold. Ask which lender will be reviewing your credit application and documents. You may elect to send any confidential information, such as your financial data and tax returns, *directly* to that bank or finance company. So, if you're dealing with a dealer or service company, make sure you work this through them. If you don't feel comfortable sending your financial information directly to the dealer or service company, it can be arranged for you to send it directly to the bank to which they're sending your application.

Robin: Very interesting! You'd think that if you're going to apply for a boat loan, whether it's at the boat show or on your own individually, that you would want to submit it to as many banks as possible to see who could come up with the better deal. But you're saying that actually hurts your credit score.

Jim: Yes, that's right, it does. "Excessive inquiries"—you don't want to have them on your credit record. They can drop your credit score down a few points and you don't want that to happen. Here's another thing—if you send your application to three banks and the first bank gets a hold of it and the second bank gets a hold of it a few minutes later to run their credit bureau report and they see that the first bank has an inquiry in there, now they're going back to the dealer or the service company saying, "Hey, what's going on? This application has been sent to other places." It sometimes sends up a little bit of a red flag. Again, one at a time, and make sure you let your dealer or your service company know that.

Robin: Great advice. **Where are the best sources for getting your boat financed and who can make these recommendations?**

Jim: If you are buying your new boat or your used boat from a boat dealer, I recommend that you talk to them about the financing—just talk straight to them. Many dealers have their own finance departments and the ability to offer financing through qualified marine lenders. They will likely have the relationships with those banks that you need. Obtaining marine financing through your dealer can be a very convenient way to purchase your boat. It is, in effect, "one-stop-shopping."

Another quality source of financing is through a service company. They specialize in finding or doing boat loans for you. Service companies, by nature, often finance larger loans, and have great experience with direct, person-to-person transactions, and with yacht brokers. If you're not purchasing your boat from a dealership, I would recommend that you consider contacting a service company to do the financing.

You can also contact banks and financial institutions directly. They provide good programs, but it might entail a little bit more legwork on your part to transact the deal. This is typically done by contacting a bank's local branch and simply requesting an application for a boat loan. Again, they might have you chasing some title work and paperwork around, where it's a little bit easier with the dealer and the service company.

In my experience, dealers and marine service company specialists tend to offer the best rates and usually have the best working relationships with banks and finance companies. The bottom line is always to do your homework and make comparisons.

I have another tip on this too. Be sure your boat lender is a National Marine Bankers Association (NMBA) member. The NMBA is a U.S.-based marine financing association. Their members are specialists in marine lending. They understand your needs and can deliver the best financing products available. Go to www.marinebankers.org for a list of qualified marine lenders—banks, finance companies, and service companies.

Robin: **What are some of the typical hidden fees that boaters need to look out for?**

Jim: That's a good question because there are some. Some boat loans might come with application, contract execution, or early payoff fees. Those are the ones that you see the most.

Financing a Boat Purchase   Jim Coburn

I suggest that you ask about fees, as there are some lenders that won't charge the fees and there are some that will. Ask about the source of the fee—who's actually charging that fee? Is the fee coming from the dealer? Is it coming from the service company? Or is it coming from the bank? Bear in mind that it's not always the bank or lender who is requesting or charging these additional fees.

One other thing—always avoid paying points on a boat loan. I mentioned this earlier when we were talking about residential mortgages. When fees are charged, they really should all be reasonable, maybe even flat fees, and not based on a percentage of your finance amount or loan balance. Again, watch out for application fees (ask about them), contract execution fees (which may come from dealers and service companies), and early payoff fees (generally directly from banks).

Robin: **What are some questions boaters should ask in regards to getting financing?**

Jim: Being a boater myself and dealing with my own loan, I think they should ask about the interest rate on the loan. That's pretty important. It's conveyed to you by the bank or the finance company as an "APR" or annual percentage rate. The higher that rate, the more cost or interest that's going to be charged to you on the loan. A lower APR, conversely, saves you money on interest costs and charges.

When buying certain boats, particularly used or pre-owned boats, you might want to consider obtaining a marine survey from an accredited marine surveyor. You'll want the survey to inform you if the boat is navigable and free from major problems or defects that could ruin your whole boating experience.

Information about marine surveys can also be found at www.marinebankers.org, the National Marine Bankers Association (NMBA) website. A marine survey is a very detailed appraisal of your boat and helps mitigate your risk in buying that boat.

Robin: You have a lot of information on www.marinebankers.org.

Jim: Yes, we do. It's a pretty comprehensive site and we've just changed it to make it easier to navigate. It's a lot of good information for banks, lenders, and, more importantly, boat buyers.

Robin: **How long does it normally take to complete a boat financing process?**

Jim: The banks call the time it takes to get your boat loan answer 'turnaround time'. It's surprisingly short. In the last two years since the financial crisis, the average turnaround time has increased by a few minutes, but it's still pretty good.

Generally, boat loans under $50,000 may take as few as 30-60 minutes to approve, provided the application information is complete and properly received by the bank or financial institution. Larger loans might take a little while longer. That's in part due to the review of the additional documentation that I mentioned earlier, such as tax returns or financial or income statements that are a little bit different for larger boat loans. Again, the key to fast turnaround with most marine lenders is a complete application and the timely receipt of other documents that are requested. The meter runs on turnaround time when these things are submitted.

Turnaround time does vary from company to company, depending on their experience in the marine finance arena. The more experienced your lender is in marine lending, probably the faster your turnaround time is going to be. One other side note here—if you're doing business with a service company, the turnaround time will be measured from the time *they* submit your data and application to the bank, not from the time *you* submit the information to them. My advice is, be sure to ask how long the process will take and how quickly they'll get the information you just gave them to the bank for a decision.

Robin: **If boaters were going to go through a service company, could they expect the loan decision to take up to a week or just a couple days?**

Jim: In some cases it could take up to a week if all the documents weren't there, but, with a service company, it could take a matter of minutes. Provided they have all the information right there to give to the bank, a service company will get the same turnaround time as if an individual went directly to the bank or through a dealer. Again, it all depends on the bank and the financial institution having the right documents. So, when doing business with a service company, you want to be sure they have all the stuff they need, ask when they are going to submit it, and then you'll know what your turnaround is going to be.

Robin: **Does the amount of financing also determine the amount of insurance a boater needs?**

Jim: Lenders vary in their requirements for you to carry proper insurance coverage. They are most interested that their company is listed as a "loss payee" in case there is a casualty or a claim.

Banks do have requirements for your insurance deductible. Generally—and you have to look at the contract or ask your dealer, service company, or bank directly about this—those requirements may be that the deductible is 2-5 percent of the amount insured. A boat must be insured for its full value. This is called agreed value and is usually for the retail or purchase price of the boat. That amount should be greater than the loan or finance amount, for sure.

You are—*we* are—as boat financers and boat loan borrowers, by contract with our lenders, required to maintain the boat and to keep up all premiums to the insurance carriers, so bear that in mind as well.

Robin: **Which comes first? Do they get the financing first or the insurance first? Or do they need to look at them both basically simultaneously?**

Jim: Remember, that's all part of the preplanning and prescreening we talked about earlier. You should shop around for insurance just like you do for your home or your car or other things you insure at your home, because rates vary from insurance carrier to insurance carrier. Shop around. You're going to need proof of insurance to be able to close on the loan. You don't need it when you apply, but you *do* need it when you sign your contract to close the loan. The dealer, service company, or bank won't transact the funds until the boat is insured and they have proof of that.

Financing a Boat Purchase — Jim Coburn

Robin: **Have you ever run across a situation where someone is being financed—they're about ready to close the deal on the finance—and then the bank looks at the insurance policy and finds out that they really didn't have the proper coverage so they have to go back and change the insurance policy to get the right coverage before they can have the papers signed for the note?**

Jim: That rarely happens—either you have the insurance or you don't. Those are the biggest detriments to stopping a closing. You're going to be in good shape if you use a U.S.-based insurance carrier. I can send you right back to that www.marinebankers.org website. There's also a piece about insurance there. Many of the NMBA associate members are insurance companies that specialize in marine insurance. Your dealer and service company will know of these folks as well.

Robin: **Is it a good idea to have both the bank and the insurance company talking to one another?**

Jim: Ultimately, that's going to have to happen because they're going to need to. To make it easier in this process, the insurance company will probably email or fax over the verification of insurance, so that it can be there for the loan closing. Otherwise, it's up to the borrower—up to you and I—to go out and grab the documentation from our insurance carrier or local agent and carry it over to the closing when we transact the loan.

Robin: So, anything that's easier is better?

Jim: Always, sure, and your dealer and service company can really help you with that process.

Robin: **Let's talk about refinancing for a minute. Is this just as involved as getting financing originally?**

Jim: Yes it is. You're going to need to submit a new boat loan application with your current data including your current financial picture. It's getting involved with the same things we've been talking about. The finance company or bank will also obtain a new, fresh credit report and review your application in the same manner as for a new loan. It was maybe a little easier a couple years ago before the financial crisis, but again, remember I said 'back to the future?' This is the way it was done 15 or 20 years ago. It's not different, it's just different recently.

Robin: **Do you see the challenges of obtaining boat financing changing again any time soon?**

Jim: Probably not, and probably it shouldn't, because we want the banks in our country to book good, solid, paying loans. That keeps our whole country and our whole financial process properly stimulated and energized and it keeps lenders lending, so I'm a big fan of due diligence in doing loans.

Robin: **Do you have any additional tips for boaters on getting financing?**

Jim: Sure. A person buying a boat and wanting to get financed needs to:

- Expect to make a *down payment* on the boat purchase. This is viewed as a good faith payment when you're applying for a boat loan. Down payments vary slightly between lenders and according to the amount of the loan. Fifteen to 25 percent down is usually a good rule of thumb to go by.

  From time-to-time, there may be some programs available called "zero-down-payment" or "no-down-payment" options. They are *extremely* rare now, particularly since the advent of the financial crisis we are going through. If these are available, qualifying for one could be based on such variables as your credit score (the higher the better, obviously), a special dealer or manufacturer incentive program, or a special lender program. These are rarities; they are not everyday occurrences.

  When you encounter a no-down-payment offer, you should always investigate what the ultimate costs would be. Those could include higher monthly payments, higher finance charges or costs to you, a higher price for the boat, and so on. So, watch those zero-down-payment specials and do your own due diligence on them.

- It's a good idea to ask about your *"commitment time."* Commitment time is how long your loan approval is valid and how long the bank or the financial company is committed to your quoted interest rate. We don't usually think about that, but commitment times do vary from lender to lender. They are typically 30 days from your application approval date for your interest rate (we'll call it a rate lock) and 60 days that your credit application approval is good. So, 30 days for your rate and 60 days for your credit (before you must have your credit rerun). This is especially important when you might be ordering a new boat that hasn't come from the manufacturer yet. So, always ask about your commitment time.

Robin: Is commitment time something you should be getting in writing?

Jim: You can get it in writing, but it's usually a standard policy or guideline with each bank, so the bank or the service company or the dealer should be able to tell you. Again, typically look for 30 days for an interest rate lock and 60 days for your credit approval.

Robin: If they pass that commitment time and have to rerun a credit check, is that another point off of their credit score?

Jim: No, time has gone by at that point. What you'd want to do—if, say, a boat is coming from a manufacturer and there's some sort of delay in getting it from the manufacturer to the dealer that takes you over the 60 days—is let your dealer, service company, or bank know that you need to get your loan credit reinstated. A bank can do this very quickly.

As far as the rate goes, they should tell you up front that that's good for 30 days. Now, your rate may change—it could go up or down. It's not always an up situation during that period. So, after the 30 days, whatever the market is, it might be up or down. You need to be in contact with your bank, dealer, or service company about the commitment time.

Some lenders might be willing to make an exception for interest rate commitments depending on whether the economy is a rising or falling rate environment.

- *Consider buying a new boat at a boat show.* Not only is it exciting to buy a new boat at a boat show (for my last boat, my family did this, and it was pretty exciting!), it is almost always the best time to buy. What I mean is that lenders sometimes offer dealers and service companies special financing rates and programs that are tied to a particular show in a particular region. Dealers will often have special pricing on boats during these shows, and this could offer potentially substantial savings for the borrower.

Robin: We talked about a lot of different things today. **Is there anything that you'd like to reiterate for the boaters?**

Jim: Yes.

- Whatever you do in life, particularly with boat financing, use common sense and make good judgments.
- Know how much you can afford for a boat by prescreening yourself and running a quick analysis of your own financial situation—it's really easy to do.
- Make sure that you ask questions about things like commitment time and what your rate interest rate will be.
- And remember—a lot of people forget this—you don't have to take the longest term (length of the loan) on this. If you can afford a little bit higher payment, go for it, because it will save you a lot of money in interest. Remember, interest charges are on your unpaid balance so they're more at the beginning of your loan than toward the end of your loan.

Wrapping it up, those are common sense tips that I'd recommend to anybody.

Closing

Robin: Well, Jim, I want to thank you for being so generous with your time today. You've given both boat owners and buyers a lot to think about with regards to financing either their first boat or their next one. You've certainly opened my eyes to the world of financing. Most important is that boaters should pre-qualify their own bank accounts first (before looking for boat financing).

If someone has further questions, what's the best way for them to get a hold of you?

Jim: Anyone is welcome to call me directly at my line: 586-530-3935; or, if you prefer to write, my email address is coburnassociates@sbcglobal.net.

Robin: Thanks again, Jim.

Key Points

1. The first step when thinking of financing is to do your homework.
2. Finance your boat for the shortest term you can afford.
3. Typical loan documents include a credit application, personal financial statement, completed and signed contract, proof of insurance, title, bill of sale, delivery receipt, and proper legal identification.

4. When financing with a dealer or boat service company, be sure your credit history and lender options are discussed before your loan application is submitted by them to a bank. Follow up to see that they send your credit application to only one bank (at a time).
5. Don't allow shotgunning—excessive credit inquires lower your credit score.
6. Your credit score is your payment history, it determines your loan approval and often what your interest rate will be.
7. The best type of loan to get is fixed-rate, simple interest.
8. Recreational boat loans are made by a consumer loan department, while financing for commercial boats is generally performed by a commercial loan department with different guidelines and terms.
9. You must disclose up front if your boat will be a live-aboard, commercial, or recreational.
10. Beware of hidden fees and avoid paying points on a boat loan.

Notes

Rent Your Boat
An Interview with Brian Stefka

Introduction

Robin: Hello everyone. This is Robin Coles and it's my pleasure to welcome you to the 2010 Nautical Lifestyle Expert Series brought to you by TheNauticalLifestyle.com. During the next hour you'll be learning how to rent out your own boat from my special guest Brian Stefka if RentbyBoater.com. Hello Brian!

Brian: Hey Robin, how are you doing?

Robin: Good! Brian, thank you so much for joining me today. Brian is the founder and president of RentbyBoater.com. Rent by Boater has been advising individuals for the last two years on how to rent out their own boats and provides the necessary tools to do so. Now online at Rentbyboater.com, they are an online marketplace that brings boat owners and boat renters together. Prior to renting boats, Brian spent that last six years involved with a community bank in Florida working in commercial lending. Brian has a bachelor's degree in marketing with a concentration in e-commerce, coupled with an MBA in finance.

Rent Your Boat

Robin: **What are the advantages of someone renting out his or her boat?**

Brian: Instead of advantages, we like to call them objectives. One can have three different objectives in renting their boat, each with its own advantages. The first objective is to *make a profit*, the one that everybody likes. This is the most risky and time consuming option, as the owner of the vessel is looking to create a maximum occupancy or number of rentals per year. This objective also will limit the amount of time enjoyed on the vessel if the owner is still planning to use it personally.

Another objective is to *supplement ownership costs*—a less risky and time consuming option. The owner of the vessel typically still wants to enjoy the vessel on their terms, while renting it out to supplement and/or help with the costs of ownership.

The third way is to *assist in the sale of a vessel*. If you're trying to sell your boat, renting your boat can not only supplement your cost of ownership, but it can increase the number of prospective buyers and marketing exposure for your vessel. The extra marketing exposure may be word of mouth through renters or the extra advertising created through a rental ad as opposed to just a sales ad.

Robin: **Are you saying this last one is a great way for someone to actually sell their own boat? Giving the new prospective buyer a chance to try the boat out first? If so, how long would you suggest they allow the prospective buyer to take out the boat? And if the buyer says yes, do you have to take the money they paid to rent the boat and apply it toward the purchase?**

Brian: Absolutely, Robin—renting your boat is a great way to turn a renter into a prospective buyer with a test run of the boat. The rental time is up to the owner. We typically recommend that you treat it like any other rental with an hourly, half-day, full-day, weekly, or monthly rate. Renting the boat to prospective buyers also provides a pressure-free sales environment. All sales tactics are up to the owner of the boat. The sales tactic that you mentioned—to apply deposits and rental fees toward the purchase price—is a great idea. Another great idea is to let people know that the boat is for sale. Create a binder or brochure with pictures of the vessel, feature descriptions, pricing, and contact information. You can neatly place this in the galley, leave it on the table, or hand it to the renter as they head out or return. Your creativity is pretty much limitless when getting a renter's attention about the sales status of your boat.

Robin: What are the different types of rentals they can offer?

Brian: When deciding to rent out your boat you have three primary rentals to choose from. The packages or options you offer to your renters can be a combination of these three.

The first option is a *bareboat rental*. This is a rental with no captain or crew. The party responsible for the vessel and for the individuals aboard will be the person renting your boat. For example, you take out an 18-foot boat, and you and your wife, friends, and/or kids just head out on your own.

There's also a *charter rental,* where a captain, and sometimes crew, operate the vessel, directed by the renting party as to where they would like to go.

The third one is the *dockside rental*—a newer concept. This option would allow you to rent your boat while it is sitting at the dock, just like a hotel room. The boat is not allowed to be started or leave the dock. The renters can still enjoy the features of the vessel and the amenities at the marina.

For other sources of revenue, besides just renting out your boat, you can also rent your fishing poles and/or fish finder, and sell bait, ice, and supplies. It's completely up to the owner of the vessel.

Robin: The dockside rental sounds really interesting. As you know, more and more boat owners are using their boats as condos on the water, and not going anywhere (which is a little sad). I think this is happening partly because of gas prices. **Can you do a dockside rental if the boat is on a mooring? Would there be any reason a marina would not permit dockside rentals?**

Brian: To be honest, I have not personally worked with a rental on a mooring, but that sounds like a great idea, assuming you have a dinghy or some form of motor transportation back and forth from land to the boat available to the renter. I would imagine down in the British Virgin Islands, there are some nice waters and that would be pretty nice. Always check with your marina, and check your marina contract if you're a slip owner, to ensure that renting your vessel is allowed wherever you're at. Typically the slip contracts you see only stipulate that subletting is not allowed. In other words, you can't rent out the dock to another boat. It's always good to check with your marina before you decide to rent out your own boat.

Technically, in renting your boat, renters will use the amenities, spend money in ship stores, eat at restaurants, and shop in local businesses. So, it's pretty much a win-win for everyone in these marinas.

Robin: **Let's go back to bareboat rentals for a minute. Isn't this a bit dangerous, just renting the boat out to anyone?**

Brian: There's definitely risk involved, just as there is with any investment. Your boat is an investment. The trick is to mitigate those risks by following all your local rules and regulations. Do your scheduled maintenance. Set operating procedures and risk-avoidance policies, such as a minimum age that you don't want renting your boat—say, someone under 25 you wouldn't want renting your boat, or under 40. Set a minimum amount of boating experience—for example, you don't want to rent to someone with fewer than ten years of experience. It's up to you. You could require certification—basic boating, a captain's license, etc.—or local knowledge of the waterways. For example, we live down in Bonita Springs, Florida. The water down here is really shallow, so when renting to somebody, I want to know that they understand the local waterways and the rules of boating before I rent to them. You're not obligated to rent to anyone who makes you feel uncomfortable. With any risk policies that you set, take the time to interview your renter and collect any documentation necessary to support their claims.

Robin: **If I wanted to rent my boat out (I don't have one yet, but in the future) to a company for a party, or even a dockside wedding, would this fit better under a bareboat or dockside rental?**

Brian: Say I'm a renter and I have a wedding on a dockside or charter rental, I don't know if I'd be fit to pilot the boat. In a case like this, if you're going to charter your boat, you'd want a separate captain and crew. You wouldn't want to be sending a whole party out on its own with a bareboat rental.

On a serious note, renting for a party should require a captain and crew. If the boat is being chartered, dockside is always a great option to hold a function if the boat is big enough and you don't want to take it out. I would not recommend a bareboat rental for these situations.

Robin: **So, a dockside rental might be nice as a honeymoon? Would that be considered dockside?**

Brian: For a honeymoon, I guess it's a nice place to stay. If *I* was on a honeymoon, I would like to have a charter boat that could take me from island to island. If I was experienced enough, I would just take the boat out myself with my significant other—that would be a bareboat rental.

Robin: **Let's say the boat owner has decided to rent out their boat based on one of the objectives you mentioned before. Should they have someone manage the rental, such as a broker, or can they do it themselves?**

Brian: This depends on the owner's available time. It does take some time renting out your own boat—there is some investment. Everything a rental company offers can be completed by an owner. There's nothing hidden or anything that a rental company does that an individual can't do. If an owner rents their own vessel, they can save the charge incurred by rental management companies—10-15% of each rental booked. A rental management company will provide a good captain and crew, if needed, along with any cleaning of the vessel upon return. A good company will also ensure that the boat is maintained, insured, and report any problems or maintenance required in order to provide a safe rental.

Robin: **Before a boat owner turns his or her boat over to a rental management company, is it wise to have the boat inspected by the Coast Guard? Or does the management company take care of this and give you some kind of report?**

Brian: All boats should have an inspection sticker from a certified organization. The federal and state laws differ and boaters are required to abide by both set of laws in any state. Management companies should know their local and federal laws and ensure the boat meets these before any type of rental goes out, whether it's charter, bareboat, or a dockside rental that they're helping you with. It would not hurt to have the vessel inspected from time to time. You might do a surprise inspection of the management company just to ensure that they're keeping everything in place and keeping you as up-to-date as necessary. Safety is always number one—as an owner, it should always be your primary concern.

Robin: **Are rental agreements expensive? What do they need for them?**

Brian: Rental agreements are expensive using a typical law firm. They really need to be customized. Let's talk about the different types of agreements you need when renting out your boat.

You need an *acknowledgement agreement*, stating that the renter understands how to use the equipment on board and how the vessel works. This is acknowledging that they have sufficient knowledge to do what they're doing.

You'll also need a *standard rental agreement* for the charter or the bareboat vessel—the basic terms of the rental. This is where you would spell out your costs per day, any additional, non-boat items that you're renting, the time that it goes out, the time that it comes back in, etc.

You also need a *waiver and release* from the renter stating the owner is not responsible for the renter's actions. You need to cover yourself, saying, "You're taking out my boat and you're responsible for anything you do out there. You're waiving me from any liability associated with your actions."

Robin: **Are these agreements state specific or are they generic documents written by a law firm? Do you have any on your website that boaters could get a feel for first before they go to their attorneys?**

Brian: We provide documents on the website that are available after an individual posts a boat. These agreements should be designed to abide by state specifications. They need to be customizable, fill-in-the-blank, so you can adjust them to your specific boating needs, ensure they protect your rights as an owner, meet the needs for your type of rental, and satisfy your insurance company.

Robin: **Can you specify in the agreement that a renter is not allowed to take the boat past a certain place—for example, they can't go from Florida down to the Caribbean?**

Brian: Yes, absolutely—there are navigational terms in agreements where you can say, for example, that the boat can't go further than 25 miles offshore or past the bridge from the rental location. There's a section in the agreement where you can identify the limitations of the rental—whether it's a bareboat or a charter—it's up to you. You can tell the captain not to take the renters to a specific area and you can specify that on the charter agreement as well.

Robin: **What are some of the risks boaters might encounter renting out their boats?**

Brian: Your boat is an investment and it is easy to identify risks you're going to experience using typical investment terminology.

The first type would be a *passive risk,* where you have limited control of what's going on on the vessel, such as actions your renter or captain take while they're on your boat. Say Joe rents my vessel as a bareboat. I give Joe a tour of the boat and show him how to use all the equipment. I interview Joe and collect the necessary documentation—I feel he knows the local waterways. After that, what Joe does on the boat, the way he operates the vessel, or the way other people operate other vessels is not under my control anymore. That would mean that I'm passively involved with the risks that Joe is taking.

Robin: So you've interviewed him as far as you can and you feel comfortable. Then, if he does what you don't want him to, that's his business.

Brian: Right. I'm passively involved at that point.

Another type of risk you can experience is *non-passive risk*—the opposite of passive risk—where interviewing, collecting documentation, and knowing your renter are ways to mitigate your risk. Non-passive risk is generally where you have full control of the situation—you maintain your boat, comply with regulations and laws, and know who your renter is—you have every control over what's going on.

You also have *systematic risk*. This is completely uncontrollable risk. Nobody can control this, not the renter or you; this is weather, unforeseen circumstances, or an act of G-d. It happens; there is nothing you can do.

Let's talk a little bit about mitigating some of these risks. Understanding your risks for your vessel is the first line of defense against them and will help you mitigate these risks in an effort to create a comfortable, enjoyable rental for all parties. For example, to mitigate passive risk you need to use the right tools. The right tools are the agreements we talked about, protecting yourself against what other people are doing—the waiver and release, acknowledgement, and rental agreement—and getting renters to abide by any operational procedures that you set. On our website we provide forms that help people do walk-arounds with their renters to identify any issues with the boat before it goes out. If there are any, have the renter sign off on the situation and make sure they understand it. Use check-in and check-out lists, go through all equipment and safety gear with your renter, walk around the boat again and show your renter how to use things. Anything you can do to educate your renter will provide for a safer rental while you are not on the boat.

Robin: Suppose it's a friend of yours or someone who's been out on the boat quite a few times with you in the past and they want to rent your boat. Would you still make them sign these papers?

Brian: Absolutely. I cherish my friends deeply and if they were truly my friends they would abide by my policies and operational procedures. Just because they're my friends doesn't mean they're exempt from that. This is especially with insurance companies—they're going to expect you to treat everybody the same. I definitely want to continue being insured and I want my friend to be insured while he's out there. Does that answer your question?

Robin: It does.

Brian: Another way to mitigate passive risk is to know your customer. Create a set of rental or risk management policies, interview your customers to make sure they're comfortable renting, and make sure you're comfortable renting your boat to them. I might repeat myself here, but you're not obligated to rent a boat to anyone that you do not feel comfortable with. So make sure you set limits for yourself, such as a certain age, years of experience, required certification, to name a few. There is no limit to your requirements to feel comfortable. Once you set these risk policies, make sure that you stick to them! That goes back to a question you asked before—don't deviate from your policy. When you deviate from your policy—I mean by making exceptions—you're increasing your risk. Just make sure you are complying with your local and state laws—which are really easy to find on the internet—as some states require a renter to have a basic boating certificate before even renting.

Robin: I think the key is to be comfortable with the whole feeling and trust your intuition with anybody that you're trying to rent your boat to.

Brian: Absolutely. A lot of the major problems that people have—you know there are a lot of horror stories that the boat's come back damaged and what not—I can guarantee you that a lot of these people didn't interview their customers. They got an inquiry on their boat, they ran out there, and they just wanted to make a buck without really knowing who they were renting to. Minimize your risk by taking those fundamental steps to having a safe rental for everybody.

Another way to mitigate some passive risk is to develop a relationship with a professional captain. This is a great idea no matter how big your boat is; get somebody who's willing to come out there and drive your boat for you. And, let me tell you, it's not hard to find somebody to drive your boat for you. You still want to interview them, just like you would any renter. Make sure he or she is a professional captain and is insured for personal liability as well. Their insurance typically doesn't cover your boat's damage—that's why you have your own insurance. But you definitely want somebody who is a professional captain who's insured. Also, when you hire a professional captain, the renter pays for this expense; it's typically reimbursed. It doesn't hurt to get somebody out there you know for a fact has great experience and is very professional about what they do. And it doesn't hurt to have somebody watching your boat either, while it's out there.

Robin: **They need to have the right size license as well, right? They can't have a six pack if your boat is bigger than that.**

Brian: Absolutely—know your boat's limits and the certifications required to have a captain aboard.

One last way to mitigate passive risk is quite simple—keep your vessel ship shape; be proud of what you own! When you're dealing with customers, make sure you collect security and reservation deposits. If your boat comes back damaged, you have some kind of retribution for the damage that was done by the renter. The reservation deposit would be to ensure that the renter is serious about taking out your boat, just like cruise lines take deposits. Have a cancellation policy in place; for example, if they cancel within 10 days, they don't get their security deposit back. Make sure that once you're committed to renting to somebody, they're committed as well. Abide by all local and state rules and regulations while renting your boat. Keep all the safety equipment on board and make sure all your equipment is working—nothing is rusting out or anything like that. Use basic common sense to ensure that once somebody is out on your boat, everything's going to be okay.

Robin: **Regarding passive risk, you said the boat owner should hire an experienced captain to help minimize the risk, and that the renter should pay for this. Why?**

Brian: It is the obligation of the renter to abide by the owner's risk policies. If the owner requires a captain, the renter must pay for a captain to operate the vessel. There are three different ways you can charge for something like this.

- You can add the charge to the rental fee itself and tell the renter that a captain is included.

- You can charge separately from, and in addition to, the rental fee. Sometimes the captain will charge the renter directly.

- You can allow the renter to find their own captain. But, get in touch with your insurance to see if you need to pre-approve the captain. Some renters have their own captain/crew that they take around—they like being around them and I guess it's part of the ambience. It's also important to the owner that any captain they allow should have their own liability insurance. This covers the captain personally, but will not cover any damage to the boat. Consult a licensed insurance agent before accepting any captain that comes on.

Robin: **What other expenses are renters expected to pay for?**

Brian: There are three primary sources of revenue charged to a renter: a basic rental fee for use of the boat; a fee for gas usage (obviously, when the boat goes out full, you want to be reimbursed for the gas they use, especially considering today's prices; upon their return, gas usage is usually refunded through a deduction in deposits, before any deposits are returned to the renter); and a captain and crew fee. There are other fees, such as for fishing poles; some people charge an insurance reimbursement fee for taking out their boat, say $50, if anything happens, you still get your deposits back—it's a risky way to go about it, but some people do that; also supplies, drinks, and food are just some examples; but it is completely up to the owner to charge for whatever equipment or miscellaneous fees they deem required.

Robin: **What type of insurance is available for rental boats?**

Brian: Insurance should be the last resort in order to mitigate all our risk that we talked about—passive risk, non-passive risk, and systematic risk. This insurance replaces your personal insurance, it continues to allow you to operate the vessel personally if you want to go out for the day—it still acts as a normal insurance—but also covers others renting your boat or a captain taking others out on your boat. Typically rental agreements, a simple business plan, and financial projections—even if it's just one year of guess-timation of what you're expecting to make—is required to obtain this type of insurance. I'd be more than happy to refer anyone to a quality company to help them acquire a quote. Quotes are always free, so if you are interested in renting and you're curious about insurance….This is usually the number one question that I receive—is there insurance out there? Absolutely, there's insurance out there. It's not easy to find, but I'd be more than happy to get you to a company that does do this, gets you insured.

Robin: **Can't you have an umbrella policy on your homeowner's insurance to cover this? Or, if you already have rental insurance on your apartment, will that cover the boat rental?**

Brian: I'm not an insurance agent and I'd have to defer a question like that to the professionals for personal insurance. I do know that accepting revenue from rentals creates a commercial situation. That contains a specific risk and requires a different type of insurance from your personal insurance. Sometimes your insurance rates are based on the amount you earn or are expecting to earn in revenues, but it's totally different from personal insurance.

Rent Your Boat — Brian Stefka

Robin: This next question came in from someone in one of my Yahoo groups, who writes, "A few years ago I considered a timeshare or rental for my boat, since it was not being used a lot and the costs were significant. My insurance company said they would continue the insurance if I co-owned the boat with someone else, but that I could not rent it out or timeshare it without an additional policy. They also said that my personal umbrella policy would be cancelled if I rented or timeshared without co-ownership, since they were concerned about liability. **It seems that there are legal distinctions for liability purposes in these two scenarios. Is there another way around this?**

Brian: I'm not an insurance agent, but more than likely this is because you would need commercial insurance in conjunction with renting. It would be a waste of money to have both because, as we talked about before, commercial insurance usually replaces your personal insurance. Concerning the umbrella and canceling that, you would definitely have to talk with your own insurance company. I couldn't provide you with any advice on personal insurance.

Based on my experience, renting your boat presents totally different risks to an insurance company. If you are looking for a quick commercial agent or you need some help, just visit my website. There's a commercial insurance agent on my sponsor section to make your search easier for someone like that. They can give you a whole lot more details than I'd feel comfortable giving.

Robin: **What about contacting a local attorney or accountant?**

Brian: Remember, renting a boat is an entrepreneurial experience. You are essentially starting up a company, whether it's a sole proprietorship or other legal entity. There are risks involved. To further protect yourself, you might want to call your local attorney and discuss setting up a separate legal entity for your vessel. Sometimes it's really quick. There's a great website out there—it's called LegalZoom.com—you can go there and get great information. It's actually relatively cheap. In most states you just set up your own entity—you pick the right entity for you—and they quickly put some documents together for you. You should definitely contact your local attorney after that.

Robin: **How can a boater protect themselves if their boat comes back damaged?**

Brian: This is one of the main reasons you should collect security and reservation deposits. If the boat is damaged, you may need to use these deposits for an insurance claim deductible or to repair the boat. You should still hold the renter fully responsible for the damage they created. All of that stuff should be in your rental agreements. It should be your primary avenue before filing a claim with the insurance company. In the worse case scenario, you have enough deposits for a deductible, assuming that the damage is over the deposit amount.

Make sure you have your renters sign agreements, don't let anybody go out without protecting yourself—without them waving your liability while they're out there on your boat and agreeing to pay for any damage they commit. If it does come in damaged, make sure you take pictures of the vessel and collect any evidence upon return. Make sure you have the renters' contact information, so you can keep in touch with them. If any other vessels are damaged in that case, make sure that the police have been contacted. Just do all your due diligence that you possibly can when the boat comes back in.

Robin: **Who pays for the costs of repairs and upkeep?**

Brian: The owner of the boat is still responsible for maintaining the safety of their vessel through routine maintenance and upkeep. Renting your boat will pay for or help supplement these costs. You, as the owner, you're obviously still responsible for them.

Robin: **I know technically, the boat owner is responsible for having lifejackets and a flotation device on the boat. Can an owner request a head count before releasing the boat? If there are little ones going on board, does the boat owner then become responsible to provide lifejackets for them? Or are the parents responsible? And the same with pets (because we want to keep them safe also)?**

Brian: Sure. The boat owner needs to be cognizant of the passenger and weight limit on their vessel. It shouldn't be exceeded. When the renters are going out and the boat owner is there casting them off, they definitely should make sure they're not exceeding these limits. Life jackets for all passengers should be required, obviously. But the owner should have an understanding of the renter's party coming aboard through interviewing them. If the owner doesn't have life jackets for this specified party, then he needs to let them know that through the interview process. If he's not willing to purchase extra life jackets, and the renter's not willing to bring his or her own to meet the party's needs, it's best that the owner not rent the boat out to this party or these individuals.

Concerning a dog life jacket, I've never looked into whether pets are required to have their own life jackets. But I would imagine if your pet jumped overboard, you should want him wrapped up in a nice little life jacket.

Robin: You would. Actually, I have a pet store down the street here that is giving discounts to anybody that goes through my website to buy life jackets for their pets, because she feels that strongly about it. I think that's pretty good.

Brian: Absolutely—we don't want anybody drowning out there.

Robin: No, and I know the Coast Guard doesn't require it yet.

Brian: But they should, right?

Robin: Yes, they should. **How much money can someone make renting their boat?**

Brian: This is pretty much dependent on four factors. It's just creating a simple income statement.

Your revenue would be your estimated rental rate and fees per rental. Estimate your rental price and take a look at similar rentals in your area to help gauge this. Estimate your days per year that you'd like to rent the boat—ask yourself, "How many days do I really want to rent my boat out per year. What's my objective? Am I trying to make a profit or am I just trying to supplement my costs? I might be happy just renting it out four or five times a year to help pay for my insurance and some of my dockage. I think that'd be great and just rent it out to people that I know." Some of the other income options that we talked about with the gas and other things that you can rent, such as fishing poles, include that in your revenue too. These are best guess, but base your estimates on the basic factors, such as the rental price and how many days you're going to be renting it out per year.

When estimating expenses, you should consider these basic expenses that I'll go over with you. You should consider them anyway, even if you're purchasing your own vessel, so you'll have an idea of how much this thing's going to cost you per year. You should get insurance, obviously, which we've talked about in some detail. Take a look and see what it costs to register your boat, including any business licenses you would need to rent out your boat. For example, in Florida there's the business occupational license ($80), and then the registration. When I started renting out my boat, it was actually less than $3 to change over my registration number to a registration that would allow rentals. Just check with your DMV, tax collector, or wherever you usually go to register your vehicle—they can help you with that—there are usually very nominal fees. Don't forget storage—there are different types: wet slips, dry slips, condos, trailer storage, storage units, on the trailer. There are all different kinds of ways that you can store your boat. When I started renting my boat, I kept it on a trailer and stored it in a unit. I'd actually keep it mobile and meet people at the boat ramp, go through the boat there, and launch it. That was a cheap way for me to do it—it definitely helped pay for the boat. Your repairs and maintenance, a lot of times just getting a company to do scheduled maintenance. If boat's big enough, they'll come out once every three months change the oil, check everything on the engine, make sure everything's working right; if something's broke, fix it. Set aside a little bit of money to be able to fix broken items.

Towing services are probably the cheapest, most valuable thing you can have. You've got to be careful though with towing services when renting out your boat. If you go through a company like BoatUS, they usually only cover an individual, they don't cover the boat. SeaTow, a great service, actually covers the boat, so no matter who's out there on the boat, they'll tow it back in. When choosing a towing service, make sure you actually look at whether they cover the boat and not just you, as an individual.

Robin: That's great to know.

Brian: A lot of people don't know that. Individual coverage is great if you're on somebody else's boat, then you can get towed back in, kind of like how AAA works. But if you're renting your boat out, go with somebody like SeaTow that covers that boat exclusively.

You're also going to pay for gas. I usually estimate a full tank of gas used per rental, but then I also assume that it's going to be reimbursed by the renter. It's kind of zeroed out. But, even if you own your own boat or you're looking to buy one, estimate how much you're going to use it. The statistics say most people use their boats 20 to 30 days out of the year. Gas prices are expensive, but if you're not using your boat, it's not too bad. That's a great reason to rent—if you're not using it, it's just sitting there collecting dust. You might also want to estimate the cost of oil for two stroke engines. You can get as detailed as you want here. Another cost to estimate is cleaning. Call a local cleaning company and figure out how much it would cost you. Usually it's $5 a foot or something like that for them to come out, maybe $10-15 a foot if you want them to do a full wax job. I usually have a cleaning company do my boat. You can save a lot of money just by running out there and cleaning your own boat after it comes back in.

There's also the rental management fee to consider when renting out your own boats—that could be 10-15%. That's a pretty hefty fee, especially if you're renting your boat out quite a bit. In renting the boat out yourself, consider that rental management fee that you don't have to pay a salary on top of what you already make. Also, if you have any mortgages out there, make sure you put your debt payments into your cost estimates, so the expenses come off your bottom line.

When estimating your income, remember to abide by the objectives you set. Do you want to make a profit or do you want to supplement your costs of ownership? Do you want to sell your boat? Do you need assistance selling your boat and want to supplement your costs of ownership at the same time? Keep your goals in mind when estimating your expenses and revenue. You'll come out to a number on the bottom line of what you're looking to make. There's a lot to this, a lot of expenses. To make things easier, on our website we provide a free calculator to help you do this. If you need to, just register on rentbyboater.com, go to the tools, and check out the calculator—it's really useful.

Robin: That's good to know. **Is it better to rent by the day, week, or season?**

Brian: This is up to the owner of the vessel, his or her comfort level along with the type of rental he or she is offering. A bareboat rental is typically just hourly, half-day, or full day. Insurance companies won't let you have a boat go out overnight with a bareboat rental, so it's usually a daily thing.

A charter or dockside rental can be hourly, half-day, weekly, monthly, or seasonal. If somebody wants to come live on your boat for the entire winter down here in Florida, that's great. It's a lot of money in your pocket, just a dockside rental—they're not even taking it out—your risks are pretty limited.

Robin: Wow, that's good, I didn't even think about it as a live-aboard.

Brian: I run into a lot of people going to boat shows, with their booths, that tell me, for example, "I've been living on my boat for two or three years." I say, "That's great. You should be renting that boat out for somebody else to be living on and getting a second boat for yourself somewhere." It's definitely a good way to rent out your boat with limited risks. A lot of companies we deal with do sailing charters down in the British Virgin Islands and down here on the west coast of Florida—they take people out for a week, a month, or whatever they want.

Robin: **How would I determine what my boat rental prices should be?**

Brian: You're calculating your income looking at different revenue streams and expenses. The calculator that we have on our website will help you determine a breakeven price based on your specific scenario. Your breakeven price is a great place to start, where revenue from your rental is equal to your expenses on a per rental basis. For example, based on my expenses I would need to rent my boat out 30 days out of the year at $315 per rental day, it's an 18-foot boat and if I did that then everything would be free for me. Then I could use the boat however I wanted ongoing, with some nominal expenses. Your breakeven price is a base line. After you figure out your baseline, take a look at other rentals in your area. Chances are they have a lot of the same expenses as you and they're coming out to pretty much the same price, but they rent out their boat on a more frequent basis, so they can offer a lower breakeven price. Consider that when you're looking at it. When you come up with your breakeven and compare it to the rentals in your area, come up with a price that you feel is fair.

In renting other people's boats a couple of times, in my own personal experience, I found that those boats were much better maintained than boats from a facility that's renting out boats constantly. Frequently-rented boats just have bare-bones electronics, no cushions, etc. People who truly value their boat as an investment really take care of their boats—you're going to have great equipment on board and the boats are going to be clean. One of the boats I rented had a great stereo system and we just had a great time on it.

Through my own experience renting out my own boat and taking care of it, people compliment me when the boat comes back—they tell me how nice it was to have a clean boat out there. Even if your price is higher, if you're providing a more quality product, people are going to recognize that. So, don't get discouraged if your price is higher than some of these rental facilities because you're getting your money for what you're providing.

Make sure you're meeting your objectives with your price and the number of days you want to rent out your boat, that your estimates are accurate and your goals achievable. If you don't feel it's achievable, then maybe renting is not for you. But developing your income statement will help you better understand what it takes to rent out your boat and whether it's something you're even willing to take the time to do. If you don't want to take the time, there are always management companies out there if you're still interested. If not, if you're not committed, then just don't rent. That's my best advice to you.

Robin: It's a great exercise to go through, even if you have just the slightest inkling to do this. Nothing ventured, nothing gained.

Brian: Absolutely. If it doesn't work, it doesn't work.

Robin: Do you have any tips for a boat owner who wants to rent a larger boat from someone else for three or four days during the summer months because the boat they have is too small?

Brian: On the renter's side, make sure the company or person you are renting from has insurance—it doesn't hurt to ask. As a renter, you want to feel protected while you're out there on the boat. If something does happen, you know there's something backing you. Don't over-do it if you just want to go out fishing for the day. If you're going in the back water, don't get a huge boat, get a boat that's going to meet your needs—a little skiff or something like that. If you're going off shore and it's wavy, you're going to want a bigger boat to get you out to where you need to go. If you don't have the experience, admit that you don't have the experience and get a captain to take you out there. Don't take any risks that are unnecessary. If you get out to the boat and it's damaged, don't drive it or take the vessel. Walk around the vessel with the owner. Have them show you all the equipment and everything like that. If there's something wrong with the vessel, don't go out on it. They can't hold you to the rental if there's something wrong, especially with life jackets and other safety equipment. Make sure the safety equipment is on there—you don't want to head out on a boat that doesn't have safety equipment. Interview the owner as the owner would interview you, whether it's a rental facility or just somebody that has a boat and is renting it out. Feel comfortable renting from them. The more you are comfortable with each other, the better the experience is going to be for everyone. And don't forget to have fun, because that is what boating is all about!

Closing

Robin: Brian, I want to thank you for being so generous with your time today. You've given boat owners a lot to think about with regards to renting out their own boats. Hopefully those who decide to go that route will take the necessary time to weigh all their options first and be successful.

Brian: Thanks Robin. I always enjoy sharing this great opportunity that exists. A lot of people don't really realize the opportunities or are scared to jump into renting their own boat. By setting a financial objective, understanding the risk of renting, and mitigating those risks to a comfortable level set by the owner, renting can be fun and easy for anyone. It's a great experience in sharing your passion with people—it's priceless. If there are any questions, please don't hesitate to contact me through the website rentbyboater.com. We are always here to help, so contact me even if you just want to talk about boating. I always love doing that too. Thanks again for having me.

Key Points

1. Three reasons to rent your boat are to make a profit, supplement your ownership costs, and/or to assist in sale of your vessel.
2. Three primary rental types are bareboat, charter, and dockside.

Rent Your Boat

3. Three forms of risk you might encounter when renting out your boat are passive, non-passive, and systemic.
4. Understanding the risks to you and your vessel is the first line of defense.
5. Three primary revenue sources/costs charged to a renter are gas usage, captain and crew fees, and basic rental fee for use of the boat.
6. Rental agreements include an *acknowledgement agreement* that the renter understands how to use the equipment on board, a *standard rental agreement* for a charter or bareboat rental—the basic terms of the rental, and a *waiver and release* from the renter stating the owner is not responsible for the renter's actions.
7. Protect yourself, in the event that your boat comes back damaged, by collecting a security and reservation deposit.
8. Always take pictures of your vessel upon its return for proof of any evidence of damage.
9. Four factors in determining your rental income are rental rate, fees per rental, estimated number of rentals per year, and estimated expenses.
10. Use common sense when renting out your boat. If someone doesn't seem like a good fit, they probably aren't.

Notes

Notes

Bad Storms/Heavy Weather
An Interview with Timothy Wyand

Introduction

Robin: Hello everyone. This is Robin Coles and it's my pleasure to welcome you to the 2010 Nautical Lifestyle Expert Series brought to you by TheNauticalLifestyle.com. During the next hour you're going to learn about boating in bad storms. Bad storms, or heavy weather, as they're known, can sneak up on you, turning that perfect boat ride into something extremely stressful. With me today, I am honored to have Timothy Wyand as my special guest. Hello Timothy!

Timothy: Hello Robin. It's great to be with you today.

Robin: Thank you so much for joining me. Timothy is a retired U.S. Coast Guard chief warrant officer (boatswain) with 22 years of service, 12 of which were at sea on both U.S. coasts, the Alaska/Bering Sea, Mediterranean Sea, Persian Gulf, and coasts of South America. Timothy is also a senior marine inspector (U.S. Coast Guard surveyor) specializing in wood and composite construction and repair. He's a long-time sailor and has raced dinghies, catamarans, and keelboats. Timothy presently owns a 31-foot pontoon boat and sells power boats and yachts in Houston, TX, and Richmond, VA. Timothy also writes for the *Richmond Boating Examiner* on examiner.com. He's been married 24 years, has four children, and has just returned from visiting one of his sons who recently came home after serving in Afghanistan. Timothy, it sounds like you've done a lot of traveling around.

Timothy: Yes, indeed, quite a bit—I've seen a lot of the world.

Robin: I can imagine. I bet you have some favorite spots.

Timothy: Probably my favorite spot that I visited is Bermuda. It's an amazing little place out in the middle of the ocean with pink sand beaches and wonderful sailing weather—nice consistent breezes. The water's a little cool for my liking, but it's a great place to sail—absolutely beautiful.

Bad Storms/Heavy Weather

Robin: **What exactly is heavy weather?**

Timothy: Heavy weather is a relative term. What we consider heavy weather, for example, on my pontoon boat, wouldn't even be noticeable on a large merchant ship or even on a good cruising sail boat. Basically, heavy weather is when you have to start doing things differently from what you normally do—when you have to start taking the weather into consideration—maybe having a shorter sail than you'd planned or deciding it's too rough to go fishing. It depends a lot on the boat—how it's designed—and on the crew's experience. A larger boat would normally be more seaworthy than a smaller vessel in the same conditions, but if the crew of a larger boat isn't experienced or capable, then they still might not be able to handle these kinds of conditions.

Robin: **Is it different for a power boat versus a sail boat? You said it differs by boat size, but what about by type of boat?**

Timothy: It's less an issue of whether it's power or sail, and more the design of the boat. A boat that's intended for open ocean—power or sail—whether it's fully decked or enclosed and a self-bailing cockpit or not are more the factors that determine when the weather becomes too rough for you. There are a lot of open sail boats appropriate for sheltered waters that would be perfectly fine in protected areas, but a heavy cruising boat, fully decked, with a self-bailing cockpit, lifelines all around, would be able to go through weather like that with no trouble at all. There are some open runabouts—powerboats 26 and 27 feet long—that may not be as seaworthy, per se, as an open cockpit, center console 20- or even 17-foot boat, that has a self-bailing cockpit and a closed transom.

I grew up primarily on the Chesapeake Bay where a summertime storm coming out of the southwest was an almost daily feature. We weathered some fairly good storms on a 17-foot MAKO® we had because it was self-bailing and had some good design features for more open waters. Some people with 21-foot runabouts that didn't have self-bailing and had a lot of loose gear, such as wakeboard towers, were having a rough time. Primarily whether the boat, power or sail, is designed for dealing with the weather—the strength of the boat, whether you can keep water out, and whether you can get rid of water once it comes in—will determine how well it can handle heavy weather. If all else is equal, size does matter. A larger boat will be able to withstand some higher waves and give better protection to its crew. Then again, the crew experience also has a lot to do with it.

Robin: **What's the worst type of storm to be in when you're a boater?**

Timothy: If you're on a lake or river, my experience is that a thunderstorm is by far the worst. They tend to be pretty severe—strong winds, with lightning always a hazard. The other issue is that storms can approach very quickly. They can form with very little warning and move rather rapidly. The worse part of dealing with that, as a boater on a small lake or river, is you have very little room to maneuver to deal with it. Storms can easily come between you and shelter, between you and the boat ramp where you have your trailer, or between you and your marina. You don't have a lot of room downwind to run before having to go around it. You may be stuck having to deal with it. That makes it a big issue on the smaller waterways.

On coastal waters and offshore, probably the worst, in my experience, is what they call the extra-tropical cyclone. On the east coast, we tend to call these nor'easters, primarily because they're large storm systems, even though you have good notice that they're coming, they cover such large areas, it's all but impossible to get out of their way. They tend to bring strong winds and large waves because they have more open water to work with and build up some waves. The other issue that tends to make them bad is the storm surge. A storm coming through during a high tide period can raise water levels several feet, which can inundate your piers, making your safe harbor inaccessible or unusable for quite a while. It can damage your boat even if you're not out on it. The issue, too, of course, is that when the winds and the waves are

Bad Storms/Heavy Weather   Timothy Wyand

in opposition to the tides, it tends to make the waves even steeper and closer together than usual, which makes storm conditions even worse. When you're on tidal waters, having a storm system like that tends to be the most dangerous because of the strong conditions. As far as getting out into the Chesapeake Bay, for example, when we have a nor'easter, it's not unusual for the water levels to rise quite a bit, which helps in avoiding going aground, but the waves tend to be very short, steep, and close together. Instead of being able to ride up one wave and down the other, which is a gentler ride for the crew and the boat, it's more of a pounding where you're just getting off of one crest and getting into another and getting hit, as opposed to being able to sail up a hill and then sail back down the hill. If you take the seas on the beam, the roll is much faster, you get more stress on the boat, and it's really stressful on the crew. The nor'easters are a good thing to watch out for in terms of weather pattern. The only good thing about extra-tropical cyclones is that usually there's at least a day's notice that they are coming. If you were planning on going out and found out about one on its way, it would probably be a good day to stay home.

Robin: **Extra-tropical cyclones, aka nor'easters, are more dangerous than hurricanes?**

Timothy: Most of the time, people have several days' notice about a hurricane and can avoid being out on their boat at all in that kind of weather. If you're further offshore and not in a position to avoid a hurricane, there are several steps you can take to mitigate your risk. But, they all pretty much depend on having one of two things—a shelter to get to fairly quickly or, if you can't, a lot of sea room in which to ride it out. Hurricanes can be pretty dangerous as well, whether you've got a power boat or a sailing vessel, just by virtue of the fact that they move relatively slowly. You can be sitting in that storm for 24 to 48 hours easily. I had the great fortune to be stationed on a ship out of Key West, FL, during 1980 to 1982. I rode out every single named storm in the Caribbean from 1980 through 1981. It's just the luck of the draw. Some of those storms, when you're waiting for them to pass by, can take 20, 24, 48 hours, depending on how slow-moving the storm is. Somewhere in my files, I have a picture taken from an Air Force storm chaser with a ship in the eye of one of the hurricanes. We had seized a couple of small boats as part of a drug enforcement action and we were towing them behind us. Because we were towing them, we couldn't go any faster than 2 or 3 knots, so there was no way we could avoid anything. We moved the crews from the seized boats onto our ships and had them with us while we rode out the storm. It was a good experience. We bounced around quite a bit. With proper handling, even the 26-foot boat we were in and smaller ones we were towing behind us—we had three of them in a nice little row, one after the other after the other—all made it through ok. The experience of the crew has a lot more to do with your survival than just the overall size of the boat.

Still, all being equal, I'd try to avoid those nor'easters if I could, mostly because you see those a lot more frequently and you have less notice than you do with one of the tropical storms coming up from the Caribbean.

Robin: Here in Boston we get a lot of them.

Timothy: Absolutely. I had the great fortune of sailing on the Coast Guard's Eagle, a Tall Ship operated by the Coast Guard Academy. One year we were doing sailing training with some cadets and we received a May Day call from a 36-foot sail boat that was having some trouble in a storm. To them it was a big storm; to us it was a good sailing breeze. As it was, the main issue was that the crew was very inexperienced and not equipped for an ocean crossing to Bermuda from New York. The winds were strong, the waves were big, but their boat should've been able to handle it. The crew was inexperienced and ill prepared. They had never encountered weather like that and weren't sure how to deal with it. It became an emergency for them. Imagine their surprise when they called the Coast Guard and a tall square-rigged ship pulled up to them and said, "We're here to help." It was quite interesting and a good experience for some of these Coast Guard cadets who had never seen a search and rescue done before. We tossed them a line and towed them to Hamilton, Bermuda, where they were safe and sound after that. They believed that since they were experienced sailing around the Long Island Sound area, sailing across to Bermuda during the summertime would be fairly uneventful, but they failed to check the weather. They didn't notice that the approaching storm system coming up from the southwest had a lot more wind than they were prepared to deal with. It wasn't that bad of a storm, but it did bring some gale force winds and they just weren't prepared for it. Their boat made it through just fine—had very little damage—and they really weren't in any danger, but their inexperience made it seem a lot worse than it was.

Robin: One of the things I've learned, while I've been out there sailing, is don't assume that because you can handle your inner harbor, or wherever you do most of your sailing, that once you get out into the wide open ocean it's going to be the same, because it's not.

Timothy: Absolutely right. There's no substitute for experience. Having an experienced crew or at least one experienced person on board who can provide some knowledge, skills, or leadership, can really make the day. Most of the boats today are a lot more seaworthy, I think, than people realize. It's not unusual after a large storm or hurricane to see a lot of boats washed up on beaches; but a lot of them are found miles and miles off shore. It's interesting how sometimes in some of these sail boat races—in say the southern ocean down off of Australia, or one of the Fastnet races (some of those had some pretty interesting storms up in the British Isles)—crews had requested to abandon their ships because they were in danger of sinking. Helicopters would come by and pluck the crews off the boat and the boat would be abandoned, but it would turn up safe and sound somewhere else three days later. It's interesting how sometimes we think a boat's not as seaworthy as it is. A lot of that is due to the crew not handling it properly. It's funny how the boat, left to its own devices, survives the storm just fine.

Robin: How much increase in the shift of wind should you allow before changing course or even shortening sails?

Timothy: That depends a lot on the boat. You really have to have some experience, to know your boat's handling characteristics. Some boats are more tender than others; some respond well to being driven hard in bad weather. It depends on your experience level, too; what you're comfortable with. When the boat begins to heel excessively, to the point where you're not comfortable with it—when it starts feeling sluggish, even though you've got all this wind power; like it's being knocked around a little bit—it's not as responsive. A boat's response comes from the water flowing over the rudder. A lot of times when you are overpowered, it doesn't want to handle properly—you've got too much weather helm, too much lee helm, depending on how you have your sails configured. When you have to ease the sheets a lot, to the point where they're luffing constantly, then it's about time to reef or change course. A lot of that depends on your experience level and boat time. For example, if you're sailing something that's a one-design, you're going to have to deal with that one way or another. Some of these one-designs don't handle well if you drop one of the sails or another; they don't handle well under jib alone. That's a function of knowing your boat. I've seen some J24s out in some absolutely horrid weather and do just fine. In fact, when they sail properly, they can be very exciting to sail under those kinds of conditions. That's where experience and knowing your boat is a big plus. Again, when the boat feels overpowered, too much heel; you have to constantly slack the sheets to keep the boat up, you have to pinch up too much to where you're losing speed, and you're steering as opposed to easing the sheets, then it's about time to shorten some sail. If you can't reef because of how your boat's rigged, maybe it's time to take one of them down—either the main or the jib.

Robin: **Are waves more dangerous than the wind?**

Timothy: It's been my experience that waves are much more dangerous. If you're talking about a sailing vessel, sure the wind can cause a knockdown, or, in a life boat, it could be capsized, but for the most part that's on an unballasted boat. It's not the end of the world—you're going to get wet. On a larger boat, with the keel, you're going to take a knock down, but eventually you'll come back up. And, if you've got the boat closed up like you should if there's that much wind, you're not going to take on any water or very much. That's not an issue. But, water's 700 times denser than air. So, when a wave hits, it hits with a lot more force than people realize. One popular show on the Discovery Channel was "Deadliest Catch"—you see these guys plowing through some of these waves and getting hit with them—it's like being hit with a fire hose only a lot wider. It's not unusual for waves to knock people across the deck, same thing on a small boat. Another thing to keep in mind is that a gallon of water weighs about 6½ pounds. Now, 50 gallons of water doesn't seem like a whole lot, but it weighs more than 300 pounds and it's easy to get 50 gallons of water into the bilge of a boat just from waves sloshing over if you don't have self bailing or if something is not closed up. Leave the hatch boards open and get a good wave down in the cockpit and you can get 50 gallons of water down there. Well, that water is now free surface as it sloshes around. Imagine 300 or 400 pounds of people running back and forth from one rail to the other at the worst possible times, and you can see what that would do to your stability. Now you have an issue, because a boat that was stable through its design before now has all this free weight sloshing around and causing issues. If you're already heeled over and you've got a bunch of water ballast and, of course, it always goes to the lowest part where you don't want it to be when you're heeled over, that's a big stability issue. And, of course, that extra weight tends to make the boat more sluggish and not handle as well. If you're a power boat and you take 50 pounds of water down the bilge, now you've got a problem with the engine. If a battery gets submerged in salt water, even if only for a short period of time, it tends to fully discharge. So, you've lost that battery and now you can find yourself without power—no engine, no steering—completely at the mercy of the winds and the waves. In my opinion, the waves are a lot more dangerous than the wind—they affect your stability. Water needs to stay out of the boat, not in the boat. If it gets in, you have to have a way to get it out. I would take a strong wind over big waves any day.

Robin: **What are the worst types of waves?**

Timothy: The worst types of waves, in my experience, are the ones that are short, steep, and close together, with a very short time between crests. Normally, in open ocean, you can have very large waves. Going back to that TV show, because a lot of people have seen it, some of the waves in the Pacific are very large, maybe 20 feet high, but, because the crests are a couple hundred feet apart, it's like driving a car on hills—you sail gently up, around/over the top, and gently back down. These waves can actually be fairly comfortable to ride, because they're far enough apart that you're not on one wave and cresting on another. Now, I've ridden on some 20-foot waves in the Atlantic off the eastern coast where we were. It was a nor'easter, we had about 40 knots of wind out of the north, so the air was blowing to the south, and we were riding the Gulf Stream, which is a strong northerly current. In this setting the seas were entirely different. We had waves that were about the same height as those we have in the Pacific, but now they were only about 100 feet apart—much steeper and closer together. Now we're slamming into these waves. Instead of being like a gentle hill, it's more like hitting a brick wall each time—as soon as you hit one, you're getting through that one and the next one hits you. When they're real close together, instead of being able to drive up one side and down the other, it's more like you hit a barricade and you start falling down and the next wave falls on top of you. And, because they're short and steep, there's not much give to them. It's more like hitting a wall, than driving into a wave. Again, talking about the 700 times difference in density, this is a lot more difficult on the structure. It's a lot more difficult on the crew too, because the motion of the boat requires a bit of effort. It's amazing how tiring rough weather is, even if you're not doing much except sitting there and holding on—holding on takes quite a bit of energy after a while, and it doesn't take long before you're exhausted. I spent about three years out on a ship in Hawaii, which wasn't in Hawaii very much. We spent nine months of the year up in the Bering Sea, up in that deadly catch area up there. Our ship was quite a bit larger, but waves are still waves. You don't realize how tired you get just trying to get around on a boat that's moving and pitching and heaving—it's very tiring for the crew. So, the worst types, for sure, are those waves that are short, steep, and close together. They almost look like a line of dominoes. You can see them coming, but they don't have breaking tops. They're very hard on the crew and they're very hard on the boats.

Robin: **Are those rogue waves or is a rogue wave something different?**

Timothy: A rogue wave is different. A rogue wave, by definition, is a wave that comes out of period or from a different direction. Most of the time, waves are generated by a strong wind or

Bad Storms/Heavy Weather — Timothy Wyand

even a current or a current acting on them. Waves tend to be pretty much from one direction—usually the direction the wind is coming out of or near to that. There's some predictability to those—you know the waves are going to come out of the east pretty much or whatever. What happens with a rogue wave is that another storm system a long distance away, or some other event, has caused large waves. The rogue wave either crosses or comes from another direction, and it's not in either the same period or cycle. Because they're waves, they tend to form cycles where they're one right after the other after the other—about the same time or distance apart. When a wave gets out of that cycle or comes from another direction, now you have a rogue wave. What happens then is that all of a sudden you've got another issue to contend with. You may have your boat set up and expecting waves off your bow and you're riding to them gently. Now, all of a sudden, this huge wave comes up from the stern. You may not be able to just ride right over it, depending on when it arrives, you could be at the trough of the regular set of waves and this wave comes out of your stern and breaks on top of you. Well, that's great—you've got that one to deal with. Now the regular storm system wave comes up, and the two of them added together could really cause some issues.

One time, I was the officer of the deck of a Coast Guard ship and we were heading north in a nor'easter, riding the Gulf Stream because we were trying to make the best possible time we could for a mission. It wasn't a search and rescue, but it was some other issue. We were heading north, trying to make the best possible time and save some fuel, of course, so we were riding where the waves were the steepest and closest together. Well, my ship was fairly long and narrow, so we were riding into these waves fairly well. I found a speed where we were able to kind of crest one wave and slide into the next without having to drop into the trough too bad. It was actually a fairly comfortable ride even though the waves were fairly large. Because we were going pretty fast, things were going pretty well. Well, we had a rogue wave—it came in and the waves got out of synch. Instead of making one big wave, what we had was a huge trough form, so instead of bouncing along gently from crest to crest—because our ship was large enough to stay between the crests and ride two crests at once—all of a sudden this huge trough opened up and we literally fell 30 feet. It was like being in an elevator that all of a sudden drops three floors. It was great seeing 3,000 tons of ship all of a sudden fall. We had solid water hitting the pilot house windows. Our pilot house windows were about 45 feet above the water line. The entire forward third of the ship went under water. Now, because we were in relatively clean water (in the South Atlantic, off the coast of Georgia or South Carolina somewhere), even though it was windy and stuff, I remember seeing the bow of the ship basically submerge like a submarine. I could see about the first 100 feet of the boat under the water from the pilot house windows, right before the solid water came up and hit us. I really thought we were going to break out all the tempered glass windows in the pilot house.

Robin: It's a bit too scary for me.

Timothy: When I saw we were getting ready to fall in there, I knew we had to reduce our speed and try to limit the damage. We cut the speed back and went through there and submerged and came out the other side. But it just about stopped the ship. We went from doing about 24 knots down to three in just a few seconds. It was a big stop and a big drop.

Everyone's like, "Whoa, what happened?" We didn't have any damage—that was ok. We had a couple fire hoses that came off the racks and we put them back on, but that was about it because we were well secured for rough weather. It's just amazing how the conditions can change—we had found a comfortable ride in, we were doing really well—it just took one rogue wave to all of a sudden change that. We had a chance to really sustain some damage, but we were well prepared for that. That's were the situational awareness comes in. Because we were prepared, we were able to take some action, slow the ship, and our ship responded very fast. If we had tried to continue our speed, we probably could've caused some damage, but we were well prepared for that. Again, the main thing on the rogue waves they come from another direction, unanticipated usually, or they can just get out of synch—all of a sudden, instead of having two 20-foot waves, you have one 30-foot wave or, in our case, we didn't have a big wave, we just had this huge hole we dropped into. So, rogue waves are definitely an issue out on open waters. Situational awareness—being aware of your surroundings—really pays off in those situations.

Robin: **What does the size of a wave depend on?**

Timothy: The size of a wave depends on three factors.

1. First is the wind speed—obviously the more wind you have the bigger the waves get.
2. Another issue is what the old-timers call 'fetch.' That is basically how much time or how much area the wind has had to work on the water. The more fetch you have, the bigger the waves get. That's why you tend to see larger and higher seas out in the Pacific than you do in the north Atlantic, because the Pacific Ocean is longer and wider. As a storm goes across there, it has another thousand miles of time and distance to build waves. You can have some big waves in the north Atlantic too. The perfect storm that took place back in the 1970s, that was covered in the movie, was particularly bad because it had a lot of time to move up the east coast. And the more time it had to move up the coast, the more time it had to build the waves. That's where a nor'easter or extra-tropical cyclone, as they call it, because it's not a hurricane, has the potential to be worse the further it goes up the coast—as it moves up the coast it has more time to work on the ocean water. When it first crosses over onto the water, you know, around the Carolinas or Virginia, it's not too bad because it's just getting started over the water. But by the time it gets up to New England, it's had a few hundred miles to work on that water and build those waves up. That's why, though you can have a really strong storm on a lake, it may only hook up a two-foot wave, even if it's blowing 60 miles an hour. But, if that same 60-mile-an-hour storm, or even a lesser storm blowing 30 miles an hour, is going across a large body of water, say part of the Atlantic, if it has a day to work on it, you could have 10- to 15-foot seas out of that. The fetch has a lot to do with how large the waves are.
3. Another thing that has a large effect on the size of the waves is a change in water depth. Anybody that's been to the beach has seen how the waves don't look too bad out in the ocean, but when they get to the beach they get steeper and higher, and all of a sudden they fall on you. It's the same out on the ocean, or anywhere else, for that matter. If you have good-sized waves, even a tidal wave, a tsunami, out in the middle of the ocean, you

Bad Storms/Heavy Weather   Timothy Wyand

wouldn't even notice it. It may only be a foot—you just don't realize it, but the majority of that wave action is in the water. But once that wave action starts running into shallower water, then the only place for that water to go, because it's constrained by the bottom, is up. These waves, that are fairly benign out in open waters, once they get in shallower water, they start getting steeper and higher. And because they are steeper..., you can only stack water so high before it starts to fall over. That's what happens with a breaking wave. A big soft gentle rolling wave is a lot safer than a steeper breaking wave, keeping in mind that it's 700 times denser than air and how heavy that water is. It's not unusual for a 15-foot wave to be able to drop several tons of water on top of you. Avoiding shallow waters in areas where there are large waves is a good idea—you're better off in deeper waters. The waves will be more rollers, softer and gentler, but in shallow waters, they'll get steeper and more breaking.

Those are the three factors that determine the size of your waves—your wind speed; fetch, or how long it has to act on it; and the depth of the water.

Robin: That explains a lot. **When is sailing in a blow the most dangerous?**

Timothy: The biggest danger you have when sailing in a good storm is when you have limited sea room, when you don't have much room to maneuver. That's assuming you don't have a safe harbor nearby. If you have a safe harbor nearby, or some protected water you can duck into, that's one thing. But, if you're out and having to deal with the storm, when you have limited room to maneuver, to find a more comfortable course or something that's easier for your boat, that could be a big issue. Keep away from a lee shore, and I'll probably mention that a few dozen times before we're over, too, because it is an issue—make sure there's no shallow water downwind from you, because that's when your biggest danger is.

Sudden thunderstorms can also be an issue, because they move quickly and because the winds tend to come downward, hit the water, and fan out in more than one direction. There can be very sudden and violent wind shifts with these thunderstorms. That can be just as bad, if not worse, as the wind speed itself. For example, if you're close hauled—got your sails strapped down and maybe a reef or two in and you're doing pretty good—but all of a sudden, a storm goes by and shifts the wind. Now it's off your quarter at the same speed, your sails are pinned in too tight; you're going to take a knockdown. Depending on how the situation is, you could end up taking some water—that could be dangerous.

That's the two things we have to worry about: 1) limited sea room, when it limits your options for dealing with the weather, whether you're power or sail, it won't make any difference there; and 2) a fast-moving thunderstorm where you have to watch for a sudden change in wind direction that can overwhelm you if you're a sailboat or a small powerboat (they have to be concerned about wind directions, too).

I run a pontoon boat and you talk about something that's affected by wind, it's unusual that my big, heavy pontoon boat would get caught out in something like that, but if a violent thunderstorm came by, the wind would be one of my main concerns. Our boat's aluminum and we have a lot of sail area. It has an upper sundeck which can catch a lot of wind when docking (trust me I know). There was a pontoon boat used as a harbor excursion boat in Baltimore Harbor several years ago that was capsized by wind action during a thunderstorm. Several people lost their lives in that.

Robin: **You'd think a pontoon would be safer.**

Timothy: In most cases it is, because of its wide stance. But the boat was fairly light, the wind was able to get underneath the pontoons and lift it somewhat. Again, a big, sudden wind shift, they were heading into it and doing ok until as the storm went by at about 30 miles per hour. All of a sudden, they were hit with a strong beam wind and all the passengers had gone to one side to avoid the rain. Once the wind got underneath that wide flat bottom that connects the two pontoons, over she went.

Robin: **Is that because the weight was all on one side?**

Timothy: Correct—that had a big effect on it. We talked about directing the crew and their experience. The captain, the master of the boat, had told the passengers that not all of them should be over there, but they didn't listen. He didn't have enough crew to get them to get out of the way. The passengers didn't want to get wet, you know, it was just raining. Then that sudden wind gusted about 60 miles per hour. The boat was not designed to operate in those kinds of conditions.

Robin: What a shame!

Timothy: It was very unfortunate. Of course, being in an excursion boat, the passengers weren't wearing life jackets at the time. They were available, but some of the passengers lost their lives over that.

Robin: **What are some tactics for coping with strong (gale) winds when saving your and your crew's life is more important?**

Timothy: Probably the first thing you want to do is avoid a lee shore—you don't want any shallow water downwind of you. That's not just an inconvenience, it's dangerous. You don't want to run aground with the wind blowing you onto the shallower ground or rocks or whatever the situation is—now you're at the mercy of the winds and the waves, so you're just going to get battered. It's dangerous for the boat—that's when capsizings occur. Having a boat turn over on top of you when you're in the water is one thing, but having a boat turn over on top of you when there's land underneath you, that's even worse. People get washed off of decks. Sailboats tend to draw less water when they're heeled over. With most sailboats, as soon as they run aground, they pivot—they don't have any choice, that's just the physics of the matter. If you've got a little bit of a weather helm, you're going to pivot into the wind. If you've got lee helm, you're going to pivot downwind and show your stern to the waves. If you're aground, you're going to stay heeled over *and* pivot, so now you may have your deck and not just your bottom

Bad Storms/Heavy Weather — Timothy Wyand

presented to the waves and you can't maneuver. You're completely at the mercy of the weather then and there's a good possibility that someone's going to get hurt for that.

Avoiding lee shores boils down to situational awareness—making sure you know what's around you and trying not to get into that situation in the first place. You can look for an area of protected water. For example, on a river, usually there's a bend you can go around and get away from the weather or you can head closer to the shore where the trees are cutting off some of the wind. If you're in open water, head into a more protected area—up in a creek, into a bay that's got some shelter, in the lee of an island. Hopefully, there's plenty of deep water downwind to avoid a lee shore if your anchor drags or your engine quits. If that sort of thing is not available, the best thing you can do when you're dealing with strong winds is get in open waters. It seems kind of like the wrong thing to do, but having room to maneuver and to put the boat on a heading where it rides to the wind and waves best is the safest course of action. If you have some time and you know the weather is coming—your situational awareness has told you there's a thunderstorm coming, you see the clouds, you hear it on the radio—you can prepare for it. There's no substitute for experience and situational awareness. Bottom line is if you got a storm coming, try to get some shelter if you can, whether it's behind an island or behind some trees if you're on a small lake. Keep deep water downwind from you, otherwise stay in open water.

Robin: **If a boater should find themselves caught in one of these storms, what's the first thing they should do (*after* they put on their life jackets on, because we know the Coast Guard's going to ask them that question)?**

Timothy: That's always the smartest thing to do—put those PFDs on—they'll keep you safe. That should be something that the captain or the boat operator should be telling people to do anyway as soon as they know a storm's coming.

The first thing you want to do is assess your situation—look at all the factors that are going on. It doesn't mean you have to sit down and write a report about it, but you want to look at things like: There's a storm coming, where's it coming from? Where do I have safety; can I get to safety before the storm gets here? Do I have enough gas or fuel to get there? If it's a thunderstorm, is it going to pass between me and safety? If that's the case, I'm not going to head that way. What's my alternative plan? What options do I have? Assess your situation and see what your options are. Next, brief your crew—let them know what's going on and what your plan is. That way they're less likely to become apprehensive and panic when the wind arrives and it starts raining. "Oh, it's a storm!" "Yeah, we just talked about that. This is what I need you to do. This is where I need you to be. You're going to get a little bit wet, but we'll be a lot safer if you stay there." Brief the crew and answer any questions they have. Reassure and give directions for anybody that needs anything. Keep it simple and have a plan.

Robin: **When should you be concerned with using or hooking the harness on your life jacket?**

Timothy: I like to hook on when the decks are wet and staying wet. If you're taking on a good amount of water on the deck, it's a good idea to be hooked on, especially, if you're heeled over quite a bit and you need your hands to work. They have an old saying, "One hand for the ship and one hand for yourself." That's always a good thing to have, but small boats, especially some racing boats, tend to have pretty small foredecks. Those sails can whip around quite a bit. I used to do a lot of foredeck work, because I'm fairly small. I'm not a big heavy guy, and they didn't like weight up on the bow, so I got sent to do foredeck work. Sometimes you need your hands to do stuff. If you're short-handed, you definitely need to be hooked in when you're going forward. You need to have a fairly short tether too, by the way. Having a 20-foot tether on a 20-foot boat doesn't do you much good, because if you slip off, you're going over the side, and you're just going to go for a ride behind it. That's not the point. The point of the lanyard, and being hooked in/on the lifeline, is to keep you from going over in the first place.

I always hooked in if the decks were wet, if I was going to be working on the forward and it was heeled over pretty good, there was a good chance of me slipping. When it's heeled, of course, there is only one place for you to go—you're going to slide down. You don't want to go in the drink if you can help it. When I sailed on Eagle (U.S. Coast Guard Tall Ship), we were required to be hooked in all the time we were aloft, any time we started climbing on the rigging and the cross trees. On a tall ship, all the sails are handled by hand. That's why you have a crew of 150 on a square-rigged sailing ship—because everything is done with man power. The sails get furled when the wind's strong. You can douse a sail from down on the deck, but, still, up there you've got hundreds of square feet of canvas flapping like crazy. The only way to store that is to go up on the rig—a bunch of you stand out on the yards and you roll it up and tie it off with gaskets. You have to be hooked on when you do that stuff. It shouldn't be any macho thing with working on the forward and not being hooked in. Being hooked in is one less thing you have to be concerned with—for you and your crew—that you're going to go over the side. It lets you work a little more confidently. Any time decks are wet and you've got a good amount of heel going, it's just a good time to be hooked in.

Robin: **When does heaving-to become unsafe?**

Timothy: Heaving-to is a good procedure to use when the weather is bad. You can heave to in power boats or sail. Basically, it involves finding a course either directly into the waves or, usually, a little bit off to one side, where the boat just lies to the waves in its most gentle motion. You get to the point though when you have to stop heaving-to, especially on a sailboat, when you're taking repeated knockdowns, even with just your storm canvas up. You can heave-to without storm canvas. I used to heave-to on my little 470 dinghy. I found a way to get it to lie-to and I would sit there if I was out sailing and wanted to take a rest or eat my lunch or something. I could get it to heave-to and the boat would just basically sit there and drift slowly downwind even with the sails up. I didn't have to mind it for a while or worry about it turning over. Heaving-to is a good skill, but when you're taking repeated knockdowns, you need to either make an adjustment on how you've got it lined or, basically, you're done. Now you have to consider lying to a drove, where basically you take down all your canvas and you put out the sea anchor or something else to hold you into the wind. That's not a very comfortable ride, I can tell you that. Heaving-to becomes no longer an option because of wave heights, or when the wave period changes to where your boat's length or shape is not a safe ride for you anymore; if every time you come to the top of the crest of a wave you get hit with a blast of wind and get knocked down again. A lot of sail boats, when they take a knockdown, tend to have a weather helm because of the shape of the hull and tend to round up regardless of how the sails or the rudder are. If that's the case, then you can do that. If you have enough speed, you can actually almost complete a tack and you'll end up with your sails back, pinned on the wrong side and then you get knocked flat and you don't come back up. There comes a point when heaving-to just doesn't work. If you're getting knocked down all the time, it's just not safe to stay there any more. Now you have to either lie to a drove or even consider running downwind—not the best option, especially if you have breaking seas. If they're not breakers, then maybe running downwind to a drove is an option.

Robin: I read somewhere recently that if you have to stop and think whether or not you should be heaving-to, then it's already become unsafe.

Timothy: That's pretty much it. We talked earlier about knowing your boat and its handling characteristics—a big determination of your seaworthiness. If you get to the point where you have to consider it, you've probably waited too long. If you know your boat well enough, you just know that, ok, these are the conditions I should be heaving-to, and you just do it. But, if you're thinking about it, that means you thought about it somewhat as the conditions got worse, and you've gotten to the point where it's probably not safe to do so. It's always better to trust your instincts and your experience and do what you know is right.

Robin: Right. And this is one time when you definitely need to have experienced people—for knowing how to do a heave-to.

Timothy: Absolutely. You don't have to wait for bad weather to practice heaving-to. A coach in Miami, when I was racing lasers, taught me how to do this. He said, "You need to go out and practice. Just go out and do stuff that you wouldn't ordinarily do." This makes your practicing more interesting anyway. So, one of the things he taught me to do was to heave-to. He said it's good to learn how your boat handles in all kinds of weather, so we would heave-to in nice weather. Then, when it comes time to heave-to in bad weather, or even if it's not real bad and you just need a break, being able to heave-to is a good thing. Let's say you're making a transit—you and someone else's crew—and you're getting tired, you need a meal, and you're starting to feel a little queasy. Maybe some hot food would be good or you just need a break from steering and all that stuff. If you've got enough sea room, no lee shore downwind for several miles, then you can heave-to for half an hour and take a break from steering—the boat rides like a duck for a while and you get a break, maybe get some dry clothes on. You can reassess your situation, maybe decide to change course, then go back to what you were doing. Knowing how to heave-to by doing it in good weather makes it a lot easier to do it when the weather's bad.

Robin: **Besides listening to NOAA on their radio, what type of cloud formations should boaters watch for?**

Timothy: In the summertime, you want to be worried about the thunderstorms that can develop fairly quickly, especially on the east coast when the weather gets hot. You want to be looking at the cumulus clouds. The main thing you're looking for in them is vertical development—do they start growing upwards? Just because a cloud is flat on the bottom and dark, it doesn't necessarily mean you're going to get a storm. It may just mean you're going to get a cloudy day or a little bit of rain. Cumulus clouds turn into cumulonimbus thunderstorm clouds when they start developing upwards. That's caused by the hot air rising, taking moisture with it, and making the air unstable. The faster the air rises, the higher it goes and the more rapidly it cools and starts coming back down. Then you start getting that thunderstorm circulation going. What ever it is you're doing, look at the clouds once in a while. If you see the cumulus clouds are starting to develop, they don't look so much like cotton balls, but are starting to look larger and taller, then you know thunderstorms are possible. When a cloud starts building upwards and a point starts to form near the top, looking kind of like an anvil shape, you know you've got a cumulonimbus forming, which is a thunderstorm cloud. Even if you don't have rain or lightning going on, when you see the clouds developing upwards, that point shows you the direction the upper air is moving and that's the direction the cloud is moving. That's a good thing to watch and will help you decide if that storm is going to pass between you and shelter, or which direction it's heading. You might want to look at keeping that cloud behind you, if that's the only one—that's the best thing.

Extra-tropical cyclones tend to form as a front goes by. A warm front and a cold front that are normally parallel start merging together, then there starts being some circulation. Usually what you'll get with those are what are called mares' tails or mackerel scales. Mares' tails are light wispy clouds fairly high in the sky that look like a horse's tail. Mackerel scales are lots of small clouds spread out in a flat layer, kind of high, that look almost like scales on a fish—they make kind of a pattern. The sailors had a rhyme that went along with this, "Mares' tails and mackerel scales make tall ships shorten sails." What that means is that when you saw those, within 24 hours you were going to have stronger winds, a nor'easter. Usually you had good weather for the first 24 hours after you saw those clouds, but usually within 24 to 48 hours you had some bad weather coming. Those are your two big indicators over on the east coast.

On the west coast, it's another whole circumstance because your weather system is entirely different. They get the lows that come out of Siberia and come right down the coast. You tend to see those things coming a long ways off. The other systems you have primarily are the tropical cyclones that come out from down by the Gulf of Mexico. You have plenty of warning and don't have significant cloud formations for those.

Robin: I like that little rhyme that you gave us.

Timothy: I didn't come up with it—that's been around since the days of sailing ships.

Robin: **What other signs of approaching bad weather should boaters look out for?**

Bad Storms/Heavy Weather   Timothy Wyand

Timothy: One of the significant ones is a change in wind direction. Most of the time, as weather systems settle in, you tend to have wind out of one direction and that's fine; but if you have a significant change in the wind, especially over a short span of time, that means there's a big change in the weather coming. Also, if the wind varies in strength—it doesn't have to be a big change—it can mean a change in the weather. It doesn't necessarily have to be a stronger wind. You've probably heard the phrase 'the calm before the storm.' In areas where you've got trade winds or consistent winds during a season and the winds stop, it usually means there's a big change in the weather coming. So watch out for big winds coming in the other direction. With a thunderstorm, another big sign that one's coming besides the wind direction is all of a sudden the wind will get much cooler—a big change in air temperature. What happens with these thunderstorms is as they suck the air, the warm air, with all that moisture, rises very high and very quickly. Up at 30,000 feet, the temperature is actually below zero. That air is cooled rapidly (it usually forms ice crystals), then that cold air, because it's much denser, falls rapidly. When that air comes down, it comes down straight, hits the surface of the water, and spreads out in all directions. That sometimes gives you a change in wind direction, but if the wind doesn't get much harder, but all of a sudden it's gotten a lot cooler, like you're sitting in front of an air conditioner, that's not a good sign. That's usually a sign that there's a thunderstorm developing really close by, because you're close enough to get that cold down draft. That's usually a clue that you need to be looking for a thunderstorm that's really close. Even if you don't have any thunder or lightning yet, there's one forming nearby.

Most people don't listen to AM radio anymore, but strong bursts of static on an AM radio are caused by lightning. It doesn't have to be nearby—it can be somewhere in the vicinity. You'll hear it on any AM channel. If you have an AM radio and you tune it to any place on the dial and there are a lot of bursts of strong static, it means you've got lightning nearby. That's definitely your clue to turn up your situational awareness and start looking around.

Robin: There's so much to think about, to keep in the back of your head.

Timothy: That's one of the great things about boating, though—the more you learn, the more you can enjoy it. Sometimes, being aware of your situation and having all these little pieces of knowledge can help save the day. A couple weeks ago, my family and I were out on our boat on a river which is about a half mile wide, but fairly long. We had left our dock and headed about four miles down the river to one of our favorite little coves where we were doing a little fishing and some swimming. It was a cloudy day, a little bit of rain earlier, but the clouds weren't too bad. Without any warning—we didn't hear any thunder or anything like that—out of the clouds came a really strong bolt of lightning nearby. A pontoon boat is not the most seaworthy of boats because it has a lot of wind area and is fairly low to the water (it doesn't take much more than a two-foot wave before we get water coming on the deck). But it rides surprisingly well, ours does. Tracking the weather, the storm, the wind direction—we were pretty sure that this one was going to pass to one side of us. We looked around and there weren't any other storms nearby. There wasn't anything between us and safety, so we knew we could run home if we had to. So we took a chance that the storm would pass by, that it was localized. We kept an eye on it and ended up getting a couple more hours of good boating time. Some folks saw bolts of lightning and ran for home and that was it. About a half hour or an hour later it was pretty weather again. Having this information and keeping aware of your situation can help you save a day, even if there is some bad weather around.

Robin: I would probably be one of those that would run home.

Timothy: Normally we do too. It's one of those things. We go boating to enjoy it. Having to go out in bad weather as I did with the Coast Guard, that's not what I do with my family. We go out to enjoy the weather, so if the weather's not good, we don't go out. But, we were already out there. Maybe the prudent thing would have been to run home, but I relied on my experience and some knowledge to assess the situation. I was 99 percent sure that it was going to miss us and, if I was wrong, I knew I could get home because the storm was not going to get between me and safety. We chose to wait it out and keep an eye on it. I was right this time, so we ended up getting a good afternoon out of it.

Robin: You mentioned the key word—experience. Everything is based on it, but I don't recommend going out into these storms just to get experience if you don't have to. **It's hurricane season in the south, and in the north here we're getting lots of rain and thunderstorms. What should a boater do to protect themselves when they go out?**

Timothy: The first thing you should do, before you go out, is check the weather forecast. There's a lot of information available. There's TV, of course, and the radio, and there's always the internet (weather.com and weather underground, which is wunderground.com). There's more to it than just looking at the forecast—forecasts are based on computer models which may or may not be 100 percent correct. Having a little experience with your local weather can help you decide what "a chance of isolated thunderstorms" really means. If you're in the Chesapeake Bay, for example, you know that every afternoon in the summertime, about 2:00 or 3:00 o'clock, there's going to be a thunderstorm coming out of the southwest. Depending on where you are, it might pass a little south of you, it might pass well north of you, or it might pass right on top of you. But there, if you don't go out on the days they're predicting "isolated thunderstorms," you'll never go out all summer. You have to look at the forecast and take a bit of local knowledge into account with it. If thunderstorms are likely, then that's probably not a good time to go. Do not just look at the forecast, but also look at the current conditions—take a look at the weather radar on the internet or on television. If you see a big line of thunderstorms heading your way, then it's probably not a good day to go out. On the other hand, if the radar is clear, then you can probably go. Just keep in mind that thunderstorms can develop fairly quickly and keep an eye out for them.

You want to make sure your boat and equipment are maintained properly. That's a really big issue. You want to make sure that your lifejackets, of course, are accessible, that you can get to them in an emergency, that they're not all moldy and dry rotted, that the straps are strong, and that people know how to put them on quickly. You want to make sure your boat runs properly. If you're a sailboat, you want to make sure your mast rigging are in good shape and your sails are in good shape as well. You may have to rely on them to get you home. You want

Bad Storms/Heavy Weather   Timothy Wyand

to make sure you have enough gas. Going out for a day of wakeboarding, you use a bunch of gas just going around in circles. That's fine. You think you have enough gas to get home, but if you want to get home fast—you're in the way of a thunderstorm—you need to make sure you have enough fuel for that. If your engine's not reliable and you're in a powerboat, it's probably not a good day to go out, because that engine may not be there when you need it. Just make sure everything is operating properly.

Navigation lights are another big deal. We witnessed a situation not too long ago on a day with a lot of rain—they weren't real bad storms, just pockets of rain, but it affected visibility quite a bit. We were on a river and there's a lot of commercial traffic on this river, so we anchored in a cove outside the channel. Some other folks decided they were going to stop and do some swimming, but they were in the channel. When the rain came, it cut down visibility quite a bit and, sure enough, they're out there swimming. Here comes a tugboat with barges and they're not the easiest thing in the world to stop. Because of the way the river is, this guy is confined to the channel—he literally cannot get out of the channel because the water's so shallow on either side. He won't just run aground, he physically cannot leave the channel; so he has no place to go but stay in the channel. Having navigation lights on this boat would have helped the tugboat see him a bit sooner. They weren't paying attention—they had no situational awareness—so they didn't see him coming until he sounded the danger signal for them to get out of the way. People had to scramble to get out of the water before that tugboat and barges came in there. He had no place to go, but stay in the channel, so they had to leave. So, make sure your navigation lights are working properly—it's important for other people to be able to see you, even if you're in rain that just comes and goes. Make sure that your boat's well maintained, your equipment's well maintained, and you've checked those forecasts. If you know your experience level, let that be your guide as to what kind of conditions you're willing to deal with. Before you go, ask yourself, "There's a chance of thunderstorms. Am I prepared to deal with one today?" If your answer is no, wait until tomorrow. If you are prepared to deal with some of that stuff, then ok, participate, anticipate—prepare for the worst, and expect the best.

Robin: **Do you have any tips for handling a boat in a rain squall?**

Timothy: A typical afternoon rain squall, with nothing too terribly bad, still the first thing you want to do is have everybody get those PFDs on. Things can go sour pretty quick, even in the best of circumstances, so it's always a good idea to have those things on. Make sure you secure any loose gear, any hatches, the cabin boards on a sail boat—it's nice to have that breeze down there; if it's not too bad, just put the bottom two in, something like that. Close up the boat to keep any water out. Check your position. It comes under the same situational awareness thing, but know what your position is before the weather really starts getting stinky, or even if it's just a rain squall. Know where you're at, so you know where you are in relation to any navigational dangers you may have—running aground, for example.

Robin: I've done that.

Timothy: It's easy to do. On a sailboat with a deep keel, running aground can be more than an inconvenience, especially if the wind picks up, because now you're stuck, literally, and you're at the mercy of the wind and waves. You can't sail out of the way because you're sitting on the bottom. It's the same with a powerboat. You'll find yourself aground and you've got the lee shore thing going on now and you're just sitting there getting beaten by the wind and waves. If a boat's floating it can get give—it can move and dissipate some of that energy from the wind and wave action. But if it's attached to the bottom, you're kind of at the mercy of all that. Take a second to note your position, update your awareness, and play the 'what if' game. What if this rain squall turns out to be more than that? Where do I go from here? Which way do I head when I can't see my hand in front of my face because of the rain? Am I in a channel? Is there a chance that I could get run over by a barge if I stay here? What about other boats? Some guy running from a storm through here, is he going to be able to see me? Maybe I should put my navigation lights on, maybe I should consider sounding the signals (not that everybody understands what they are, but if you hear a loud noise in front of you, you can pretty much assume that there's something there that you don't want to hit). So, put the PFDs on; secure your loose equipment so you don't get water in it, and so if the wind picks up, nobody gets hurt by things moving around; make sure you know where you are in relation to any dangers nearby; and think about what you are going to do if something else happens.

For boat handling, that's a different situation altogether. For a powerboat, or a sail boat under power (the same thing), just make slow headway. If there are some significant waves building, then you might want to head into it. If the winds are strong, just head into it, making better steerage. If you know there's a safe direction you can head, then continue to head in that safe direction. Just keep in mind the fact that visibility is down—you can't see; other people can't see you either. Use that to gauge your speed. If you're in a powerboat, you'll want to be able to stop or turn in half the distance of visibility. If you can see a mile, then you need to be able to turn or stop in half a mile. That sounds like a lot of distance—it really is—but if you're going fast, it doesn't take very long to cover that distance. Some of these bass boats that folks use in lakes, they cruise at 70 miles an hour and can go even faster. One of my neighbors at my marina has a 40-mile-an-hour pontoon boat. Running from a storm, keep in mind, if you can't see very far and all of a sudden there's a boat stopped in front of you, you don't want to be the guy that ruins their whole day. Maybe you thought you were one place, but it turns out you were not, and a marina or dock or dam or buoy happens to pop up in front of you. Use your visibility to gauge your speed.

Robin: I was on a boat and we ran aground in a rain squall. It happened so fast. We were trying to bring the jib down—the mainsail and the furlings had broken.

Timothy: That can be an issue. Some of the furling gear can make it very difficult to get that jib down if its on the roller furler. That can keep you busy, that's for sure.

Robin: We're running out of time, so I have one last question. **Is there anywhere safe for a boater to be in a bad storm? I know we've talked about getting to shelter, but is there any one place that is safer than others?**

Bad Storms/Heavy Weather — Timothy Wyand

Timothy: The main thing to do is to avoid a lee shore in shallow water. You won't drown in shallow water, but it tends to be worse for the boat—you're more likely to wind up in it. The main thing you want to do is avoid being in a situation where you've got shallow water or land directly downwind of you. If anything can go wrong, it usually does; you know Murphy (of Murphy's Law) is definitely a sailor, no doubt about that. The lee shore is the worst possible situation, even if it's not really a storm, just strong winds—the kind of day a lot of people like to go sailing—if you touch bottom, lose power, rip a sail, or even something simple like getting an override. I was in a race once, sailing a J24 and we were doing really well; it was a small lake and we had a nasty override on the jib, which is surprising. This was a borrowed boat and they had jib sheet winches. Most J24s don't use them—they tend to cleat them by hand—but this one did and the guy who was trimming that day was not very experienced and he got a nasty override in it. The wind was blowing pretty hard. We had to tack—we were heading toward the seawall. The problem was that we couldn't get the boat to flip over because we were sailing with a good size overlapping jib and we had to sheet it really flat. Of course, once we got the override, we tried to pull it tighter and that just made it worse. To make matters worse, this was one of those Wednesday night just-for-fun after work races, so none of us were really prepared for anything. It was like, "Hey, I'll meet you after work and we'll just jump on the boat and go." None of us were really prepared or dressed for sailing in a squall. None of us had our rigging knives with us. The jib was sheeted so tight we couldn't pull it down, it just wouldn't move. We found a hacksaw blade down below and I was on the foredeck with this rusty hacksaw blade trying to saw through the sheet in time to get it cut through enough to where we could tack and not plow into the seawall. That lee shore danger downwind is a real problem. It doesn't take much—it just took an inexperienced guy a few turns on a crank to put us in real jeopardy. Now we laugh about it, of course, but at the time it wasn't funny.

Robin: We laugh about it too. Ours was a borrowed boat as well—maybe there's something to that.

Timothy: There's another lesson.

You want to avoid danger downwind. You don't want a navigational hazard on one side and wind and waves on the other. Other than that, try and find some protection from the wind and waves. Get on or close to the shore line on the other side; get behind something—a lee or an island. If not, open deep waters may be your best bet.

Closing

Robin: Timothy, I want to thank you for being so generous with your time today. You've given me, and probably most of us on the call, a lot of insight regarding heavy weather and dealing with bad storms.

Timothy: There's a lot of good information available. A really good reference—even if it has been around for a long time, it gets frequent updates—is *Piloting, Seamanship, and Small Boating Handling,* a book by Charles F. Chapman—it's a great resource. Another good place you can check, of course, is my web page on examiner.com.

Robin: **How do we find you there?**

Timothy: Go to examiner.com, click on Virginia, select Richmond; I'm under Sports, then Boating. My web address is examiner.com/x-15246/Richmond-boating-examiner. Apply the button and you'll get all my updates as they come out; you won't have to worry about that nasty web address and clicking through all that other stuff.

Key Points

1. Once you know bad weather is approaching, make sure everyone on board put on PFDs (personal flotation devices).
2. Check the weather forecast before you go out. Make sure your boat and equipment are maintained properly. Know your boat's handling characteristics.
3. Experience is important to making it through any bad storm or heavy weather.
4. On a lake or river, the worst type of storm to be in is a thunderstorm. On coastal waters, the worst is an extra-tropical cyclone, aka nor'easter on the east coast.
5. Watch for a significant change in wind direction, strength, or temperature—it means there's a big change in weather coming.
6. If a hurricane is heading your way, find shelter quickly. If you can't find shelter, you'll need lots of sea room in which to ride out the storm.
7. Don't assume, because you can handle the harbor where you do most of your boating, that once you get out into the open ocean it's going to be the same—it's not.
8. Waves are more dangerous than wind. The size of a wave depends on wind speed, fetch, and change in water depth. The worst waves are short, steep, and close together.
9. Avoid a lee shore when you're coping with strong winds.
10. If the decks are wet, or you're taking on water, hook the harness on your life jacket to a life line or tether.

Notes

Search and Rescue
An Interview with Alan Sorum

Introduction

Robin: Hello everyone. This is Robin Coles and it's my pleasure to welcome you to the 2010 Nautical Lifestyle Expert Series brought to you by TheNauticalLifestyle.com. Today you're going to learn the top three things boaters need to do to facilitate a search and rescue mission.

I'm honored to have a special expert with me today—Alan Sorum. Alan is an unreformed Alaska harbormaster; a boating feature writer for Suite101.com, an online magazine; and a member of the United States Coast Guard Auxiliary. Hello Alan!

Alan: Hello Robin.

Search and Rescue

Robin: **How does a search and rescue operation work?**

Alan: The system is fairly complicated, but in the United States, we break it into two different areas. On land, search and rescue is coordinated by the Air Force; on the water, search and rescue is coordinated by the Coast Guard. The Coast Guard has a system of what they call SARs (search and rescue coordinators) that pursue the cases in their geographic areas of responsibility. The country is divided up into individual areas where there are Coast Guard stations, with Coast Guard Active Duty and Auxiliary units participating in these missions.

Robin: **You said they're all over the country. Are they set up by region?**

Alan: Yes—if you look at a map, the Coast Guard has it broken into something like 17 districts. Alaska is District 17, Hawaii is its own district. Alaska is one district and it commands out of Juneau, the state capital. Then there's a couple of what they call Captain of the Port—one in Anchorage and the other in Juneau. They break it up that way to make it manageable.

Robin: **What is a good search and rescue system for boaters?**

Alan: The best thing a boater can do to facilitate a rescue is for everyone on board to be wearing their lifejackets. That's the best thing a boater can do to save lives if there's a problem on the water. But, if we're talking about *additional* things a boater can do to improve their chances of a quick rescue, the first thing they need to do is to purchase and learn how to use a marine VHF radio. That's really important. The second thing is to file a float plan with your local harbormaster or a friend. That way, people have an idea of how many people are on board your boat, where you intend to travel, and when you plan on getting back. That's really useful if somebody is trying to find you later. The last thing is that a lot of recreational boaters should consider purchasing an EPIRB (emergency position-indicating radio beacon).

Robin: **What equipment should they make sure they have on the boat?**

Alan: For basic boating safety equipment, it's really important to have the things you would normally think of—lifejackets, fire extinguishers, signal flares. In addition, having both a marine VHF radio and an EPIRB is a really good idea.

Robin: **What types of lifejackets should they have? And what should they look for to make sure their fire extinguishers and flares and stuff are up to date?**

Alan: With National Safe Boating Week coming up, the thing people are trying to get across is that there's really no excuse for not wearing a lifejacket. They come in so many different sizes and shapes, and they're a lot more comfortable now. A lot of people are starting to wear the suspender inflatable lifejackets. The best lifejacket is one that you're comfortable with and actually wearing. Here in the north, a lot of people wear float coats which offer a little bit more protection from the elements, but the most important thing is to have an approved lifejacket and be wearing it. If you have it stowed and something happens, there's usually not enough time to find the thing and don it after an accident occurs.

If you're interested in the condition of your boat and the safety gear on board, think about getting a vessel safety check from the Coast Guard Auxiliary or a member of the United States Power Squadrons®. They'll help you look at your fire extinguishers and make sure they're charged, and look at your flares to make sure they're not expired. It's a really good way to check the boat out before the season begins.

Robin: **How many lifejackets do they need on the boat?**

Alan: Under federal law, you need one approved lifejacket within reasonable reach for each person on board. They have to be the right size and they have to be approved. It's usually a good idea to have a couple of spares. The other thing they require is that you have an approved throw-able device—a floating seat cushion or a ring buoy—something you can throw to somebody in the water. Those are the basic requirements for lifejackets.

Robin: **A lot of boats now are using the LifeSling Overboard Rescue System? How important is that to have on the boat?**

Alan: LifeSlings are approved as throw-able devices. If you're out on a boat and somebody falls overboard, even if they're not injured, people don't realize how hard it is to get the person back in the boat. That's where something like a LifeSling—or other similar thing out there—is really important. For boaters, it's a really valuable drill to actually practice "man overboard"—how you track somebody in the water, how you get back to the person, and how you get him or her back on the boat.

Robin: **Some of the Coast Guard Auxiliary and United States Power Squadrons® locations have a course called "Suddenly in Command." Some of them are now changing it to "Taking Over the Boat." As a title, which is more appropriate? And are there any other courses you recommend that a boater, crew member, or even** someone who just goes out on a boat and doesn't know much about it, should take to learn about and practice man overboard?

Alan: You've done a good job listing some of the courses. Taking a regular boating safety class is always important. If the skipper of the boat has time, man overboard should be part of the safety briefing that happens when passengers first get on board. The best thing a skipper can do is show their spouse, or somebody else who's on the boat quite a bit, how to run the boat, stop the engine, and use the VHF radio. There are usually times during a trip where you can take those opportunities and they could pay off really well later.

Robin: **Why does it make more sense to have a VHF radio rather than relying on a cell phone?**

Alan: The Coast Guard's search and rescue communication system throughout the United States is based on the use of VHF radios. They've put a lot of time, money, and research into a program they call Rescue 21. They've got VHF coverage over pretty much the entire coastline of the United States and most of the major river and lake systems. The system's designed to work with VHF radios. They have repeater sites and transmitter sites and personnel strategically located throughout the country that can pick up these radio signals and do something with them.

The trouble with cell phones is—and they do work well when they work, but, like here, where I live, in Prince William Sound in Alaska—you don't necessarily have cell phone coverage everywhere. You really don't want to get out on a boat and depend on that as your only means of communication. Get a VHF radio on your boat first, and if you happen to have a cell phone along, you could try that, but the system in the U.S. is based on having a VHF radio.

Robin: **Are there any particular channels on the radio that you should be paying attention to and using?**

Alan: What they call hailing and distress—the channel that should always be on—is channel 16. It depends on what part of the country you're in. In some parts of the country, they want you to hail (when you try to contact another boat) on a different frequency. That really depends on how many people are out there, but you really should be listening to channel 16 in case you hear a distress call that the Coast Guard doesn't hear. And if you need to *make* a distress call, your radio is on the right frequency for you to contact the Coast Guard.

Robin: **Is a VHF the type of radio that also has the NOAA (National Oceanic and Atmospheric Administration) weather on it?**

Alan: Typically, it's a different system; but typically they do include a couple of different weather channels on marine VHF radios. NOAA, aka the national weather service, maintains a whole system of transmitter sites where they broadcast these kinds of routine, regular marine weather forecasts. They also transmit warnings. Almost all the VHF radios you see come with a couple of extra channels, called something like weather channel 1 and 2. Depending on where you live, your weather broadcast will be on one of those channels. You can't transmit on that, but it's a really good way to listen to the current weather for where you're boating.

Robin: **How is a rescue facilitated?**

Alan: There are quite a few different things that could happen during a rescue. Basically, you're going to call the Coast Guard or another authority and ask for help. The most direct method is for the boat in distress to make a May Day call on channel 16 and communicate directly with the Coast Guard. That's one way. On-board radio locator beacons operate in a couple different modes. The beacon transmits a distress signal, and the search and rescue satellite system picks that up and alerts the search and rescue authority to start a rescue mission. A lot of times, people will see another boat in distress or they'll hear something on the radio that concerns them—a third party can turn in a report. If you filed a float plan with the harbormaster or a family member, and you didn't come back on time, that person can call the Coast Guard and ask that they check up on you.

Robin: **Can you give us an example—pretend you're putting in a May Day call—so we can hear what it would sound like?** (Nothing like putting you on the spot. :)

Alan: It's three May Days—so it's May Day May Day, May Day—then you give the name of your boat, number of people on board, where you're located, and the nature of your distress. You *always* start off saying the May Day message three times and then the basic information about your situation. The Coast Guard then comes back and talks to you. They've actually got an entire script where they'll go through the whole situation with you and nail down all the information they need. The key is to get that first conversation started.

Robin: **You said that the Coast Guard has a script—somebody sitting in the office answering these calls, not the same Coast Guard personnel that are out on boats going around rescuing people—and they're going to be asking questions. The boater, even though he or she is making a May Day distress call, needs to have a little patience with the person on the other end, otherwise they're not going to get the help. Is that correct?**

Alan: The Coast Guard will have what they call a watch standard or, depending on where the call is received, a search and rescue coordinator that picks up the call. The trick is to be patient because they are going to ask a lot of questions. Some boaters might wonder, "Why are these guys asking all these questions when my boat's sinking?"

In case they lose contact with you or something fails later, they definitely load the conversation with as much information as they can get about the boat, the situation, where you're at, etc. Knowledge is definitely safety in that situation. You just have to be patient—take a deep breath and answer as many of the questions as you can.

Robin: **When a boater is out and, G-d forbid, they have to put in a May Day call, what are some things they should notice to describe about their surroundings?**

Search and Rescue   Alan Sorum

Alan: In a perfect world, you've got a GPS on board or you've got a good background in coastal navigation, so you can provide either latitude and longitude or a geographic location. Being aware of your surroundings is the biggest thing. If the skipper and others on board are keeping track of their position on the water and where they're at, that's very useful. The gold standard would be to look at a chart plotter or GPS and say I'm right here and pass that on.

Robin: Right, but that's a perfect world and in a panic situation we're not always in a perfect frame of mind. **Would it be safe to say that anybody on the boat should be paying attention to lighthouses they go by; any landmarks, whether they know the names of them or not; church steeples; things like that? Would those be things that would help?**

Alan: Geographic information like that is really good. For the worst situations, the Coast Guard does have radio direction finding capabilities, so to some degree they can pick up a bearing on your boat just based on the VHF radio. But, paying attention to your surroundings is always a useful thing to do.

Robin: **Are there any specific things the captain of the boat should make sure their passengers know before leaving the dock?**

Alan: It's definitely a good idea to do a safety briefing before anything happens—before anybody unties the boat, starts the engine, or leaves the harbor. On charter boats, it's a requirement that they do a short safety briefing before they even start a trip, but it doesn't have to be complicated. You want to point out, for example, here's your life jacket; here's your exit; if there's an emergency, listen to the skipper and he'll tell you what to do; the radio's located here; this is how to turn the radio on; this is how you make a call; signaling; the flares are stowed under this bench—the basics—where things are on the boat and what they should do if there's a problem. It doesn't take a long time—a quick overview of the boat and where everything's at—but it's real useful.

Robin: **I'm guessing that most people know what a VHF radio is and have one on their boats, but there seems to be confusion over an EPIRB and a PLB. What's the difference between the two?**

Alan: EPIRBs are radio locator beacons and they even carry them on airplanes. EPIRB stands for emergency position-indicating radio beacon. EPIRB is a lot easier to say.

A PLB (personal locator beacon) is a portable beacon—a radio beacon that send out a radio signal that allows the Coast Guard or other search and rescue people to pick up your location. The biggest difference is that EPIRB is a boat-based device—it goes with the boat and carries the boat's identification with it. A PLB is quite small and made to stick in a pocket of a life jacket or coat. The nice thing about PLBs is they're not just for boating. If you like hiking or skiing, you can carry one for those kinds of activities. The technology is really pretty awesome. The way it's explained to people is that it takes the search out of search and rescue—they tell the

Coast Guard right where a person is in the water. They estimate that since 1982 PLBs have saved more than 25,000 lives.

Robin: **If someone is trying to decide whether to buy an EPIRB or a PLB, does it depend on the type of boating they're doing? If a boater is doing a lot of cruising in the ocean, would it benefit them to have *both* an EPIRB and a PLB? And what's best for nighttime boating?**

Alan: For a blue water (deep sea) sailor, there's a good chance he or she is familiar with EPIRBs and already has one. An EPIRB is a really good idea, but not just for blue water sailors. For a person in Prince William Sound, in the Gulf of Alaska, off the coast of California, on the Great Lakes, an EPIRB would be really valuable. It's not so much how far out you are on the ocean, it's just the fact that you're out on the water and, if there's an emergency, you're going to be hard to find. EPIRBs are identified and registered with the boat. You can't carry one of those things around with you. PLBs are quite small and fit into a life jacket or pants pocket. If you're out at night on a boat, a PLB is a good thing to have stuck in a life jacket pocket or somewhere with you.

At night, you should be wearing a life jacket—and make sure that your life jacket's got retro-reflective tape on it—and carrying a light and a whistle. A lot of boaters actually carry a small survival kit in their life jackets. At night you should definitely think about the buddy system. You shouldn't be out there alone. If you are out on the deck at night, a PLB, a life jacket, and some of these other things are really a good idea.

Robin: **You mentioned carrying a small survival kit. What are some things that would be necessary to put in there?**

Alan: I've seen a lot of different kits put together. There's a group in Alaska called the Alaskan Marine Safety Education Association that does a marine safety instructor's course every year that takes about ten days. They actually go out and do some survival type situations. They say that everything you'll need for a survival kit will fit in a one-quart Ziploc bag—matches, some sort of fire starter, a signal mirror, a sheet of plastic, a small knife, a piece of aluminum foil, things like that. It's what would make a difference if you do happen to have a problem. It's pretty amazing how much you can fit into a small Ziploc bag and, when you actually need it, how helpful that stuff is.

Robin: I wouldn't have thought of some of those items. **How do EPIRBs work?**

Alan: When I explain this, it may seem complicated, but what's funny is it works really well and fast. There are a couple of systems out there. There's a thing called COSPAS (Cosmitscheskaja Sistema Poiska Awarinitsch Sudow—Russian: satellite system to search for vessels in distress—established in 1979) which was the Russians' first attempt at a search and rescue satellite. Russia, the United States, France, and Canada all cooperate in this satellite system. The one we're most familiar with here in the United States is called the Search and Rescue Satellite System or SARSAT for short. We were talking about NOAA a little bit earlier. SARSAT,

Search and Rescue   Alan Sorum

the actual search and rescue satellite system, actually piggybacks search and rescue on the NOAA weather satellites. So NOAA's got a big involvement in the search and rescue system. That's the reason the registration goes through NOAA when you register your EPIRB. That's an interesting tidbit.

So, you've got an EPIRB or a PLB and it can get set off in a couple of different ways. For instance, many commercial fishing boats are required to have what they call Category 1—it goes off automatically if the boat sinks. Another way, obviously, is you can flip the switch and set it off manually. The beacon sends off a 406 MHz radio signal that's picked up by these satellites that are orbiting the globe. The satellites downlink it to what they call the local user terminal (LUT)—a ground receiving station. Throughout the U.S., they have things called Mission Control Centers (MCCs) that pick up that information from the local user terminal and ship it to the rescue coordination center (RCC). We were talking about how the country is divided up into different areas. If an EPIRB went off here in Alaska, the rescue coordination center in Juneau would get this information, then they point resources/people—could be a C130 Coast Guard Auxiliary member, a Coast Guard safe boat, a helicopter—towards the position once they've identified it. The beacon also has a 121.5 MHz signal. There's a homing signal, so once they actually get a little closer they can bear in and use the radio locator to find you. It's pretty remarkable how quick these things are. I've done some safety exams of fishing boats, when I was harbormaster here in Valdez, and I accidentally set off one of these EPIRBS. I literally didn't have enough time to get back to the office before the Coast Guard was calling asking about a particular boat being in trouble. The system works really quickly.

Robin: **Did you get a fine for triggering the beacon without really needing it?**

Alan: Luckily, we get along pretty well. But those sorts of things happen and that's one reason it's important to register the EPIRB. That way they can call and check to see if it's an accident or if there's a real problem. Of course, if the signal's going off inside a harbor, they'll likely call the marina manager or harbormaster first, because it's not likely that a vessel in distress is tied up at the docks. That's a good way to double check.

Robin: **EPIRBS have come a long way—what kinds of advances have been made in the technology?**

Alan: There are a couple of advances that have really jumped out here in the last couple of years. Almost all the beacons originally operated on 121.5 MHz. The new beacons now operate on the 406 MHz band, which has proven to be a lot more effective. It's just like computers and a lot of other things—the beacons, the way they put them together and the way they operate is better now and they're smaller and cheaper. If you look at an EPIRB that was made a while back, the things were just enormous. The size and cost of them have greatly improved. The other thing they've started doing is putting GPS receivers on board the beacons as an option, so you can buy a GPS-enabled EPIRB, giving you two different tools in an emergency. The first gives off a locator signal that the satellites can hone in on, and it's also transmitting your latitude and longitude, actually giving the search and rescue people your actual location. Each

EPIRB now has a unique code. Owners need to register them with NOAA, providing the family phone number and other contact information. That's turned out to be real useful.

Robin: **What do EPIRBs cost?**

Alan: That's one reason I've been promoting EPIRBs with recreational boaters as time has gone by. They used to be really expensive. There are several manufacturers out there—one called ACR Electronics and another called McMurdo—that do a good job of building these. There are two different kinds of EPIRBs. A Category 1 EPIRB usually comes in a bracket, is mounted somewhere on the outside of the boat, and goes off automatically if the boat sinks. The other style, called Category 2, you have to trigger manually. Obviously, a Category 1's got a lot more going on with it, so it's going to be more expensive than one that's manually deployed. A GPS-enabled beacon is going to cost a bit more than one without it. For recreational boats, a Category 2 EPIRB with GPS would be a good thing to have. You can probably buy one for around $500. For a GPS-enabled PLB that you can carry in your life jacket, you're looking at around $350. You can obviously spend more than that but those are good planning numbers.

Robin: **Where would be the best place to get these? You mentioned two manufacturers—ACR Electronics and McMurdo. Can they get them at West Marine? Can they get them online?**

Alan: You can get them at West Marine and if you Google EPIRB, a ton of choices pop up. You could go to a Chandlers or other marine supply shop in your community and ask, "What do people use around here? Who's servicing these things in our neighborhood?" That's where talking to other boaters can be helpful. It's not real hard to track one of these things down with the way the internet is now.

Robin: **What if someone has one on eBay? Is purchasing a used one a good idea? Not a good idea? Say your friends don't do boating anymore and they have this equipment. Is it worth getting an EPIRB and/or a PLB from them?**

Alan: I wouldn't be too worried about buying a used beacon. There are a couple of provisos. The beacon will carry a decal somewhere on it that says when the battery's going to expire, and it's going to have a sticker that says it's registered with NOAA. The thing to look for if you buy a used beacon is will the battery last for a while; then you need to re-register it. ACR Electronics have service representatives throughout the United States. If you do get a good deal on a beacon, it would be a good idea to just take it in to the service people and have them take a look at it—then you're definitely good to go.

Robin: **What are the chances of it breaking and what would be a good backup?**

Alan: I don't know if people would be carrying a backup to an EPIRB, but it's one of those things where I'd say get a VHF radio first, and, if you can afford it, get an EPIRB. If you're doing well, you have an EPIRB for the boat and have a PLB for your life jacket— that's certainly not unreasonable.

Search and Rescue   Alan Sorum

Robin: **I do a lot of searches on the different online forums and I've seen a lot of questions about changing the batteries on these EPIRBS. How difficult is this, and what is the proper procedure?**

Alan: That's another complicated question. The batteries on EPIRBs are pretty long lived. If you buy a new beacon, the typical expiration date's going to be something like five years after you put the beacon into use, so it's not like you have to change the battery every year, it lasts for a long time. If the expiration date printed on the beacon is past, you should replace the battery and if you actually use it during an emergency, then it's a good idea to get the battery replaced afterwards.

If we're talking about changing the batteries, it's going to vary quite a bit depending on the manufacturer, because the company's going to tell you that for them to guarantee that the beacon's going to work properly, if they're going to stand behind it, they're going to set out standards for what they want. I know ACR Electronics would prefer that you take the beacon—they've got a number of battery servicing locations if you look at their website—to one of these places and have them do the battery change. If you think about an electronic device that's been sitting possibly on the outside of your boat in a marine environment for five years, then it's a good idea to take it into a service station and have them change the battery and check it anyway. It would be a prudent, good maintenance thing to do to begin with. If you change your own battery, depending on the beacon, the key is to make sure you buy an original equipment battery. It would probably be best to buy it right from the manufacturer. The Coast Guard has even reported a couple of instances of counterfeit batteries. They look like the real deal, but they're not made to the right standards and you really don't know what's going on there. If you have a beacon that you can change the battery yourself, you just need to make sure you go to the source for the battery.

Robin: **You mentioned that it's important to take the beacon in and have it checked to make sure the battery's ok. Would you put this on your list of things to do every season?**

Alan: I don't know about every season as far as a service station. Before you start the season, take a look at your EPIRB and see if there are any obvious problems. Most of them will have a self test position where you can actually check them. So, obviously you'd be looking at the registration, NOAA's current, and that the battery is current and in good condition. I haven't tried it yet, but I know ACR has started a thing called 406Link. They've actually got it setup where the EPIRB can send out a signal using a satellite-based communications system that will tell you the beacon works. It's set up so you can basically subscribe to a text or email system where you punch a button on your EPIRB that sends out a message saying, "I'm ok" and gets your GPS coordinates. So if, for example, a person is following your movements and you're making a long trip somewhere, you can hit that 'I'm ok' button every once in a while and they'll get an email saying you're ok and your position. That's kind of a handy thing, but it also tells you that the beacon is working.

It looks like a pretty neat service. I haven't had a chance to try it yet. You don't need it for the EPIRB, but if you sign up for it, the price is pretty nominal. I can't remember if it's $5 or $10 a month, but it's not real expensive. It's not required for the beacon to work, but it's nice to have.

Robin: **It's great to be able to check in at home to let them know where you are and that you're ok. Do you have any other comments on the use of EPIRBs or on search and rescues?**

Alan: I've been involved—because of the harbormaster business in Alaska—with commercial fishing vessels for a long time. They've been required to carry EPIRBs for many years. With the price and technology now of EPIRBs and the cost of a commercial fishing boat out there working for a living, having an EPIRB shows they value their safety. Recreational boaters could definitely benefit from their example. The beacons are affordable, they last a long time, and they can make a real difference. If you wanted to buy somebody a nice Christmas or birthday present, an EPIRB or a PLB might be a nice thing to do for the cost. The only other proviso, maybe it sounds obvious, but you can only use an EPIRB in an emergency, so you definitely have some legal down sides to playing with one of these things. They're only supposed to be used in real emergencies and then just—we talked about NOAA earlier—make sure the beacon is registered to the boat or the boat user so if there is a signal, people can double check that it's not a false alarm.

Robin: **Can somebody get a fine from, say, the Coast Guard, or even the harbormaster's office, if they're caught playing around with this?**

Alan: It wouldn't be a harbormaster thing, but there are definitely some legal downsides to making a false distress signal. It would be the same thing that happens, when you listen to the news every once in a while somebody will get on and have a hoax distress call. It's the same concept and it's definitely not a really good way to get along with the Coast Guard.

Robin: **It's something you don't want the kids playing around with, but they'll need to learn how to use one in an emergency.**

Alan: At some age, at least with our kids, there's some point where you know you can trust them and they'll do the right thing. It's a matter of maturity really.

Robin: **What about PLBs and other radio locators?**

Alan: It's the same thing—it's definitely a violation of the law to set one of these things off unless it's an emergency. It's simple—they're not toys, they actually work really well. When you think about all the people involved in the search and rescue system, it's not a good idea to get them involved in a false alarm because they could be out dealing with a real situation.

Closing

Robin: I want to thank you for being so generous with your time today. You've certainly given me, and probably most of us on the call, a lot of insight regarding search and rescue missions.

Search and Rescue

Key Points

1. On land, search and rescue in the U.S. is coordinated by the Air Force, on water by the Coast Guard.
2. The best thing to do to facilitate a rescue is to wear a life jacket; the next best thing is to have a VHF radio.
3. File a float plan with your local harbormaster and/or a family member or friend.
4. Basic safety equipment includes life jackets, fire extinguishers, and signal flares.
5. Under federal law, you need one approved lifejacket within reasonable reach for each person on board, a couple of spares, and an approved throw-able flotation device.
6. The best way to place a distress call is to use channel 16, stating May Day May Day May Day (three times), then give the name of the boat, number of people on board, the boat's location, and the nature of the distress.
7. Always be aware of your surroundings, especially in an emergency situation.
8. Do a safety briefing with your crew and passengers before you untie the boat, start the engine, or leave the harbor.
9. A small survival kit should fit into a small Ziploc bag and include matches or some sort of fire starter, a signal mirror, sheet of plastic, small knife, and piece of aluminum foil.
10. Register your EPIRB through NOAA.

Notes

Notes

Digital Selective Calling, the Automatic Identification System, and Automated Radio Checks
An Interview with Chris Kourtakis

Introduction

Robin: Hello everyone. This is Robin Coles and it's my pleasure to welcome you to the 2010 Nautical Lifestyle Expert Series brought to you by TheNauticalLifestyle.com. During the next hour you're going to learn all you need to know about digital selective calling (DSC), the automatic identification system (AIS), and automated radio checks (ARCs). With me today, I am honored to have Captain Christopher Kourtakis as my special guest. Hello Chris!

Chris: Hi Robin. I'd really like to thank you for giving me this opportunity to speak with you today about this topic and hopefully making more people aware of what's available out there.

Robin: Thank you so much for joining me today. Chris Kourtakis has been boating for over 20 years and has been working in the marine industry for over 15 years. Chris is a licensed U.S. Coast Guard captain. He owns and operates H2O Limos which offers yacht rentals and on-water boating courses. H2O Limos has been nationally recognized for its boating education. You can find articles written by Chris in numerous marine trade magazines around the world. Chris holds a bachelor's degree in business and an MBA. When Chris is not working, he can be found somewhere on the water with his family.

DSC, the AIS, and ARCs

Robin: **What exactly is digital selective calling (DSC)?**

Chris: Digital selective calling (DSC) is a new VHF radio-based safety tool that came out in the late to middle 1990s. It is a dedicated digital channel—channel 70—on all your receivers. What DSC does is create a safety net on your radio. It allows you, if you are in an emergency situation, to just press and hold one button on your radio. This will automatically send a message with your boat's information—description, current location, and radio call name—directly to surrounding boats and to the United States Coast Guard, who monitors this channel. With DSC, you don't necessarily have to get on the radio and hail May Day or try to get someone's attention. If you hit this button, the cavalry is coming.

Robin: **What is the biggest advantage of using DSC today or in the near future?**

Chris: The biggest advantage is it hooks to your GPS and automatically, when you hit the DSC button or the red button on your VHF radio, sends your location. A lot of times people get into a panic. They think, for example, that they are near a lighthouse at Point Pleasant, when in reality they've drifted a mile, two miles by the time they actually make the distress call and they're at a different location. What DSC does is continuously send the message to local surrounding boaters with your actual location. If you're drifting or waves are taking you out to sea, it'll automatically take the guess work out of where you're at. That saves time, so if a search is out for you, the U.S. Coast Guard won't go to the location where you *thought you were*, they'll go to the location where you actually *are*. The biggest advantage is it's a safety net—you hit that button and you know that someone is coming. You're not sitting on the radio going, "May Day, May Day, May Day," trying to get somebody's attention, and hoping somebody will respond during your emergency.

Robin: **What if there was more than one emergency at a time—multiple people using VHF channel 16?**

Chris: That's one of the biggest issues with channel 16—it gets tied up. If there are multiple emergencies or times when more than one person is using the radio on a consistent basis, it will tie up channel 16. A lot of times the Coast Guard, if you are in an emergency situation, may ask you to switch to something else if yours is not deemed a life threatening emergency. That's where DSC really comes in, because it doesn't tie up channel 16 or anything else like that. You hit the button and you've got a dedicated channel on your radio that goes through and is received by someone who is monitoring the other side. They will automatically send help to you. You always know your call is going through, versus sitting there hailing May Day May Day May Day and hoping somebody can respond. The odds of having several or multiple instances at the same time, where the other stations can't respond, are slim to none, but it does happen when people get caught in storms or something like that. There was an issue over the weekend on the water and three different Coast Guard stations picked up the response. The closest one responded, then allowing the channel to open up for other people. It's based on distance too, so if there are a lot of people in the area using channel 16, it could potentially tie it up. Where somebody may or may not be able to get their information through, the DSC will automatically get that information through.

Robin: **You mentioned a dedicated channel, is that channel 70 that DSC and the radios are now going to make available?**

Chris: Yes—it's automatically programmed into your VHF radio and when you hit the DSC on your GPS, it automatically will transmit on channel 70 through your radio and then transpond directly through. You'll notice this when you're flipping through your VHF radio. You can't get on channel 70—you can't dial to it to use it as a speaking station. It is designated strictly for DSC emergencies. Only certain U.S. Coast Guard receivers will actually receive that information. I also have a DSC radio myself, so if a DSC emergency does come out and I am within the area, my receiver will pick that up so that I can potentially respond to the emergency and help someone out. I will get that broadcast on channel 70 and my radio will automatically switch. That's another great feature of the DSC—it doesn't tie up a line. You know it's always going to go through because nobody can be on that line using it for conversation with other people.

Robin: **What happens if someone is trying to put a scam out there, trap you, or to lure you over to get onto your boat? Say they want to rob you or something. Does that happen? What's the likelihood of that?**

DSC, the AIS, and ARCs   Chris Kourtakis

Chris: It's very unlikely. I'm not going to say it doesn't happen. In all my travels and adventures, I haven't heard too many stories like that. The reality is if somebody's hailing an emergency, you're going to be getting the Coast Guard or some other law enforcement agency that's going to respond to it. If somebody hails in and says, "I have an emergency," he or she has already given the boat information, the boat description, details about how many people are on board, and things like that. If I'm responding as a civilian, I'm looking for, for example, a blue center console boat that has three people on it. While I'm looking for that boat in the area, I'm going to go right to that blue center console with three people. The likelihood that the U.S. Coast Guard or local law enforcement is right behind me to respond to that emergency is very good. So, the likelihood that somebody can rob me or hold me up and get away with it is pretty tough. I haven't heard of too many scams or people trying to do this. On a global level, it's a little bit different.

Robin: We have the pirates.

Chris: They're not necessarily hailing for emergencies—they are just coming up on ships and taking control of the vessels.

Robin: **Can you talk about the FCC's ban, effective March 25, 2011, on selling radios built to the RTCM SC101 standard. And can you explain what that is?**

Chris: There are a couple different classes of radio out there. The biggest thing this ban covers is that a radio now has to have a separate channel for channel 70. Before, it did not. An older, similar class radio may not have had a dedicated channel for DSC, whereas all new radios being built must have a dedicated channel for DSC or a strictly digital channel. Therefore, there can never be any interruption or anything that's going to block that channel with incoming or outgoing calls. A DSC distress call will come directly from a dedicated channel on the radio and be sent directly to somebody who can respond and help.

Robin: **Nowadays you can buy a radio with or without that. You're saying that in the future that will no longer be the case.**

Chris: This ban means the creation of a separate channel on the radio. Currently, your VHF radio has one channel coming in and one channel going out. This is mandating that your radio has at least two channels—one that you consistently use and one that you kind of put to the side until you absolutely need it. When you hit that button in an emergency, there's going to be a channel out there that's available for your radio.

Robin: **What's going on with the Coast Guard's safety alert on radios with DSC?**

Chris: This is a great feature that the Coast Guard's finally offering. If somebody hits their DSC button in my area, my radio will automatically switch to channel 16 (the DSC response channel) to see if there is something I can do to assist. It's the law. Most boaters know that by law you must respond in an emergency as long as it doesn't put your vessel in harm's way. Meaning that if I'm a quarter mile away and I can help somebody who's drowning in the water, and it's not near rocks or anything that's going to harm myself or my crew, then I have to respond; I see a flare go up and I'm near it, I have to respond. The reason I like this Coast Guard Marine Safety Alert so well is that it automatically switches my radio whether I'm talking to a friend on channel 72, monitoring channel 16, or listening to the weather on channel 2, it will automatically switch me to that DSC broadcast coming through, so I can respond if needed.

This is a great improvement compared to what we used to have even five or ten years ago. The radio's come a long way and these safety features make it easier for people to go boating feeling safe and secure in their ability to get the help they need.

Robin: On the other hand, it's not going to hold too well if there is an emergency and you don't respond to it. If the Coast Guard questions you, you can't say you didn't hear it.

Chris: If your boat has a radio in it that's DSC equipped—especially if it's going to receive that radio broadcast—you're going to be held responsible for your actions.

Robin: **What are the costs associated with owning a radio equipped with digital selective calling (DSC)?**

Chris: One of the great things about this is that you can get a DSC/VHF fixed-mounted radio for about $100 from your local boat and accessories store, so everybody can have DSC on their boat. It's not just for the big yachts any more, like it used to be. With DSC, you must have a GPS on board your boat, and that GPS has to be tied in to the DSC radio so it can broadcast the boat's location. It can be a small GPS for a couple hundred bucks or it can be one of the new outstanding navigational ones for several $1,000s. It just depends on what you want and what your budget is.

Robin: **What about registering your DSC equipment and updating that information when you sell your boat?**

Chris: The service I always use is www.BoatUS.com/MMSI. When you go onto their website, it gives you everything you need to know about registering your MMSI (Maritime Mobile Service Identity) number. The other thing people need to know about the MMSI number is, once it's put into your DSC radio, it stays in there. There is no taking it out or putting it into another boat, or things like that. Once you register this number with that specific radio, it stays with that boat for the life of the radio unless you send it back to the manufacturer and have it physically wiped and reset. The reason they do that is when you register for your MMSI number, you fill out all the information such as a description of the boat (what kind of boat it is); the name of the boat; its size, color, etc. It will also ask for your radio call name, your cell phone numbers, and another number they should contact in an emergency situation when you're going to be on the boat. All that information gets logged in with your MMSI number, and once that's in the radio, it's there for good and cannot be taken out. When you sell the boat, you need to let the new owner know to go to www.BoatUS.com/MMSI or wherever you have it registered, give the new owner your password, and have him or her update the contact information. But the boat information will always stay the same—it cannot be edited.

DSC, the AIS, and ARCs — Chris Kourtakis

Robin: **What happens if you rent your boat out for a season?**

Chris: On my boat, the contact information is for my company and the MMSI number gives the boat description and things like that. If you're renting your boat out as a daily rental, you don't want to change it, you just leave your contact information the way it is. But if you're someone who rents your boat out for a season to another owner/operator, you should change that MMSI number to the renter's name, address, and cell phone numbers; and maybe leave yourself as the emergency backup contact.

Robin: **Is there someplace boaters can go if they have questions about using DSC?**

Chris: A great little website dedicated to DSC is www.vhf-dsc.info. It answers a lot of questions on how to use it, how to get your MMSI number, why you need it, what to do in an emergency, and things like that. Other great resources include www.BoatUS.com, both the U.S. Coast Guard and Department of Homeland Security cover this briefly, and there are several great videos on YouTube if you just type in "DSC." It explains what DSC is, how to register yours, and how to use it. One thing people need to understand is that watching these videos and reading about it is going to be the best thing they can do.

A lot of people need to realize that DSC is for life threatening emergencies only. Running out of gas is not considered an emergency, so if you hit the button and the Coast Guard responds and you're out of gas there's going to be a pretty significant penalty in fines. I have known of people who have gotten up to $25,000 fines for falsely pushing that button. That's a pretty expensive tank of gas.

You can't necessarily test this system to see how it reacts. There's no way to know for sure that it's up and running. It's a matter of assuming that it's hooked up and functioning properly. You hope that when the time comes that you need it, and you hope it never does, but if you do need to push that button, that help will be there.

Robin: **It sounds like there's an opportunity there for somebody who can do some programming and figure out how to do this testing without calling the Coast Guard.**

Chris: Yes, that would be a great feature for a lot of people.

Robin: **What is the automatic identification system (AIS) and how does it work?**

Chris: The automatic identification system (AIS) is one of the fastest growing areas in marine navigation today. Basically, an automatic identification system is an onboard transponder unit. Whether you're a small or large boat, this radio beacon continually transmits your boat's speed, course, location, and other information. It's been used for several years on larger shipping boats that operate in the shipping channels so that they can be monitored online and by various people and safety committees that monitor the shipping channels. But it's only recently—probably within the last two or three years—that it's become affordable and available on smaller ships. And they've come out with a Class B.

There are two types of transponders currently. Class A is for commercial shipping—that transmits two channels. The smaller Class B transmits for personal vessels, such as yachts. This system will let you know if your path is going to cross that of another ship within two miles that also has AIS. It's going to let you know whether you need to change course and if there is the potential that something dangerous could happen.

Robin: **Do they have AIS devices at lighthouses?** You know the stories that so many times boaters have come through, received flash signals, and not known that they were coming from a lighthouse telling them to get out of the way.

Chris: Some lighthouses are monitored by people actually using AIS devices. I have spoken with some lighthouse operators looking into the investment of getting set up with this equipment. It is an initial investment for somebody like a lighthouse that has to get all the onboard equipment and physically set it up at their place. But once they do, as an AIS boater, you'll be able to literally take a cursor on your GPS, move it over, click the icon for that unit and it'll give you all its information. That information could be that it's a lighthouse, 350 feet tall, off shore one quarter mile. Or, if it's a larger boat, it'll say, for example, 350 feet long, the name of the boat, the fact that it's an oil tanker heading from Boston Harbor to New York City, and the path that it's taking. It'll have its course logged in, so you'll know exactly where that boat's heading, what it's carrying, and everything else about it.

Robin: **How soon will either of these—DSC or AIS—be required to have on board?**

Chris: With AIS being so new, I think it's going to be several years before it's required. At this point, GPS and navigational systems are not required in boating situations. Until you have a required GPS, you can't expect to have AIS. And that also goes for DSC. It's not, at this point, required to have a VHF radio on a boat when you're boating in larger waters, it's just highly recommended. I think we're still several years away from required DSC or AIS but, as a boating educator, I'm all for both systems being on board all boats at all times.

Robin: **How compatible are these two systems (DSC and AIS) with each other?**

Chris: These systems are compatible in the sense that they act together. The AIS uses the VHF antenna for transmitting and response and that's why it's a great combination to buy a VHF radio—if you're looking for a new one—that actually has AIS built right into it. It's a receiver more than a transponder, so you'll be able to receive and see where other boats are, but they still won't be able to see where you're at. These two systems act simultaneously in a sense. With DSC, it's an emergency response calling, whereas AIS is an avoidance or identification system where you can avoid a dangerous situation. Ultimately, if you have AIS, you never have to push that DSC button.

Robin: **There are different types of AIS. Is one better than another for either a power boat or a sail boat?**

DSC, the AIS, and ARCs   Chris Kourtakis

Chris: There are two types—Class A is commercial and Class B is for the smaller vessels (sail boats, power boats, anything noncommercial). The biggest difference between the two is the transmissions. A commercial Class A will transmit every two seconds, whereas a Class B will transmit every 30 seconds. That way you can see more precisely where the larger commercial vessels are at, versus the smaller. With this, there's also a feeling that's been looked at, that the smaller vessels move a little faster so that 30 seconds can be critical to navigation. They're looking at whether they need to shorten or lengthen that, but until then, it's 30 seconds. A Class B is the only one you can get for a pleasure craft.

Robin: **How much, approximately, does an AIS radio system cost?**

Chris: I've equipped one of my boats with an AIS receiver only and I picked up the radio for around $300 and that was a VHF radio which had both DSC and AIS automatically built into it. There are some larger systems where you can get AIS only, which is a receiver. A receiver and a transmitter can go for $400 to $500 retail on the low end. And then you can get in the upwards of $5,000 to $6,000 range, depending on whether you want to get your own screen specifically for AIS, whether it's color, if you're looking for updates, and things like that. It really gets indepth. It depends on the level of information you want to get. But for the basic, simple ones, a couple hundred bucks gets you started, gets you on the water, and will hopefully help you avoid any situations out there.

Robin: **Is an AIS system something boaters can install themselves?**

Chris: Yes, absolutely—when I installed my VHF radio, it took me about 15 minutes to connect it to my GPS and get everything up and running, including hooking in the antenna. Another separate AIS box is being offered by different manufacturers such as Garmin, Raymarine, Simrad, Shine Micro, and others out there. If you have the Raymarine GPS, then you definitely want to get the Raymarine AIS—it's a plug and play. You literally plug it into your GPS and plug it into a power source and you're all set, ready to go. Garmin's the same way. The Shine Micro is not an off brand, but it can be mounted in any boat—it's just a matter of wiring it into the back of your GPS and wiring it into your VHF radio—you're talking 15 minutes to a half hour. It's definitely something that the average handyman or average boater should be able to do in a relatively short amount of time.

Robin: **Do you need to have electronic navigation charts to use with the AIS?**

Chris: Yes, absolutely—the electronic navigation charting system is reading the GPS coordinates of where these ships are at and where they're heading. The VHF radio-equipped boats that are sending the information need to be hooked up to a GPS unit also in order to broadcast their coordinates to help avoid a collision. Without a GPS, an AIS is almost non-functional and doesn't do anything. You'll be able to receive some of the information that's coming in, however, if you don't know what to do with that information and read your own charts, it's going to be pretty difficult. For example, you know it's coming in and it's at 42.8113, and you're sitting at 42.8113 and don't have a GPS to know that, then you've defeated the purpose of having the systems. You need to be able to look at where that ship's coming from on your GPS, be able to click on it and see where its actual course/path is, and, hopefully, avoid that collision situation. Without it, you'll get the information, yes, but by the time you look at a chart and everything, it could be too late.

Robin: **Some boaters are using the charts on their laptop computers. Will that work?**

Chris: Yup, absolutely. You can plug AIS into a laptop. There's a USB cable adapter that'll plug right into it. I always use my laptop with satellite internet connection for backup radar and GPS systems. If you get that broadcast to come across your AIS, if it is hooked up to your GPS, it should show that information directly on your screen. If not, and you use it separately on a VHF radio, then you'll be able to get the coordinates that are being broadcast by that ship from their AIS system, and you'll be able to look at them and look at your coordinates real quick and decide whether you're in the way or you're safe.

Robin: **Is there a specific identification number given with these services? If so, how can boaters get it?**

Chris: There is no specific service or number per se. It goes back to having an MMSI number—*that's* the information that gets plugged in through your VHF radio and the information that actually gets broadcast with your AIS system. It's going to tell the name of the ship, the color of the ship, what the ship looks like, the radio calls for the vessel, and other information.

The AIS will not give out your personal information; it'll just give your boat name. When you're inputting that MMSI number information, make sure you *do* put it in, and you don't avoid it, saying to yourself, "I don't want the boater next to me having my information and my cell phone number." They're not going to have it. All they're going to see is your MMSI number coming across their screen. They will not know your location and course information until it is an emergency and you actually hit that broadcast button. When AIS does show up and you click on the icon for the information on your GPS or other screens, it's going to tell you the name and size of the boat, and, with a commercial vessel, it's actually going to state their course. That way you can avoid crossing paths.

Robin: **Do these systems replace the big clunky radio equipment that some boaters have?**

Chris: It's not going to replace it, it's in addition to. The AIS is something you put under your dash and you never see it. It's kind of like the little black box in airplanes. You know it's there. You know it's helping you. It's providing information but, again, you never see it. So, it's not necessarily going to replace radio equipment. It is my recommendation that if somebody is going to make the investment into an AIS system for a couple hundred bucks that he or she also looks into upgrading his or her GPS unit and possibly his or her VHF radio in order to help all the systems on board the boat communicate. I'm not saying that the older GPS units don't work—they work great. However, there are some compatibility issues. For example, if you

DSC, the AIS, and ARCs — Chris Kourtakis

bought the Raymarine AIS system, it may not communicate properly with an early- or mid-90s GPS radar unit. You may have to do a little bit of updating there. If your radio doesn't have DSC, then there's no reason to have an MMSI number. With AIS, you're going to want to upgrade your VHF radio so you get an MMSI number and the information is broadcast correctly.

Robin: **In a search and rescue, normally someone from the Coast Guard office will respond. Does the DSC or AIS replace that comfort of talking to a live human and knowing help is on the way?**

Chris: Both systems will really help the Coast Guard identify where you're at. If you have AIS—and they can read that you have AIS—it's going to specifically give them the coordinates of your exact location. If the U.S. Coast Guard has to deploy, they will send somebody directly to those coordinates versus coordinates that you may have given. With the DSC, it's a matter of lifting or breaking the plastic on your little red box or red button on the radio, pressing that button, and holding it down for five seconds. You know that once you hit it, in essence, the cavalry is coming. You don't need to talk to or respond to someone or anything like that. Truly, if your ship's going down and you hit that button, they'll be able to go directly to it. The DSC is hooked up to your GPS unit, so it's continuously broadcasting your location. It avoids the potential of human error—somebody getting on the radio saying that they're a quarter mile southwest of Beacon Point—or at a point where they thought they were—but by the time they really made the radio transmission, they were a mile or two away from where they thought they were, in a new location. That's going to save the Coast Guard time, because they're not going to go to the old location, they're going to lock in on your current GPS information that's being broadcast by your AIS and DSC. In a nut shell, it's going to become a real life saver and time saver. Everyone knows, seconds and minutes are vital when doing a rescue on water.

Robin: Good point. **But in a search and rescue, wouldn't you actually want someone live on the other end, just to know they received your message?**

Chris: You want somebody live, you want to know somebody's there for you. But there are other situations such as a boat fire. Your boat's on fire, you need to get your lifejackets on, you hit that DSC, and you have to go overboard. There's that confidence knowing that you don't have to respond via the radio, that somebody is coming to help you.

In the past, without DSC, you literally had to stay on board, give your coordinates, and put yourself in danger. A lot of people actually lost their lives because they were trying to give coordinates, tell rescuers that the boat was on fire, and what kind of help they needed, and at that time, the boat either exploded or it sank. With this, as long as the DSC is operational, they will continuously move with the DSC signal. If that boat does go down or the radio is finally disconnected because of fire, they're going to go to the last known signal location. If it's right where the boat goes down, that's where they're going to head, versus where you said it was going to be. I really feel a lot more comfortable than knowing that I have to get a live human on the radio. A lot of times you're sitting there, a lot may happen at night or during bad storms and the reality is you might be the only boat on the water during that period. That fear in your gut, knowing that you can't get a hold of somebody—I don't even want to imagine what it feels like. Knowing that you can just push that DSC button and that somebody's coming has got to be a lot better and more comfortable in a situation like that.

Robin: **There's less possibility of human error too—there's no chance of somebody transposing the latitude and the longitude numbers either.**

Chris: You're absolutely right on that. It'll eliminate everything. It's a digital signal. When it's received by somebody else with a DSC receiver, they get all the information you need them to get, they just don't know the extent of the emergency. But they're guessing worse case scenario, so they're sending what they need to send.

Robin: **There's a lot of talk lately about a new automated radio check (ARC) system. What exactly is it?**

Chris: ARC is a great system. Both Sea Tow and BoatUS have been at the forefront of trying to develop this. As a boater, every time I leave the harbor, I want to do a radio check to make sure my equipment is working properly. In doing that, I tie up a radio station for a second or two. Most people don't know that channel 16 on your radio is not the place to do a radio check. It is actually illegal. Most of the time when you do it, you'll hear the U.S. Coast Guard come on and tell you that channel 16 is not the place to do it and prescribe a channel for you to use for the check. A lot of people use channel 80 or channel 82. A lot of times, I go out early in the morning and I don't get a response on my radio check, because I'm out so early. People may or may not be out there—you get a few fishermen that may respond on the radio, but a lot of times you don't get a radio check back. The other thing is, I boat late at night and I may not get a radio check back as I'm leaving one of my port of calls. With this new automated system, I turn to, I believe it's channel 27 or channel 28, depending on my location. I send a radio check and I get an automatic message back stating that my radio check went through. I am no longer tying up channel 16. I'm actually leaving that channel open so the Coast Guard can monitor it for somebody that is having a distress or May Day call.

Robin: **You said you get a message back. What is that message? I've heard boaters say that there's some kind of commercial radio advertisement that comes with it.**

Chris: I've heard about both situations. This is such a new service that it's not available in every location around the country. Here in the Midwest, we don't have it yet and they expect to have it here either by the end of the season or by next year, according to the U.S. Coast Guard here. The problem is—well, it's a good and a bad problem—that Sea Tow and BoatUS might be broadcasting back, yes, we received your radio check along with a commercial stating that, for example, West Marine's having a special on life jackets. I've also heard that there's a specific message, "Your message has been received. Thank you for using channel 27 (or 28). Over and out." That's a simple, quick message. I have heard of both circumstances. From what I understand, it's up to the local person that's responding to your radio check. Most likely either Sea Tow or BoatUS will do this (broadcast advertising following a radio check received message) as part of funding that they are getting to help offset their costs. Either way, whether I hear the commercial come through, at least I know that my radio check was received. I get the automatic message and I either continue to listen or turn to channel 16, which I'm supposed to monitor anyway when I'm out on the water.

Robin: Are there any other benefits to using this automated system?

Chris: The biggest benefit is freeing up the chatter on channel 16. It allows channel 16 to be dedicated to security messages, May Day messages, and actually what it was designed for; and that's distress—a distress channel that the U.S. Coast Guard monitors on a consistent basis. It allows the Coast Guard to free up and listen to those messages versus every day getting thousands of radio checks coming across. By the time you start looking at all the boats out there, if everyone used channel 16 (to do radio checks), a distress or May Day call could potentially be missed. If there are five or six radio checks in a row and the Coast Guard has to respond and say this is not the channel to do that on, somebody in a dangerous situation could be overlooked—he may not have a DSC and he's actually out there using his radio—he's in trouble.

When it comes to my area, I'm going to use channel 27 or 28 as a courtesy. Whether I hear a commercial or not, I know my radio check went through, but I want to use one of those channels so it'll allow the Coast Guard to monitor the channels they need to monitor and allow boaters that potentially need assistance to have the open channel they need.

Channel 16 is also monitored by Sea Tow and BoatUS, so somebody out there might do a quick call and say, "I'm out of gas," and Sea Tow or somebody else will pick up the message on that channel and move them to a different channel to figure out what they need. That way the call is picked up and the channel isn't tied up by a radio check somebody nearby is doing.

Robin: What happens if people continue to use channel 16?

Chris: What everybody needs to understand is that channel 16 is continuously monitored and continuously recorded. So, they are going to monitor somebody that is abusive or is not using the channels correctly. Ultimately, that could mean a fine or worse. The reality is that people are still using it. You're still going to hear the U.S. Coast Guard saying that you need to move to another channel. Radio checks are not good for channel 16. For years in the past, there was a lot of radio chatter on channel 16. This system has been designed to alleviate and clear up some of that. Until then, channel 16's going to be a busy channel.

Robin: When do you think that clearing up the use of channel 16 will start to happen in the United States? I'm assuming it's not being used in Europe either, correct?

Chris: It is not being used in Europe yet. Even for myself, who boats in international waters, being close to Canada, their regulations for radios are different from what we have here in the U.S. I think it's going to be quite some time before everybody catches on. It needs to be proven in the United States. Once it is, SOLAS and some of the other people are going to grab onto it.

SOLAS stands for the safety of life at sea. They're going to want the international channel—channel 16—clean, clear, and available, so that somebody can use it for responses. But more cities in the U.S. need to get it. I think Boston was one of the first, along with New York and a few others on the east coast.

Robin: Rhode Island has it.

Chris: There are also few places in Florida—Miami, Fort Lauderdale, and a few others—that have it. Until it starts hitting the mainstream areas along the coast, in the Great Lakes, and on the major shipping channels, it's going to take a couple of years for everybody to get on board with it. A lot of people don't even know about it yet. Once it's communicated and marketed properly, so people know about it and start using it, then more and more locations will hopefully get it and help alleviate this problem. I think we're a few years off from Europe getting it, and even Canada itself who's our friendly neighbor here.

Robin: That's a problem—there are not a lot of places that have it. We have a lot of boaters here in the Boston area that go south for the winter. They're not going to have the service down there. We no sooner get them trained up here, then they go down there and have to go back to using channel 16 again.

Chris: You're absolutely correct in that. It's kind of like when DSC first came out. There were a lot of locations around the United States that didn't even have bases on land that monitored DSC. So, even though you had it, you could hit that button, there was no one out there to respond. It took a few years for the U.S. Coast Guard bases to get everything and for the local Sea Tow and BoatUS locations to actually get DSC responders and transmitters in various locations. We get people that, like myself, boat all over the country. I go to Boston for the weekend and use channel 27 and 28, then I go down to Wilmington, NC, and try to use it and I don't hear anything. I forget that they don't have it down there yet. It's going to take some time. But once it's in, we'll be trained to immediately turn on our boats, turn on our radios, turn on channel 27, and do our radio checks even before we leave the docks.

Robin: That's another good habit to get into.

Chris: It has added another routine to our pre-launch checklist.

Robin: **Do you have any additional tips on using DSC, the AIS, or ARCs?**

Chris: The biggest thing that I want to remind people is that you have to get online and get your MMSI number. Without that, the system is completely useless. In fact, until you load your MMSI number into your VHF radio, the DSC will not work. Another thing for people to remember is you must have it hooked up to your GPS unit. The DSC is automatically going to send out your coordinates and tell everybody where you are. There are specific radios out there—such as the one I got with AIS—that have built-in GPS navigation. But it's also drawing from a GPS. Without my GPS, a lot of times that radio could be dead. People just need to understand that it's a total system—a team effort from your electronics to get everything working. But it all stems from that MMSI number—you need to have that information in there. If you don't have the MMSI number information logged in and you hit that button, it either doesn't work or it does broadcast, but they come out and you're in an area where there are 15 or 20 boats and they don't know which one to respond to.

With AIS, a lot of boaters still don't know what it is. It's early—only in the last couple of years has it been available for pleasure craft. It's just a matter of time. I highly recommend it for somebody in Boston Harbor, the New York channels, or the Great Lakes (which are around shipping channels). It's a must—$500 is going to save me half a million dollars if somebody's going to run through my boat. To me it's a no-brainer on getting it—ordering it and getting it installed. Even if it costs me $100 bucks to have them install it, it's quick, easy, and painless. Once it's in, it's always there, and nobody can take it away—you always have it, you don't have to remember to turn it on or anything. If your radio's on, your GPS is on, and you're getting the broadcast. Where I boat, I can pass 15 or 20 freighters on any given day. Sometimes when you're boating, the freighter's coming down the channel and you have skylines on either side, those freighters can blend in—until you hear the horns, and sometimes those horns can be too late to realize what's behind you. But if you have an AIS that picks up their message saying they're in the channel and they're within 500 or 1,000 yards of you and your alarm's going off saying you're on a collision course, it's a lifesaver.

Robin: Here in Boston Harbor, the police will actually come after you and tell you to get out of the way.

Chris: However, if they're not there, I've seen too many times in a shipping channel that people don't realize there's a boat behind them. A freighter's coming through—it's international waters here—these freighters are 300, 400, 500 feet long and 20, 50, 100 feet high with the cargo they're carrying; and when you have background, such as the buildings around Boston Harbor, those ships are lit up and blend in and you don't realize it.

Robin: We get a lot of the LNGs (liquified natural gas tankers) coming in here, so it's not something to mess around with.

Chris: No—absolutely not.

Closing

Robin: Chris, I want to thank you for being so generous with your time today. You've given me, and probably most of us on the call, a lot of insight regarding better use of digital selective calling, the automatic identification system, and automated radio checks in helping with distress calls and search and rescue missions.

Chris: Robin, I really appreciate you giving me the opportunity to speak with you and your listeners. Regarding boating safety, the more people that know about the tools that are out there and educate themselves on what is available, the fewer fatalities we're going to have and more pleasurable boating's going to become throughout the course of time. But, until then, we just need to keep plugging along. Hopefully people are doing the right things out there and hopefully we'll get to a day when we don't need these systems. Until then, they're out there—they are essential, in my opinion. They may not be required, but I feel they are essential. Like GPS when it first came out, people were hesitant, "Oh, I have my charts and everything else." Well, how many people today don't even know how to read a chart, but they can operate their GPS very functionally. It's just a matter of moving forward with technology. We have it, let's embrace it. Let's use it and avoid bad situations.

Robin: It's for our own safety. Chris, how can someone find you to get more information?

Chris: Get a hold of me through my company website, which is www.H2OLimos.com, or email me directly at Chris@H2OLimos.com.

Key Points

1. Channel 70 is the dedicated channel for DSC on your VHF radio.

2. If you hear an emergency on the radio, it's a law that you must respond as long as it does not put your vessel in harm's way.

3. Channel 16 is to be used for emergencies only.

4. Make sure you register your DSC equipment and update that information if/when you sell your boat.

5. DSC is for life-threatening emergencies only.

6. If you're renting your boat out for a season to another owner/operator, you should change the MMSI number registration to reflect their contact information.

7. The biggest difference between Class A and Class B AIS is the transmissions—Class A transmits every 2 seconds and Class B transmits every 30 seconds.

8. AIS depends on a GPS unit and the electronic navigation charting system.

9. AIS and DSC are life and time savers in emergencies.

10. Don't forget to go online and get your MMSI number.

Notes

Multihulls
An Interview with Jim Brown

Introduction

Robin: Hello everyone. This is Robin Coles and it's my pleasure to welcome you to the 2010 Nautical Lifestyle Expert Series brought to you by TheNauticalLifestyle.com. During the next hour, you're going to learn about modern day multihulls, their advantages and disadvantages over monohulls, and what sets catamarans apart from trimarans (besides the obvious number of hulls). With me today, I'm honored to have Jim Brown as my special guest. Hello Jim!

Jim: Good morning, Robin.

Robin: Jim, thank you so much for joining me today. Jim Brown is marine architect, multihull pioneer and builder, author, sailor, and teacher.

In the 1950s, Jim helped build the first large model molded fiberglass boats in the US. Jim built the first modern cruising trimaran and sailed it on a 2,000-mile ocean voyage with his lovely bride, Jo Anna.

In the 1960s, Jim designed the Searunner series of ocean cruising trimaran sail boats for amateur building. These designs attracted some 1,600 builders worldwide. Several of these boats have completed world cruises.

In the 1970s, Jim sailed the coasts of Central and South America with his family. He was inducted into the *Cruising World* Hall of Fame. Jim's personal yacht was selected by *Sail* magazine as one of the 100 Greatest Sailing Yachts in North America. He authored *The Case for the Cruising Trimaran,* published by International Marine Publishing Company in 1983, which sold 11,000 copies. He also developed and patented the "constant camber" method of producing compound curved plywood modular boat components.

In the 1980s, Jim transferred constant camber technology to peasant fishermen in several remote locations in Africa, the Philippines, and the Central Pacific Islands, where it is now used to produce sophisticated working watercraft for fishing and transportation. He has written often for *WoodenBoat* and *Cruising World* magazines. He has taught wood-epoxy technology at WoodenBoat School in Brooklin, Maine.

In the 1990s, Jim was a guest lecturer on yachting history at Mystic Seaport museum and gave architectural seminars at the University of North Carolina. He designed small multihulls for mass production in rotomolded polyethylene, with thousands sold for rental and expedition service. He has voyaged to Cuba. He designed several large catamaran excursion craft, built with constant camber technology and certified by the US Coast Guard for carrying passengers on offshore routes.

Since 2000, Jim has been the recipient of an award for outstanding achievement by the New England Multihull Association. He is a cofounder of OutRig!: The Modern Multihull History Project, which collects, preserves, and disseminates the history and lore of modern seafaring. Jim is now in his late 70s and has two grown sons who are both boat designers and builders. He writes, sails, kayaks, and travels all over with Jo Anna, his wife of 51 years. They are based in rural Tidewater, Virginia. Wow, Jim, you have done a lot!

Jim: Well, that concludes my remarks for today. We don't have to go any further. (laughter)

Multihulls

Robin: **Where do modern multihulls come from? What made them happen?**

Jim: There are three basic multihull configurations available today. The catamaran, the trimaran, and the proa (pronounced **proh**-*uh)* all come to us from the ancient people of the South Pacific, the Indian Ocean, and even as far west as the East Coast of Africa—all multihull territory. There are still literally hundreds of thousands of these boats in daily service on a Stone Age level. When I say that, I mean no metal parts. The ancient multihulls, which go back some say as far as three or four millennia, were made entirely of vegetable fiber. There was nothing in them that wouldn't go away with time, so there's not a whole lot known about the really ancient multihulls. There's no doubt that they've been around for a long time and the way it looks now they're going to be with us for another two or three millennia, no doubt.

The thing about these boats that a lot of people don't realized today is that they were probably the first real seafaring vessels known to mankind. Today we think of multihulls as being something new. In fact, most people think of them as just happening yesterday, but the truth is, well, if tradition means old and time tested, the multihull watercraft is probably the most traditional of all surface vessel types in the world.

Multihulls are an Asiatic concept. They began in what we would call Island Asia now and they were used in all three configurations in order to explore and eventually populate the entire Pacific basin as far north as Hawaii. It's quite something when you think about the fact that these boats were making planned ocean voyages—out one year and back the next—thousands of miles offshore at about the same time that the Venetians were just beginning to fiddle their way down around the hump of Africa always within sight of land. The ability to use the multihull was very much dependent on the early multi mariners being able to lie on deck, look up at the sky, and almost empirically locate themselves on the face of the planet.

Multihull boatbuilding is an amazing technology that goes back a long way, while our own nautical heritage is very much monohull. The multihuller was doing it before, perhaps long before, it was done off shore in monohull vessels. When you think of multihulls today, you really can't consider them something new. They've been around for a long time.

There was something that happened right after World War II. It was a classic case of reinvention that was applied to the basic configurations and I think that reinvention was

Multihulls   Jim Brown

materials driven. We found that a lot of materials science had advanced during World War II to the point where things like plywood and fiberglass and light metals and synthetic fibers for sail cloths and for cordage and all of those things became commonly available in the years shortly after World War II. That led to a reinvention of the multihull. These modern multihulls are not reproductions or emulations of the ancient vessels in any way. They're an entirely new breed of watercraft. The thing that really makes a modern multihull modern is light weight. There were attempts to utilize the multihull configuration by westerners going back as far as the 1600s, but the light weight did not appear until right after the war. The ancient multihulls were wonderfully light, don't get me wrong. They were wonderfully light for the materials and the tools that were available to their builders, but nothing like what can be achieved with modern materials.

So something really happened post war that made the modern multihull happen. It was not just materials driven. As I see it, the global context at the time tended to encourage the development of new stuff. After the war there was a great buoyant optimism in the developed countries. We had managed to quash the despots in Europe and Asia. We felt ourselves to be a special people, like we could do anything; with enough wealth and will, we could change the world. I think that stimulated a smattering of inventors who were working with new vessel types using modern materials in places like Australia, New Zealand, England, and, particularly, in California and Hawaii. That's really what made multihulls happen—that 'can do' generation.

I guess we began to lose that by the early '70s. We were not so buoyantly optimistic anymore. We were taking a licking in Vietnam and we had sort of given up on the idea of trying to do away with poverty and bigotry and all of that. We had a different thing enter into the multihull fold at that time—what I call 'escapism.'

Most of the early multihulls during the '40s, '50s, and '60s were built by owner-builders, not all but most of them were backyard operations by what you'd call mad scientists experimenting. Some of us saw the potential and really invested substantial portions of our lives in making this thing happen. The enthusiasm, almost hysteria, that accompanied the emergence of these boats, was definitely a result of the context of the times. I have to say, hats off to those experimenters—the guys that really led the way, the real trail blazers.

I was not one of them; I was rather a Johnny-come-lately. I got into multihulls when I was in my early 20s. I was standing on the shoulders of the guys who had really blazed the trail, who had made most of the basic discoveries in both catamarans and trimarans at that time. I was younger than most of those guys and that's one reason I'm still around. That's why I sort of feel obliged to tell the story of this incredible burst of energy and creativity that went into developing these boats early on in the postwar period. I'm delighted to be included among those guys like Woody Brown, Rudy Choy, James Wharram, Arthur Piver, and Dick Newick—those guys were the real trail blazers. I'm now trying to make sure that that legacy, the legacy of that time, doesn't become lost.

Nautical historians aren't paying much attention to multihulls because they're too new. They're not curatorial yet (laughter), but we're saving the stuff.

As I see it, that's the way modern multihulls happened.

Robin: **When and how did you get into sailing?**

Jim: I was schooner bumming around the Caribbean in my early 20s. I didn't know quite what else to do with myself. I pretty much failed at everything else I tried and I was a skin-diving nut. The whole underwater world was just beginning to open up at that time. This was the mid-1950s and Jacques Cousteau had really made so many of us aware of 'the silent world,' as he called it.

I got myself a job on a big schooner that was carrying diving parties around the Caribbean. There was a Bahamian boatswain in the crew—we had eight guys in the crew on that boat, plus the skipper, and they were all Bahamians except for me—the boatswain, a man named Fred McKenzie, was the guy that really got me into sailing. He taught me the ways of a windjammer and it came at the right time. It just stimulated the living daylights out of me to the point where it's been one damn boat after another ever since. But it was a strong traditional background—I didn't start out in multihulls; I came out of conventional boats.

Robin: **How did you become attracted mostly to multihulls?**

Jim: It was a blind luck, pure happenstance. I found myself in the company of two very influential mentors—people that really shaped the rest of my life. One of them was a guy named Wolfgang Kraker von Schwarzenfeld. He's very little known in the annals of multihull history these days, but he was actually one of the first. He was a German guy that had been through the living hell during the war in Europe and built himself a catamaran out of tin and sailed it across the Atlantic. He was even ahead—maybe only by a matter of days—of James Wharram (British), the other real pioneer in the Atlantic. But Wolfgang crossed to the Antilles in 1956 and made his way up the islands to Miami where I met him. He was looking to join the crew of this big schooner that I was working in, the Janine, a 151-foot steel stafle schooner, a marvelous thing.

The captain of the schooner, this guy Mike Burke, who was soon to become famous as the proprietor of Windjammer Barefoot Cruises, which really opened up the charter business in the Caribbean, needed a bunch of photographs to prepare a brochure. Wolfgang was a shutterbug, so he came into the crew. It took me a while to find out about all the circumstances that led him to cross the Atlantic in this catamaran. I later saw the boat in Miami and I must say it was the first multihull I ever saw and it offended me roundly. I couldn't get over the gruesomeness of the thing and I couldn't understand how a guy could cross the ocean in it.

So, I was interested and one thing led to another and Wolf and I and this great gal, Jeannie Miller, joined us. She was a passenger on one of the diving trips and she hit it off with Wolfgang. The three of us ended up forming a nice tight diving and sailing team. We left the schooner and took off for South America in another yacht, had some big deal adventures and all that, and finally came out of it figuring that we were going to build ourselves what we called a triple cat at the time. Wolfgang said, "The only trouble with my boat is she needs another hull in between," and that's how the trimaran came in to my life.

We ended up getting stuck in Columbia with an immigration snafu and we finally built ourselves a triple cat out of oil drums in order to get out of there. We somehow managed to make it to Panama and so on. Not long after that, I found my way to California. When I left Wolfgang and Jeannie, we were all going off to do our separate things in order to accumulate the cash we needed in order to build a boat for ourselves.

One of the things we decided was we were going to build it out of fiberglass, a very new thing at the time. I learned that there was a company in Sausalito, California, a town I had never heard of, that was building the first large fiberglass products in the United States. The British were way ahead of us at that time in fiberglass technology. But, I bought a motorcycle and rode it out there and got a job at this place and learned about fiberglass. The whole thing became a sort of lead-in to bumping into the next mentor—the guy that really played a great role in my life, this man named Arthur Piver (rhymes with diver, as he used to say). Piver is now known pretty much as the father of the modern trimaran.

This was getting into 1957-1959. The catamaran had already been developed in a very modern sense by the Hawaiian catamaran concept (that's another whole story). The catamarans were ahead of the trimarans, no doubt, in the 1950s. I had the chance to try out a couple of Hawaiian catamarans and I was quite dismayed—flummoxed by so much speed with so little control. I learned later that the reason they were not all that controllable was that they were intended to be operated from the beach. They had very shallow rudders and no center boards and all that stuff. They were for carrying joy riders off the beach at Waikiki and were not really sea boats. They would just go like stink in a straight line, ripping across the ocean like a sea plane on take off. I was just flabbergasted by the whole thing.

When I got back to the Sausalito, I bumped into this guy Arthur Piver. He had a little trimaran that he'd whacked out in his garage. It was also rather offensive looking—just a collection of plywood boxes—but it did everything that the catamarans of the day didn't do. It would tack dependably, come about like a sailing dinghy, and really go to windward. You could really steer it down wind in big waves. We were sailing in San Francisco Bay and the Golden Gate. We had a chance to really test this thing.

So I became a protégé of Arthur Piver and that's really where I came into the multihull fold. With these little boats of his—this was a 16-footer and he had another one, a 20-footer—we'd take them out into the Golden Gate and just go blasting through conditions that would break an ordinary boat. I couldn't believe the sea-keeping properties that these things had. They were also beachable. Furthermore, they were unsinkable. I had had the experience in my schooner bumming days of sailing in a boat that was going down and I'd never gotten over it. It was obvious that these little trimarans of Arthur Piver's had the potential to be capsized but, at least, they wouldn't sink.

I figured if I had one that was a little bigger than the one we had at the time—let's put three sheets of plywood together instead of two so we'd have a 24-footer instead of a 16-footer—that I could put a little cuddy cabin on it and undertake a coastal voyage back to the Caribbean. I wanted to go back to the Caribbean—part of another long story—I'd lost track of Wolfgang and Jeannie. It would be 35 years before I would find Wolfgang again. Another thing that really attracted me to Piver's little trimarans was their low cost. Multihulls are generally more expensive to build than monohulls. But in the early days they were easy to whack out by an amateur builder. Even if you'd never even built a bird house, you could build a collection of plywood boxes and go out in the big briny and really have yourself an adventure.

I discarded the first trimaran I built before I finished it. I needed that experience to start again. I was definitely self-taught when it came to building. A lot of the builders at that time were buying plans from Arthur Piver. A lot of them were absolute green horn wood butchers—no idea what they were doing—but the boats worked. At least some of them worked, not all of them, it's true. Many builders in the early days did extraordinary improvisation in finishing off their boats and some of the craziest, wackiest floating contraptions you can imagine resulted, but the ones that were built to the plan worked pretty well. I figured that because they were beachable, that I could make a coastal voyage in this thing. Even if I got in real trouble, I could always run it in onto the beach.

That's what I eventually did with my wife Jo Anna. We built this 24-footer that Arthur Piver called Nugget and sailed it out the Golden Gate in August of 1959 and turned left and headed off for Mexico. It was nuts—absolutely the dumbest thing we ever did. Jo Anna was five and a half months pregnant by the time I got the boat built, but we decided to go anyway. It was absolutely nuts, but we pulled it off….

Robin: What a story!

Jim: I guess it's a story, but there are thousands of them, Robin. There are thousands of stories out there like that. That's what we're trying to collect now with our multihull history project. I'll tell you about that later.

Robin: What are the advantages and disadvantages of having a multihull over a monohull?

Jim: (laughter) In the early days, multihulls were very countercultural. There was a rather dreadful schism between the multihull people and the monohull people.

Robin: Like the sail and the power boats today?

Jim: It was worse than that. It was almost like the stand-off between science and religion. People that were really devoted to their boats, no matter what the type, could find plenty of ammunition to argue the issue on both sides of the table.

Is a multihull better than a monohull? I think maybe we'd better start with the disadvantages.

Multihulls   Jim Brown

Disadvantages of multihulls over monohulls

What's happened to multihulls since the modern multihull early days is that they have become astronomically expensive. That was not the case in the beginning. The reason for that is the multihulls cost more to produce. The owner-builder has pretty much faded out of the picture. All these boats are being produced by front yard operations that require high investment. There's a lot of regulation involved and high expectations on the part of the clientele. They want a boat that comes out looking smooth and shiny like an automobile. It certainly does not have to be in order to sail it around the world. This has been driven partly by the clientele and the designers. There's been what Dick Newick calls this 'greed for speed.' It has driven multihulls toward high tech and high cost to the point where they've almost been driven into obscurity, particularly in today's market place where most people just can't spend the money on a modern production multihull. Of course, all of the production yacht builders today are in deep yogurt...

Robin: ...for the same reasons too—because the clientele want all these expensive fast-going boats and they're forgetting about years ago when it was just go out, relax, have fun, leave the comforts of home at home.

Jim: A lot of the stuff that's come down to us in the name of, here's another Dick Newick term, 'modern inconveniences,' has not necessarily enhanced the sailing experience.

Another part of the high cost of modern multihulls is not just their purchase, but also their maintenance. The berthing and haul-out costs and so on are usually greater than with monohulls.

That's really put the bite on the business to the point where, in fact, the entire recreational boating industry is being driven down onto trailers. Anything you can trailer is of great interest these days—you don't have to pay berth rental and you can bring it home to work on it yourself. That relates the multihulls in this way: it's pretty hard to trailer a very wide boat. There have been a number of clever means of developing trailerable trimarans and catamarans, those that fold up in order to get them onto the highway legally at their legal trailering beam. There's a lot of activity in that area today. I'm very interested in that area myself, because if you can trailer it, it also means you can build it in your garage.

At least with a smaller vessel, the age of the owner-builder is coming back. The editors of *WoodenBoat* magazine are telling me they're seeing an absolute explosion in the owner building of small wooden watercraft. That's mostly kayaks, canoes, skiffs, and stuff like that, but it's also happening in multihulls.

Robin: I've gone to the **Wooden Boat Show** and they have a **section called "I built it myself."** The boats entered into that contest are unbelievable, but there's a waiting list of over a year to be entered into that now. They can only take 50 people.

Jim: It's wonderful. It looks like the economic squeeze that we're all feeling, is driving a reemergence of the can-do generation. I love it myself. I may be just an old timer, but I love it.

There are a couple of other disadvantages now to multihulls. A major one, to my mind, is limited load carrying ability. Multihulls are not good load carriers. If the ancient Pacific multihulls had been able to carry cannons, we might be speaking another language today. The boats were so much faster and more maneuverable than the big British blunderbuss things. The European explorers that first showed up in in the Pacific in 1600s were just agog at the performance of the ancient multihulls. And they had them that were big enough, like the Fiji Ndrua, the real juggernaut of the South Pacific—90-feet long, carrying 200 warriors, at 20 knots—but they couldn't carry cannons.

The trouble with multihulls is that, particularly the cruising vessels, cruising tends to encourage the pack rat. Your boat gets just stuffed full of all kinds of stuff that you think you're going to need and maybe you will someday and you'd like to be able to reach for it, but it tends to overload multihulls. The reason for that is the multihulls have narrow hulls. That's the real essence of the multihulls. Whether it's the main hull and the floats of a trimaran, or the twin hulls of the catamaran, those hulls are very narrow. That's why they're so fast—they don't cause that wave making phenomenon that monohulls do. Monohulls have to be wide enough to stand up on their own and multihulls don't. In fact the design of multihulls is kind of a cop-out in a way, because the designer doesn't even have to consider what we call form stability when designing the individual hulls. You can make them narrow enough so that when you put them in water they fall right over on their sides. But when you hook two or three of them together and spread them wide apart, you have something that is geometrically more stable than a monohull could be, but as the water sees the hull forms, they're still narrow. They can break through what they call that hump in the resistance curve and really take off. They just don't push a wave ahead and drag a wave behind like monohulls have to in order to be wide enough to keep from falling over, especially sailboats.

There's a real difference here in the two types. The narrow hulls just won't carry the weight. The shape of the hole that they're making in the surface of the water—when you put the narrow hull in the water, it doesn't have to push as much water out of the way to come down to its water line—that's why they go, but it's also why you can't just keep asking them to push more and more water out of the way. The real Achilles heel of multihulls is the under-wing—the underside of the bridge structure, or what we call the wing, that holds the hulls together. Whether it's two hulls or three, you've got to join them all together somehow. That structure reaches out like a big arm and holds on to the other hull, it has a surface that has to be kept up out of the wave tops. In most cruising catamarans, in particular, that under-wing surface is the real Achilles heel of the boat. If the waves get big enough, or you push the boat fast enough, or if you push it down in the water deep enough, that under-wing starts to take a real licking by the wave tops.

Multihulls   Jim Brown

That pounding on the under-wing and the limited load carrying are the real disadvantages to multihulls. You can work around them. You have to change your mind about what you're going to take along with you and sometimes you have to change your mind about which way you're going to go against the wind. You'll slow down or bear off or do something to reduce the pounding, which is particularly bad in the big catamarans. The hulls are spaced wide enough apart so that they can actually straddle a wave crest. Let's say the weather hull passes over the crest and starts down the back of the wave, and the crest is still there and it slams on the under wing before it lifts up the leeward hull to get over the crest. That pounding business is a real limitation. It means you just can't take everything you want to. It also means that the modern catamaran is at a particular disadvantage. I'll try to talk about that later, but let's get to the advantages, ok?

Advantages of multihulls over monohulls

Speed: personally, I never have thought that speed was the primary advantage of the multihull, but a lot of people think of them as being fast and of course we now know that they can do such wonderful things. The latest big French trimarans are crossing the ocean in three or four days—faster than ocean liners. The America's Cup vessels recently were able to turn in speed in the recent contest between the big catamaran and the big trimaran, the Oracle and the Alinghi. Those boats in their practice sessions, were regularly flirting with 50 knots of boat speed. They can go very fast, even in very light airs. They can be driven hard in light airs because their rigs are so powerful. Those things can sail almost four times faster than the wind is blowing.

Speed is one advantage, even in the cruising boat that's overloaded and was never intended to go fast. There's nothing wrong with just darn well getting where you're going. Some sailors that buy big pudgy monohulls are saying, "The last thing I want to do is hurry. I go out, I'm going sailing to relax and float." But you're going to expose yourself to a lot more discomfort out there than if you had a boat that would lope along at half again as fast. That's about the kind of speed I talk about—a cruising multihull should be able to knock out speeds about half again as fast as an equivalent cruising monohull. Some multihulls will go a whole lot faster than that, but they've come up with some very fast monohulls these days. Multihulls have driven the advance of sailing technology. The potential for that speed that was demonstrated by early multihulls have driven a lot of marine architecture ever since World War II.

The next advantage of multihulls is motion. The multihull *can* have a motion that's less comfortable than the equivalent monohull, but most of the time it's far *more* comfortable. If you have an equivalent monohull and multihull anchored in the same roadstead and it's a quiet day, but the harbor is all chopped up with motorboat wakes, the multihull is going to jump around more than the monohull. But if it's an open roadstead and there's a real swell running through, it can easily cause the monohull to roll its rails down—just roll your eyeballs out. Whereas, the multihull sits there like a duck and bobs up and down over the surface and has to conform to the shape of the wave. It's definitely not immobile, but doesn't develop that residual pendulum type roll motion that monohulls do. While underway, particularly at speed, they can be marvelously smooth riding—not all of them are, that's for sure, but they can be.

Then the interiors—the modern cruising catamarans, in particular, have these glorious accommodations. They can be so much like your recreation room at home that inexperienced people look at them and say that's what I want. Most of the bridge cabin catamarans of today have this wonderful communal space in the bridge. It might have the whole galley there, together with lots of lounging area, the navigation station, entertainment, books, the whole thing, is there in this bridge cabin that is held up by the hulls of the catamaran. But here comes the problem, there is so much space in them, that sometimes the design is not intended for real seafaring. The designer is encouraged to reduce the under-wing clearance that I was talking about before to gain standing headroom in the bridge cabin. If the boat is any good, the crew that's waltzing around in the bridge cabin has its feet well above the waterline. That means you have to push up the superstructure, the house top begins to develop a lot of what a sailor calls top hamper—it's very well named. Many cruising catamarans have, in my view, unacceptable top hamper. It's what my friend Joe Hudson called the school bus effect, done in order to provide these glorious accommodations, but it tends to push the under-wing down and the house top up.

When the multihull gets big enough—some say 50 feet, I think 60 feet is a better number—you can deal with that; you can have enough under-wing clearance *and* enough headroom in the bridge to make a good boat out of it without it becoming excessively school bus-y. In so many cruising catamarans, the helmsman's position—the actual pilot seat of the boat—has to be on a double-high bar stool behind the school bus so you can see over it. The helmsman is perched up there in a fighting chair. If he falls out, he's got a long way to get down to the under-wing. You see a lot of modern multihulls that are designed that way and many of them are good for just what they are intended for—lakes, bays, rivers, and sounds—protected water. But if you're going to go out in the big briny, you've got to have under-wing clearance and that's hard to do in a small catamaran. All the exhibitors showing their modern cruising catamarans at the boat shows should provide a kayak in the water, so that the prospective buyer can get into the kayak and see if he can get his way under the wing of the boat. If you can paddle a kayak through the tunnel of a catamaran, you got a pretty good boat. For a small cat, you might have to scrunch down, bend and put your head between your knees, in order to get through there. But you see some of them at boat shows where you can barely see through there. A lot of them have these big protuberances that stick down and out of the bottom of the wing or out of the side of the hulls that really detract from their seafaring nature, in my view. Normally speaking, the modern catamaran can have wonderful interiors, but the trimarans can too, it's just a different sort of interior. You don't have that big block of space in the middle of the boat that resembles your living room at home. The accommodations are more like in a monohull—maybe we can speak to that later.

The other real advantage to a multihull over monohull, in my opinion, is safety. That's not been their classic reputation. We were roundly criticized in the early days of multihulls. We were told that we were going to sea in a boat that would make us swim for our lives. That might well be true if one is looking only at the prospect of capsize, but you can't look only at the prospect of capsize, you have to compare it with the prospect of sinking. We've learned that the two are very similar. Sinking and capsize are both very rare in the cruising boats these days. Capsize is quite common in the racers, but no more common than racing monohulls that have their keels break off or their hulls break in half. And there are the other very common kinds of marine hazards—collisions, fire, shipwreck, stranding...

Robin: ...and running aground is a big one now.

Jim: We'll get to shoal draft, boy—that's one of the main advantages of multihulls. But just because you have shoal draft doesn't mean you're not going to run aground. You start sneaking around in thin water and you'll find yourself stuck more often than if you had a deep boat. The great thing about that is you can step off and push the boat off the bar and climb back on again and keep going. I have an old 31-foot trimaran that whenever we run aground, my sons and I just jump out and push off.

The common kinds of accidents, particularly shipwrecks where the boat is stranded, we have many examples of the crew living through calamitous shipwrecks and ending up being able to just step off onto dry land with the multihulls. That doesn't happen with monohulls, boy. The keel hits the reef and the boat lies over on its side and gets a hole poked in it with seas bursting over the upturned bilge and the crew really isolated a long way from land.

In collision, most multihulls are unsinkable and that's a tremendous safety advantage. When you start thinking about that, thousands of years of sailing have accepted the possibility of sinking. We sort of likely go to sea, try to prepare for it, and try to prevent it.

The same thing has to be done with capsize—there's no doubt about it. The real difference between capsize and sinking is the consequence of capsize is much preferred to the consequence of sinking. We find that multihulls, particularly trimarans, can provide a habitat for the castaway sailors after an offshore capsize. You compare that with a sunken monohull where the boat literally disappears from the face of the earth, and you've got to concede that non-sinking multihulls have a tremendous safety advantage if you're going to take it all the way to zero hour.

Robin: You've convinced me.

Jim: It took us a long time to convince ourselves. I had this thing about sinking because I'd almost been through it. So maybe I was little more open to the notion than most people, but, boy, most traditional sailors thought that we early multihullers were just nuts to go offshore in that thing.

The real advantage—and I'll concede that this is the one point that cannot be argued from both sides of the table (all of other points I've made in the way of advantages can be argued by a monohull aficionado)—the one thing that the multihull has that cannot be approached in a monohull is they've been developed now to the point where they have these splendid seakeeping properties. That is combined with shoal draft. In no other configuration do you get that combination to that extent. That just gives a cruising sailor a crack at another whole hemisphere of the water planet that is inaccessible to the offshore sailor with a deep boat. You can't argue against that.

If I could close the discussion of advantages and disadvantages, I might say that the real difference between multihulls and monohulls is in their people. The people who are willing to embrace the multihull concept are really embracing a different attitude toward the sea, Robin. It's another way of looking at it. I'm not saying that one boat is better than another, I'm not. I still love monohulls. I think a sailing dingy is the niftiest thing around. Monohulls, in my view, get really good when they get big—50 feet's okay, but 150 feet is great—you've got a great thing there. It's just that I could never afford one.

But this attitude toward the sea is based on a new generation of humanity. Many of today's water people came out of swim fins and masks and snorkels and surf boards and wind surfers. It's a whole different thing. These guys look at a big wave as not a threat, but as something to be enjoyed. They don't consider their boats to be a fortress to protect them against the sea. They're more like an implement that they can use in order to go out there and really get it on, really jam through the waves. It's an entirely different attitude toward the sea, I think. That's a lot of blah-blah, but that's the way I see the differences, the two types.

Robin: That is a huge difference.

Jim: Yeah, a lot of people don't think about all that stuff. I've been thinking about it a lot lately, of course, because I've been trying to write a book about it. I'll tell you about that later if you're interested.

Robin: Aside from the obvious fact that catamarans have two hulls and trimarans have three, what else sets them apart, given both their advantages and disadvantages? I know you mentioned a lot of it earlier with the multihull over the monohull. But there must be some differences between the catamaran and the trimaran.

Jim: There are some more distinctions that apply to the configurations. They really are different animals. Because the world is gone cat crazy, Robin, there are a lot of people out there that don't even think trimarans are multihulls, they're something else off the wall, some other kind of creature. But, if we want to stay with this biological metaphor, we could say that both catamarans and trimarans come from the same phylum. They're both surface watercraft. The catamarans and the trimarans are different than most other watercraft because they have more than one torso or thorax or whatever you want to call it. They're quite different creatures relative to monohulls. The difference between the cat and the tri is they're distinctly different species, but in the same phylum and the same genus.

First of all, there are structural differences because of this configuration thing. The trimaran, with its big central main hull and its two smaller outer hulls or outrigger hulls, is conceptually a little easier to deal with structurally. In fact, probably the first real multihulls that ventured offshore were trimarans—the good old double outrigger canoe. It's easy to tie floats onto a main hull, but it's not too easy to tie two main hulls together—they're bigger and heavier, you've got more going on there.

In the trimaran (let's come to the modern trimaran now), the main hull provides you with things that you don't get with the cat, structural things. One of them is the place to step the mast. In a catamaran it's pretty hard to find a place to step the mast without having an enormously strong bridge reaching across between the two boats. You also get a place in the trimaran to attach the head stay or jib stay out on the bow. You don't have a bow out there in the catamaran, not on center. The catamaran also requires two rudders, it's not strictly true, but most catamarans have twin rudders and you have to hook them together somehow. The steering linkages get to be very involved and expensive in cats. The two centerboards—the centerboard and its trunks—have to be duplicated in the catamaran, not in the trimaran.

And here's the biggie—the trimaran can get along just fine on one engine. Whereas the catamaran, well, you can run a catamaran with one engine and you can run a catamaran with one centerboard, but that's not the way to do it and most people don't do it that way. So, you can save a lot of weight and cost in the trimaran, because of its main hull to attach the jib stay, the centerboard, the rudder, and the engine.

In the catamaran, the other structural differences also come into play. You almost have to have a model in front of you to look them over in order to really get a handle on it. The bridge between the hull, these differences relate to the size of the several hulls in a single vessel—their size and their spacing, how wide apart they are. The catamaran has twin hulls, they're both the same size and they're spaced rather wide apart. It's a long way from one hull to the other in the catamaran. Whereas in the trimaran, unless you make it extremely wide, and that's what they're doing to the race boats now, the space between the main hull and the outer hull is somewhat less than in the catamaran.

These differences, well it gets to be pretty complex to talk about it, but I've already mentioned one in the big cats especially, with the hulls wide apart, they can straddle the wave crest and cause pounding on the under-wing. In the trimaran, the harder you drive it, the more you push the lee hull down and the closer to the water comes the under-wing panel.

So there are disadvantages to both types when it comes to their hull spacing. The trimaran's float hull or outer hull is not as far away from the main hull—there's not as much room in there—but you do push the lee hull down. There are other factors that we call interplay wave making. The early trimarans were not wide enough to avoid the problem of the main hull bow wave angling off and running into the float. Now they're made wide enough so as we can avoid that problem.

But, I hasten to say that all of these structural differences, all of the problems of one type or another, have now been overcome. There's no doubt that you can make a good strong catamaran, even though there's no simple place to attach the head stay. The same thing with trimarans—I mean, if you only have one engine, maybe someday you're going to wish you had two because one won't work. It's the old trade off. There are so much compromise that goes on in marine design of all types of vessels, both monohull and multihull.

Basically, we can say that catamarans are better load carriers than trimarans. They have two big hulls instead of one. If a trimaran is a good one, it's designed so that its float hulls are actually held up pretty much out of the water by the main hull. The main hull has to carry the load of the outrigger hulls in the trimaran. The reason for that is if you push the outer hulls down too deep in the trimaran, it cuts into their maneuverability. That is, you have to drag the full length of three hulls through the turn while tacking and that's when the power is turned off.

That's another difference, the catamaran has to drag its two hulls through the tack. The trimaran, if it's properly designed, basically only has to drag one hull through the tack. For that reason, trimarans are more maneuverable than catamarans. It's easier to tack them; it's easier to sail a snake wake through the harbor and avoid traffic and stuff like that in the trimaran. They're quicker on the helm, generally speaking; not strictly true, but generally speaking.

Yet the catamaran is better on the beach. If you're to beach the boat, voluntarily or by accident, the catamaran, if indeed you have a sandy beach or even if you don't, the thing will sit there like a big raft on the beach. Whereas the trimaran, its main hull is deeper and if you've got any surf running as a swash on the beach, the trimaran will lurch drunkenly from one float to the other as it responds to the surf while pivoting on the main hull, which is the only thing that's aground.

Most people would say that the catamaran has better accommodations. We've talked about that. In my view, that point is arguable. The catamaran has accommodations that are better for those who regard their boats as domiciles. The trimaran has better accommodations for those who regard their boats as vehicles. There's a real tradeoff to be made there and a lot of thinking that needs to be invested by the prospective buyer, designer, or builder, because right in there, a lot happens. So many people buy a boat because of its accommodations. Well, what kind of accommodations are we talking about here? Do you want to be a good live-aboarder in the marina? Or you want to spend months at a time in the various harbors that you go and visit? Or do you want your boat to be a gin palace where you can have all your friends come down on the weekends and hang out? If so, maybe you'd better have a catamaran. But if you want to get out there on the big briny, particularly with a small crew, and have a really good place to fix your meals, do your navigating, and all of that, in a way that is private and apart from the crew, the off-watch that's trying to rest, maybe you'd better think about a trimaran.

Trimarans are also better upwind, Robin. It's not universally true, of course, because it depends on the boat itself, but, generally speaking, trimarans are better up wind and that's because their centerboards or dagger boards are mounted in the main hull. The main hull of the trimaran is deeper than the hulls of a catamaran, so the centerboard starts from deeper and goes deeper. It can reach down there into solid, quiet water and hang on. Also, being in the center, it contributes to the steering properties of the boat.

Multihulls   Jim Brown

And there are other aspects, differences between these two animals that make the trimaran a better boat up wind. It relates to motion—I'm talking now about the comparison in the size and the spacing of the hulls. The catamaran hulls are the same size. Each one of them has to be big enough to support the entire weight of the boat if you were to stand the boat on edge. It has to be a lot bigger than that, actually. The trimaran, on the other hand, its outer hulls are of different size than the main hull. Their gross displacement, when buried to the deck, can be adjusted by the designer so as to make it possible for the sailor to see very clearly when his boat is being overdriven.

The catamaran, because it's so darn stable, especially the big ones, it's just incredible, it's like going offshore in a pool table. You've got 10-foot waves that are rolling around and you walk around the decks with your hands in your pockets. It's just amazing how stable they are. And yet, if the wind blows hard enough or the wave gets big enough, you can pick up the weather hull without depressing the leeward hull much. That makes the catamaran, in my view, less intuitive, less user-friendly.

The trimaran will communicate with the pilot in a much more direct manner. It will tell you in no uncertain terms that you're driving the daylights out of your boat, because the lee float, the bow of the downwind outrigger, will go driving right through the crests. That's normal behavior when driving the boat hard to windward. You don't push the whole float underwater, you push just the bow, and you see the crest rolled down the deck. But you still got maybe half of the buoyancy of the lee float still out of the water, and it's telling you, "Hey, man! Do you want to really do this?" Okay—you've got a good strong crew, guys that know what they're doing. You're driving for the finish mark in a race, and you got another boat that's trying to put you in its lee. Okay—strap it down and let her go. Lash that bugger—let her go. But not when you're offshore. You don't behave like that offshore, unless you're one of these hard bitten racers who go to bed while the boat is doing that.

I personally think that single-handed racing is unseamanlike because the boat has to be operated at flank speed very often with no one on watch. Even at times like that, the trimaran is more communicative with the pilot than the catamaran. They're a little more user-friendly in that way and for that reason, I think they're more like a monohull and they're less likely to become capsized than the catamaran because they tell the sailor when it's driving too hard.

The cat appeals to inexperienced sailors, but people who are coming out of monohulls can understand the trimaran a little better. You can get down in the middle and put your feet below the waterline and still have standing headroom without putting the school bus on deck.

That whole business of intuitive, user-friendly operation, I think that argument has to go to the trimaran but only for boats that are really intended for serious offshore operation. I think also that the trimarans are safer.

Here's a real distinction: not only are they less likely to become capsized, in my view, but they're also habitable when capsized and a catamaran is not. And the reason for that is when the trimaran is capsized, the outer hulls form giant airlock spaces. They are air tanks and they will hold the main hull up high enough to make the interior of the main hull habitable even when the boat's upside down. You can cut a hole in the hull or open the safety hatch in that capsized trimaran in order to ventilate, to get oxygen inside the main hull, while the vessel is capsized. With the catamaran, if you violate the airlock that's in those capsized hulls, the boat is probably going to settle too deep to be habitable inside. So, like a sunken monohull that has disappeared, the catamaran requires that the crew take to a life raft. I'm not saying that they should take to the life raft alone. It becomes critical now for the life raft to remain tethered to the mother ship in a catamaran. We've had several incidents to indicate that it's a bad mistake to take off in your life raft if you can stay attached to your capsized mother ship, because the mother ship contains all kinds of stuff that you can use for survival while awaiting rescue. There are a number of wonderful historic examples to illustrate that point, Robin. We've seen it, particularly with my great friend, John Glennie, who with his crew of two managed to survive for 120 days—four months—inhabiting their capsized trimaran in the South Pacific. When they finally got to the shore, they were in such good shape that the authorities didn't believe their story.

If you want to talk about safety, that's ultimate safety—that's zero hour—that's the very thing that really niggles the mind of the man, woman, child who is contemplating sailing offshore. "My G-d, what if the thing sinks or capsizes?" From what we know about it now, you'd rather have it capsize, and if it's going to do that, you'd rather have it be a trimaran and a catamaran, at least that's my analysis. It's pretty longwinded; I hope somebody is still interested, because I think this is hot stuff.

Robin: This is just fascinating.

Jim: We've learned a lot in the last 50 years. A lot of it we've learned the hard way; a lot of us have learned our seamanship the hard way. There have been a lot of crack ups, some loss of life, and some true tragedy in order to accumulate this knowledge. But we've got it now, and there's just no doubt, Robin, that it all points to the fact that multihulls represent an absolute sea change in marine architecture. We're going to see a whole lot more of them, both recreational and commercial, and military—no doubt in my mind.

Robin: I know quite a few people now that are actually buying cats. I don't know so many buying trimarans, but I know a few that are building their own. It is heading that way.

Jim: That could be a pretty hard nail to get into trimarans because the press these days—the evidence in the harbor and so on—is mostly catamaran. There's no doubt that, for most of what they're used for, they're just great. Cats are great. Cats are great for these excursion vessels, what we call the cattle-marans that carry joy riders off the beaches and all the warm water resorts all around the world now. Those cats are just great; they've got great big ones now. The largest I've designed was 64 feet. One of those was certified by the Coast Guard for a 150 passengers and they steam the thing right up to the beach and pick the people up right out of the surf. They drop a ladder down between the bow nets and people can walk out of their hotels, scramble up on the boat, and go out and watch the whales and the birds and the sky and the mountains. Charter catamarans are a big deal and cats seem to be better at it than trimarans.

Robin: We've come so far in boating. **Jim, we've been talking about multihulls—catamarans and trimarans—but we haven't yet talked about a proa. What's that?**

Jim: Proa (pronounced **proh**-*uh*) is one of the words used in the ancient South Pacific to describe a vessel that some people call a half a trimaran. That is, it has one main hull and only one smaller outrigger hull. To be a true proa, that contraption has to carry that outrigger hull always on one side or the other, usually on the windward side; that is, the outrigger hull—the small hull—to windward. The reason for that is that the rig of the boat is set up so that it can accept the wind only from one side.

This sounds absolutely nuts and proas really are off the wall. We're getting into some pretty zany stuff here. Keeping the small hull always to windward, let's say to windward—some of them keep it always to leeward; never in the ancient boats, but some of the modern boats, such as the so-called Atlantic trimaran, as designed by Dick Newick, carry the outrigger hull on the downwind side, but the ancient Pacific boats and most of the other proas carry their outrigger hull on the upwind side—what this means is that you can't tack. If you tack, the wind comes around on the other side of the vessel and there's nothing to hold the rig up. If you tack through the eye of the wind, the wind changes sides. Let's say you're on the port tack and the wind's coming in over your left ear, and you want to tack, so you put the boat up through the wind and come around and you're on a starboard tack and you've got the wind coming over your right ear. You can't do that with the proa, not the same way. What you have to do instead is stop and put the other end forward. They sail either end first and it's pretty hard to describe this but it's not called tacking, it's called shunting. A true proa must be able to shunt; it cannot tack. Let's say you're going along here on what you might call the port tack and the outrigger is off on your left side there and you're sailing along and you want to go off on the other "tack" (we called it the other shunt), instead of turning left through the eye of the wind, you turn right and stop and adjust the sails so as to make what was the stern now the bow.

Robin: That's a lot of skill.

Jim: It's culturally outlandish for, because we think of boats as being bilateral, having a right side and a left side, like we have a right ear and a left ear.

Robin: **How do they get anywhere? It sounds time consuming.**

Jim: It is until you get a handle on it. You get a handle on it and you realize that except in one peculiar predicament, the proa is really a lot more manageable and maneuverable than the tacking vessel. We could go on and on about this, Robin, and I'm afraid it's a subject for another time, but I'll summarize by saying that there's a lot going on in proas today. It's like the early days of catamarans and trimarans. We have some very can-do experimenters out there, pushing the envelope toward the proa. I have absolutely no doubt that the proa has a lot to show us yet. It's going to take at least as much of a mind shift as from monohull to multihull for us to embrace the proa. I'm not willing to bet on it yet, but I wouldn't be a bit surprised, I don't know that I'll live to see it, but I think that the commercial vessel of the future, the commercial sail-assisted or a motor-assisted ocean-crossing watercraft of the future, is going to be a proa.

I'll have to leave it at that unless we could sit down with some drawings or a model or I could get together some of my video footage and try to illustrate how a proa operates. I happen to have the unique experience of having sailed in a true seafaring proa and understanding them pretty well because of the work of my son, Russell. He's probably the only American who has really done a lot of seafaring in the proa. I've learned from him. I had to pass the torch to do it, but I think I understand what I'm talking about with proas. I've never designed one and I would not feel myself qualified, but there's no doubt that it has a lot to show us yet. An interesting thing, here's another aspect of the proa, it was probably the multihull type that was used for exploring the Pacific by the early island people, Micronesians and Polynesians—the proa was the vessel of exploration.

The trimaran, the double outrigger canoe, was probably the first seagoing multihull type because it was used for carrying people from island Asia out to the nearby island groups like the Philippines, for instance. They were pushed out by population pressures and other things. But when it came time that the Philippines—that's 8,000 islands—were also outstripped as far as their environment was concerned—and this all happened before Christ—the people had to push out into the open Pacific and against the wind. It was the superior weatherliness of the proa that made it possible for these Stone Age vessels to explore the entire Pacific basin and for the navigator priests to come back and tell people that, "Okay, we've had logs floating in from over there for a long time and we found the island. It's over there and we can get you back to it." Then they used the catamaran as the freighter, the vessel of colonization, in order to go populate. They populated a wider area of earth than any other race at that time. That's where the proa fits in, I think.

Proas are incredibly weatherly vessels, even the old ones that were made entirely out of sticks and string. A modern proa will go to windward like you wouldn't believe. I think it's going to be possible to develop them to be the safest of all offshore watercraft. Maybe I shouldn't say this, but the potential is there for the proa to become self-righting. If it gets knocked down, the potential is there for it to come back up. No other multihull can do that. Monohulls can do that, but they can sink. There are some interesting comparisons in there. We could talk a lot more about proa at another time if you want to.

Robin: Sounds good. **How easy would it be for a boater to switch from a monohull to a multihull?**

Jim: It wasn't easy for me. I had this strong traditional yachting background. The first multihull I saw, I was truly offended by the thing. I had to be led by the nose. My old friend Wolfie, and then Arthur Piver, they dragged me over tradition past into multihull territory. I think that would be true of many experienced sailors—people who have some sea time behind them—they'll probably have to be dragged by the nose. I've seen a lot of examples of that, particularly my dear friend Doug Jane, who had more sea time on monohulls than you can imagine and is now a great multihull proponent, but I had to work on him for years. He's now built five big ones and has done a lot of delivery passages in them and stuff like that. It *does* happen to experienced sailors, but it's easier for inexperienced sailors to embrace the multihull notion. They see that space in there, especially for wives and children and older folks—you can get around on a big catamaran with your wheelchair.

That applies particularly to the type of catamaran wherein the perspective buyer is more interested in the domicile aspects of the boat—the thing as a floating home, a cabin in the pines that you don't have to buy land for and you can move anytime you want. That's the real market for modern production cruising, recreational multihull—people that would like to have a space on the water where they can go and hang out. With this boat, they can move it. Wherever they put it, they have to pay to leave it there, and the marinas are clogged with multihulls now.

I just returned from the Rio Dulce in Guatemala which is one of the great cruising harbors in the world, I think. When my wife and my boys and I were in there in the mid-1970s, for a while we were the only cruising boat in the whole river system. It's a grand inland waterway system. I just went back with my old friend Joe Hudson. We sailed down there in his beautiful 35-foot Marples-designed trimaran. We sailed in there and learned that there are over 2,000 cruising yachts in the Rio Dulce now. It's just incredible. When you go around and look at them, which you can do—you can get your dugout canoe, put a motor on it, and run around the whole river system looking at all these boats—a lot of them are big cats and a few are tris. I didn't make a count, but I would say 20-25% of those 2,000 boats are multihulls. People park them in the Rio Dulce during hurricane season because the place is hurricane proof, and they head for the Caribbean after that.

The other great thing about the Rio Dulce is that it gives you access to the Guatemalan highlands—still the most exotic place ever I've been. My wife and I agree on that and we've been around a bit. My poor buddy Joe wants to sell his Marples now (his body has given up on him). Whoever gets it will be right in the heart of the best cruising ground in this hemisphere, I think—the Belize Keys, the Honduras Bay Islands, oh man.

Robin: Sounds wonderful. **Have any experienced sailors actually changed back to monohulls?**

Jim: Oh, I didn't talk about that (laughter). They have, yes. Some of the very most experienced sailors that I know have reversed the cycle. It's particularly true of people who are getting on in years and who don't want to have so darn much of their net worth tied up in the boat itself.

There are so very many good cruising monohulls around that are begging for ownership. You can buy a wonderful boat, spend a little money fixing it up, and have an absolute jewel of a used monohull. But you can't buy a good used catamaran that way very often, very seldom. The people that have them paid so darn much for them, they want to hang on to them. But I've had people change back, yes. I suppose we should ask them about that—why they've done that. Maybe that's a possibility for another gab here someday, Robin. I can think of a couple of people we can talk to about that—some very experienced cruising sailors who have changed back from multihull to monohull.

Another advantage of multihulls is load carrying. For the same length of boat they can carry a lot more weight and can squeeze it into a tighter spot, whether it's at the marina, the anchorage, or the boat yard.

Robin: You can **trailer it** probably a little easier.

Jim: I was thinking of larger live-aboard cruisers. A trailerable multihull is, by nature, pretty small. Ian Farrier has designed some big folding trimarans using his fascinating folding system, up to 40-footers now. They can't trailer them down the highway folded without a special permit. They have to have a lead car, a wide load sign, and all that stuff in order to get down the highway. But, just to get them into a travel lift crane for hauling out and for storing them into boat yard, it's worth it for them to fold it up.

Robin: **Is there a length restriction in multihulls, especially for racing?**

Jim: I don't think there's a restriction, except cost. As a good example, we can see, particularly in the racing boats, the big French trimarans, most of the trans-ocean speed records now are held by trimarans. They've got them up to 150 feet long—they're incredible things. The America's Cup was sailed in 90-footers. The commercial future of multihulls, which is assured now, I mean it's assured that a large part of the commercial fleet of the future is going to be on more than one hull—anything that carries lightweight cargoes—they're no good for carrying oil or ore or something like that—but, for carrying things like people and vehicles, such as in ferrying, the best of the modern fast ferries are now trimarans. They are 400 feet long and carry 1,000 passengers and 260 cars at 40 knots with unprecedented energy efficiency. That's the writing on the wall, Robin, right there. When it gets time for us to give up flying and driving frivolously, which appears now to be inevitable, the way to get across the water is definitely going to be in the modern multihulls. Look how far they've come in the last 50 years. Give us *another* 50 years and I think the trans-ocean liners are going to be motor-sailors. We can talk more about that someday, too.

Robin: We can, but we won't be around to see it. **How do things like displacement beam and sail area relate to stability and performance in multihulls?**

Jim: We're getting pretty technical here.

Robin: We have some technical listeners.

Jim: It's enough to say that they do relate. The designer uses them in the form of ratios and there's a thing we call the displacement to speed ratio, displacement to length ratio, displacement to sail area ratio, which is more to your question. All of those things are numbers that a designer can come up that allow him to compare the boat that he's designing with other boats that have known performance features. It's a fascinating juggling act.

It does relate to stability for sure, and to instability. All of that relates to performance. Without getting into a course on marine architecture, which I'm not qualified to teach, we'd just better say that there's no magic in multihulls. There's no designer mumbo jumbo that other designers don't have, because they haven't done multihulls yet. You do have to learn how to use a few things a little differently. We have thousands of prototype multihulls out there sailing around, and a lot of data on them.

Actually, some of the new ones are really beginning to gather a lot of data. We can see just how tightly integrated the subject of marine design is. In a way it's a little tighter in multihulls. If you change one thing, it seems to change everything else, and that's pretty hard to make an amateur client understand. If you're designing a boat for a guy and you say, "Now we've got to do a very careful weight study. I need to know about everything you're going to put on this boat, and I mean *everything*." So you go down the list and you come up with a total and say, "Okay, if you're going to put all of this crud on this boat, we're going to have to design it like this in order to carry that weight." And then in the middle of the construction, the guy decides that he wants a double sliding glass door.

Robin: Or he changes spouses or friends, so there's a weight difference there.

Jim: The basic ratio that speaks to your question is the *power to weight ratio*—the sail area to displacement ratio—how much power have you got held up there in the wind relative to how much weight you're trying to push through the water. You really have to push in the water. Man, you've got to push the water out of the way to get through, and water is heavy. The modern construction methods have made it possible for us to really get the weight down, at least in the racing boats, and the power way up, by building things like the rigid wing sail that was on the BMW Oracle, the America's Cup winner. It had a rigid wing sail larger than the wing on any passenger carrier in a carrying aircraft. The power that that thing generated was just astounding, and yet the boat is extremely light weight because it's all made out of carbon fiber with a great deal of very advanced engineering involved. It was wide as it was long—90 feet wide, for Pete's sake—could barely get it through the Panama Canal. That thing just had a favorable power to weight ratio—it was able, most of the time, to sail away from the competition, which was also a very advanced boat—the Swiss Alinghi catamaran. Both of those projects were splendid achievements and a lot more needs to be said about them. But the ability to manipulate these relationships, these ratios, between various factors in the design, is becoming more and more sophisticated.

It's way beyond me. I still like the idea of taking a dugout canoe and putting a couple of bamboo canes across it—a couple of little floats out there—I can understand that. Modern multihull design is becoming very advanced, no doubt. There's no magic in it, but there are a few things to learn. The biggest thing is that when you change one factor, and all those relationships, it changes everything else. The computer will tell you so. You can see it clearly when you ask, "What if...?" It's very clear. This is a red flag to the client that goes to a designer for a custom multihull design. Once you cast that thing in concrete, you damn well better not go messing with it or you're going to end up with a joke. It has happened too many times.

Robin: **How do multihulls generally hold up in heavy weather? We've already talked about capsizing and the possibility of sinking compared to sinking in monohulls.**

Jim: We used to a have a lot of structural problems, but they weren't of the sort that you'd expect. There's been very little record of multihulls becoming dismembered, that is, the crossbeam structure failing and allowing the hulls to fall apart. It's happened, but very little of that has gone on. It's been mostly dismastings and rudder failures, centerboard failures, and panel failures—that is, the skin of the hull and/or the under-wing is often designed to be so very light weight in order to make the boat go fast, that it doesn't do very well when resisting cyclic loads. They're not as fatigue resistant as the initial numbers seemed to suggest. So structurally speaking, we've had to learn to make monohulls stronger and stronger. Unfortunately, that means more weight, money, and work. But we've had to do it if we want the boats to last very long.

Many of the racers aren't really intended to last very long, though, over time, cyclic loads and slamming loads—the pounding business—can really raise hell on any structure. We've been slapped in the face about that more than once. So what we've got going on now is pretty darn good. You can really depend on your boat if you use it wisely—use it for what it was intended. If you take a big box and take it offshore, there's no doubt you can pound the under-wing out. But, there's a lot of evidence to suggest that when these fleets of yachts get caught offshore, such as when a whole bunch of boats are going off in a race, and terrible gale comes through, I mean truly terrible gales that have, at least twice now, caught whole fleets of yachts offshore, with the fleets composed of both multihulls and monohulls. The results of those zero-hour situations suggest that you're better off in a multihull. The multihulls come through just fine.

Robin: It's just mind boggling how they even survive, any of them, in those races.

Jim: It is. It's kind of nuts to go out there.

Robin: Exhilarating, it sounds like.

Jim: The Australians, even if they got a gale warning coming up, they'll fire the gun for a big race and send everybody out there in that stuff. I think it's downright poor seamanship. I'm not a big fan of racing. I've always thought that the real benefit of a multihull was that the thing was capable of such wonderful speeds, but when you're placing yourself in harm's way, you just throttle back so that you've got plenty of speed held in reserve.

Now, you've got to have a pretty safe boat. It's like having a good car that would go down the highway and be stable at 150 miles an hour…. Some of these modern automobiles—same with some of these trimarans and catamarans—are capable of such incredible speed. In the name of racing, they just sail them without reserve. If you take a good car and just throttle it back to 90 instead of 120 mph, it's a very safe machine, very road-worthy. The same thing is true of sea worthiness in multihulls. I've always thought that that was the real advantage of having a fast boat is that you could hold a lot of that in reserve, especially when you've got your wife and kids and all that stuff out there in a race.

Multihulls   Jim Brown

Robin: One thing we haven't talked about yet is the **trimarans fitted with hydrofoils**. I see those popping up in the new magazines now.

Jim: Hydrofoils have been responsible for some of these incredible record-setting dashes that the French have made across the Atlantic and around the world; the British too. The boats you're referring to are racing trimarans fitted with what are called J foils. There are also T foils and ladder foils; different types of foils. But the J foil is like a big dagger board that's mounted in the floats of one of these extremely wide trimarans. It's a dagger board that goes down through the deck of the float and out the bottom, but at a diagonal. That is, it enters through the outboard side of the deck, let's call it the deck of the outboard hull, and comes out the bottom of that hull on its inboard side, so that it angles back underneath toward the boat.

A hydrofoil is an underwater wing and accomplishes the same thing in water than an airplane wing does in air. It's just that water is 600 or 700 times more dense than air, so the hydrofoil doesn't have to be nearly as big as the airfoil in order to generate a whole lot of lift. On these big French trimarans that carry these J foils—they're called J foils because their dagger boards are not straight, they're curved in a big arc, so if you look at the end of them, they have the shape of the letter J—when you start pushing them through the water fast enough they generate enough lift to allow these sailors (and these guys are true athletes) to drive these big trimarans, some of them 150 feet long, hard enough to lift the main hull, not just the weather hull, up out of the water and also lift most of the lee hull out of the water.

Robin: I've seen incredible photos of that in some of the sailing magazines.

Jim: They're just amazing. What that does, of course, is gets most of the boat out of the water so it can go faster. But it's a real balancing act, Robin. What they are doing is balancing that whole boat—it's a huge contraption—on that foil. The lee hull is in the water just enough along the surface to provide fore and aft stability, so the boat doesn't dive its bow or its stern. That's all the lee float is for when these boats are flying on that J foil. They don't always have conditions that'll permit that kind of sailing, but when they do, the boats can just take off at an incredible speed—50 knots has probably been achieved in bursts now.

But the J foil is not for everyone. You've got to be an absolute maestro to control the boat under those conditions. When the boat comes up out of the water and heels to leeward and flies on that foil, they are even able to incline the mast to windward so as to not lose the sail power that most boats are trying to lose when they heel. The real purpose of heeling is to dump excessive wind power out the top of the sail. These things, they don't want to do that—they want to use that energy to drive the thing through the water. That's the J foil.

There's another one they call a T foil, which is the one that I think is more interesting and has a greater commercial future. It's a foil that, if you look at it from behind or coming at you, looks like an upside-down T. It has a vertical dagger board going down into the water that's also shaped like a wing, the section of that thing is shaped like a teardrop—it looks like a table knife sticking down in the water. On the end of the table knife, there's a lateral wing—that's the top of the T (in this case, the bottom of the T because the T is upside down). That foil down there, now, it's well down in the water. It can be fitted with what you might call an aileron, which is a flap on the trailing edge. That flap can be controlled just like in an airplane so that the T part of the foil on the bottom can develop lift upward or downward. What they're doing with T-foilers now, particularly those designed by Sam Bradfield and his team of genius guys down in Florida, they have devised a trimaran that has three T foils—one in each outer hull and one of them actually on the stern of the main hull, which comprises the rudder, so the vertical knife blade part of that one turns in order to comprise the rudder. Now the boat comes up out of the water, it flies on all three of these T foils. The foil on the downwind side is lifting up the downwind side of the boat and the foil on the stern of the main hull is lifting up the stern of the boat. But the foil on the upwind float, that's down in the water, it's actually pulling downwards, so they can keep the boat dead level even though the wind force is trying to make it heel. So you don't have to incline the mast to windward to keep from spilling wind. Now you've got something you can really control.

I think the future for this type of hydrofoil vessel is really great. There's a tremendous opportunity here to devise wind-powered machines that can also be engine powered, that can go fast, stable, and safe enough, but not a balancing act. So that we can really push out into the future with foil-borne multihulls that can become truly commercial, that is they can keep schedule even if there's no wind, they can motor fast enough to keep schedule.

Because of the apparent wind effect, which is something that we can get into, but it's like hanging your head out of the car window—you're going down the road in calm, but you've got 50 knots of wind blowing over your face. When a sailboat gets going that fast, it generates a lot of its own wind. That's why they can sail faster than the true wind is blowing. I think that particular concept, the apparent wind phenomenon, can be utilized in order to develop sailing vessels in the future that are very much like modern jet aircraft. They will require enormous bursts of power to get them up on foil—if the wind isn't blowing hard, they're really going to have to hit the throttle to get the boat up on foil—but after it's going, now it's generating enough of its own wind so they can throttle back, maybe even shut down, and sail fast in very little wind, at least on some points of sailing. Now we get the opportunity for, say, an ocean crossing, for example, if you're going to ride an ocean liner over to La Havre like they used to. They know so much more about weather systems, and the control of the vessel can be computerized, optimized. I really think we're looking at multihulls that are really going to speak to the energy future of humankind. They'll be a good example, not the only example, but a darn good example of how you can apply modern technology to an ancient concept and thereby find a way ahead for this really rather alarming predicament that humanity finds itself in today. Did I answer that question?

Robin: Oh, yes, you did. My mind's racing a million miles here with this one.

Jim: It's a lot of fun to talk about this stuff. What we really need to do, we're going to try to do it on our site, I think, is get a few people, not just one dude like me who's a blah-blah, but get a few people to present alternative or augmenting views in a conversation like this. But we're going to have to shorten it down, ay? (laughter)

Multihulls   Jim Brown

Robin: **I know you have a new website. Can you just tell us a little bit about it?**

Jim: It has come about as a result of my interest in modern multihull history. Because I was around a bit in the early days, I know that there are thousands of stories that are just like mine out there that are dying to be told. So, we've made a website where we can all do the telling. We're asking for submissions from the public—to send us whatever it is they want to say that's multihull related, particularly how multihulls have shaped their lives, and we're getting some neat stuff on there. We've just gotten started.

I've neglected the site in the last few weeks because I'm trying to get a book out. I guess I should tell you about that too. I've been working on a book for years. We're going to publish it on demand and online. It talks about many of the things that I've tried to address today.

The website is www.OutRig.org and everything is free on OutRig, but we have a commercial counterpart which is outrigmedia.com. We're hoping to gather some of this historical information, put it together as information products, and make it widely available.

Robin: That sounds very good.

Jim: So much of the stuff we've been talking about has been objective—comparing this with that; why you want this kind of boat instead of that kind of a boat—all of those are objective considerations. Whereas when it comes right down to it, Robin, the reason a guy or a gal chooses a boat or a boat type is not objective. It's very subjective. No matter what I say or what anybody else says, what you want is the kind of a boat that turns you on, that you can learn to love; something that will grab you right by the pit of the pituitary and say, "Yes, you can love me." If you can find a boat like that, you're going to love and hate it either way, like it is with all things, and yet, if you really love it, you're going to be able to contend with its shortcomings and be able to really enjoy its advantages. All of this stuff about monohull, multihull, catamaran, trimaran, proa, and so on, what you're really looking for in there is something that is just so darn fascinating to you that it lights the fire in your belly and you can run with it.

Closing

Robin: Jim, I want to thank you for being so generous with your time today. It's been fascinating. You've certainly piqued my curiosity about multihulls and even convinced me to try a trimaran, and I'm on a monohull.

Jim: You ought to try one, but it may ruin your life.

Robin: It can't be any worse. I look forward to seeing your new website and reading your book.

Jim: Thank you very much for providing a format where I was able to really shoot my mouth off, if it means something.

Robin: We've all been listening with baited breath.

Jim: I'd be glad to hear what people think. They can write to me—my email address is OutRig.org@gmail.com and my website is OutRig.org.

Key Points

1. The real difference between multihulls and monohulls is people; people willing to embrace the multihull concept are really embracing a different attitude toward the sea.
2. One disadvantage of a multihull is limited load carrying capacity. Consider what you're going to take with you. You sometimes have to decide whether to go against the wind or bear off in order to reduce the pounding, which is particularly bad in big catamarans.
3. A trimaran has one large central hull and two smaller outer or outrigger hulls. A trimaran can run fine on one engine. There is a place on a trimaran bow to attach the head or jib stay.
4. A catamaran doesn't have a bow. It usually has twin rudders and you have to hook them together. A catamaran's stirring linkages are complex and expensive. The catamaran has two centerboards/trunks; a trimaran has only one.
5. A catamaran's widely spaced hulls can straddle a wave crest. A trimaran's float, or outer hull, is not as far from the main hull as the two catamaran hulls are from each other, so there's less room to straddle in a trimaran.
6. The catamaran has to drag its two hulls through the tack. A trimaran, properly designed, only has to drag one hull through the tack. For that reason, trimarans are more maneuverable than catamarans. It's easier to tack them.
7. Trimarans are better upwind—they communicate with the pilot in a more direct manner. A trimaran will tell you in no uncertain terms that you're driving the daylights out of your boat because the lee floats, the bow of the downwind outrigger, will go right through the crest. That's normal behavior when driving the boat hard to windward.
8. Trimarans are safer than catamarans. They are less likely to capsize, and, if they do, trimarans are habitable when capsized and catamarans are not. When a trimaran capsizes, its outer hulls form giant airlocks that hold the main hull up high enough to make it habitable even when the boat is upside down. You can cut a hole in the hull or open the safety hatch in a capsized trimaran to get oxygen inside the main hull while the vessel is capsized.
9. A proa has one main hull and only one smaller outrigger hull on one side of the boat, usually to windward.
10. Hydrofoils are racing trimarans fitted with J, T, and/or ladder foils; hydrofoils are underwater wings that accomplish the same thing in water that airplane wings do in air.

Notes

Custom Electrical Panels and Wiring Harnesses
An Interview with Mark Rogers

Introduction

Robin: Hello everyone. This is Robin Coles and it's my pleasure to welcome you to the 2010 Nautical Lifestyle Expert Series brought to you by TheNauticalLifestyle.com. In the next hour you're going to learn about custom electrical and instrumental panels along with wiring harnesses. I'm honored to have Mark Rogers as my special guest today. Hello Mark!

Mark: Hi Robin, it's a pleasure talking with you.

Robin: Mark, thank you so much for joining me. Mark started out around 15 years old as a studio engineer at a local radio station. He tried college for a couple of semesters, then joined a band and traveled around the eastern part of the US for a few years. Mark worked for a number of years as head electronics technician for the DJM music stores, as well as doing broadcast and recording studio engineering and construction. In 1991, Mark and his wife bought a 36-foot sailboat that needed a major electrical overhaul. As Mark was working on that project, other boaters would come over to watch him. Confident that Mark knew what he was doing, the other boaters started asking for help with their own electrical issues. In 1992, Mark raised his sheet and started a side business working on boat electrical systems. In 1994, Mark left the music industry, began Mobile Marine Electrical Services (MMES) Custom Panels, formerly in Newburyport, Massachusetts, now in Salem, New Hampshire, full time, and has never looked back.

Electrical Panels and Wiring Harnesses

Robin: **What are custom electrical and instrumental panels?**

Mark: Custom panels are usually one of a kind, or a very small number of, panels designed to fit specific needs and applications, such as size, shape, number and types of circuits, metering/monitoring, remote controls, and so on. With a custom panel, we can eliminate many of the compromises one must make using a "one-size-fits-all" production panel.

We are a Blue Sea Systems dealer, so if a production panel meets a customer's needs, we can provide that as well. We are one of a handful of dealers authorized by Blue Seas to configure their 360 Series modular custom panels, so we cover all the bases.

In terms of the types of panels we do, everything from a panel with a single switch to very complex multi-voltage panels; small name or label plates to large menu boards for whale watch boats. We've done engine panels, panels to mount electronics displays like radars into, and so on. We do mostly boats, but also some other stuff. A couple of years ago we did a set of three panels, with something like 36 rocker switches on each, for a train that goes around the country spraying herbicides on the railroad bed. We also did the interface boxes and harnesses to all the motorized control valves on that system. That was kind of a neat project.

Robin: Did you go on the train?

Mark: No. Actually, they called a couple of months ago and they're talking about doing another one at some point. I look forward to working on that again.

Robin: **Why would I, as a boater, want a customized panel?**

Mark: If you need to fit a panel into a particular sized space and there is not a production panel made that would fit there; or if you want specific items on your panel that do not come on a production panel, such as an inverter, generator remote, or some other piece of equipment, then you really need a custom panel. You can have much dressier panels than most mass produced ones if you want, with the boat name and/or the boat builder's name, or almost anything else, on it. You can light the panel up for an even cooler look. We can personalize panels as much as you desire. With a custom panel, you can have more options and choice than almost any panel fabricator gives you. Some customers are just looking for a faceplate on which to install their existing engine gauges, since the panel they currently have might be cracked or broken. We can do anything from a blank panel to a fully loaded one with a terminal block back plane and the harness between the two.

Robin: **You mentioned a back plane—what's that?**

Mark: A terminal back plane is a piece of material generally smaller than the panel itself by half an inch or an inch or so, so it'll fit through the same hole. It mounts behind the panel. On the terminal back plane are mounted all the terminal blocks, bus bars, and stuff. Each terminal on the terminal block is labeled as to what device connects there. Then we build a harness between the panel and that assembly. The customer mounts the back plane and the panel, and then all he or she has to do is make connections with wires coming from the various devices on his boat to the back plane. As long as you know what the wires are, it's real easy to hook up.

Robin: Sounds complicated. My head is dizzy.

Mark: Actually, it's pretty easy. The harness between the back plane and the panel is all pre-wired and pre-tested, so you don't have to touch anything there—all the technical wiring is done.

Robin: **Are there any differences between a panel for a power boat and one for a sail boat?**

Mark: In electrical panels, not usually a lot. For custom panels on sailboats, one thing we do that's a little different than power boats is set up a selector switch for the navigation lights that is fed by a single breaker, rather than having multiple breakers for navigation lights, anchor light, strobe light, and so on. We'll have a single breaker that feeds a small rotary switch. That rotary switch has multiple positions—say, steaming anchored, sailing, and strobe and tri-colored light positions—those are fitted—and you just set the switch to whatever mode you're in. If you're motoring at night, flip it to steaming and it automatically configures the running lights to

Custom Electrical Panels and Wiring Harnesses — Mark Rogers

the proper combination. You don't have to turn on and off different breakers and try to remember which lights are supposed to be on for this—you just hit the switch.

Recreational power boats usually don't have too much—you're either underway or anchored. A pair of breakers works fine in that case. Commercial fishing boats use a number of different combinations of lights, so we can also do the same thing there with a rotary switch automatically configured for whatever mode of fishing they're doing. Engine panels for powerboats are usually more complicated—there are more parameters you're reading on the engines and often there are twin engines rather than a single one—that's more complicated than a typical sailboat engine panel.

Robin: **Can a boater take a panel from a salvaged boat and customize it to fit their own boat?**

Mark: Not usually. In a rare case I suppose you could, but you don't know what you're getting in terms of quality of the breakers and that kind of stuff. It's sort of like being stuck with a production panel in that the size is what it is and you have to make it fit or hope it fits your space.

With a custom panel, of course, we can make it any size and shape you want. If you want an electrical panel in the shape of an S, we can do that.

Robin: **An interesting wiring conundrum is how do you effectively, and safely to marine standards, connect low power instrument power leads to larger units with heavier power leads; for example, connecting 30 or 32 wiring to AWG 14 or 16 tinned copper stranded wire?**

Mark: Often, for those items, you can provide a single breaker that feeds a fuse block with the requisite number of fuse positions for those devices. That way, each small wire can go to its own terminal on the fuse block. This lets you bring in a larger cable or larger wire like a 14, 16, or 10, depending on how many fuses or the ampage between the breaker and the fuse block. You have low amp fuses for each individual small device and each little wire goes to its own terminal. This lets you get rid of the inline fuse holders found in the power leads of each unit and moves them all to a central location—that's nice. You're not looking for wires wrapped up in a bundle somewhere. For the higher current items like radar, VHF, and single side band (SSB) radios, we generally give each one of those its own breaker. It's the small current stuff for which we'll use a single master breaker.

Robin: **A number of manufacturers now make it possible to connect a PC to a chart plotter to a VHF radio, so we can get navigation software all working together. What does that entail?**

Mark: There are a couple of ways to do those type of connections—you can either use the little 22 sized heat shrink covered butt connectors and just splice the wires together, or you can use something like the Blue Seas #2408 or similar terminal block, with little ring terminals for each one. The advantage to doing it with the ring terminals and the terminal block is that you can move things around and reconfigure if you need to. With the heat shrink butt connection, if you want to change stuff you've got to cut the butt connector off and re-splice. We like the terminal blocks, but it depends on whether you're going to change it in the future.

Robin: So, we've decided as a boater that we want to get a customized panel. Can you walk me through the process of getting one?

Mark: We start by discussing the customer's needs. Sometimes the discussion can be pretty simple and straightforward if he or she only needs a small number of breakers to fit in a given space—maybe a meter or two. If that's the case, we just need to know a few other things such as the style of breakers s/he wants—flat, actuator, or toggle style. Does s/he want indicator lights? Does s/he want the labels backlit or not? We can come up with a pretty quick CAD design and price estimate and send it to the customer as a PDF file. Then they can look at it and decide if the layout is what they like and whether they want to add, change, or delete. We give them that and the price estimate, and they can make a decision at that point. For more complex panels, there are some other things we need to know, so there are a few more questions—what the overall dimensions we have to stay within are, as well as the depth that's available behind the panel face. Then we can talk about the type of circuit breaker panel—is it going to be an A/C panel, a D/C panel, or a combination of both? What voltages will it be controlling—12- or 24-volt D/C, for example, or 120/240volts A/C (maybe 120-volt, 208-volts three-phase A/C on the big yacht, or some combination of the former)? What do you want for metering and monitoring and voltage and currents? We've done panels with as many as four different voltages on them. We did one that had 12- and 24-volt D/C *and* 120-volt A/C *and* 208-volt A/C three-phase on it for a big air conditioning unit. There are a few other questions we ask. What other items are you going to want—a generator and a verter remote, tank level gauges, refrigeration controls, and so on? At that point we can start doing CAD layouts for that and actually see what we need for space, given what they've told us we have to stay within. Next we send the drawing to the customer and get their suggestions and/or approval of the design. If they want to move stuff around, it's still fairly simple at this point, because it's just keystrokes on the computer. Once we start cutting it (laughing), that's what it is, so in the CAD phase is when it's real easy to say, "I want to change this. Can we put the A/C section on top and the D/C on the bottom?" or something like that. But once all that stuff is established, we can talk about the esoteric things: the color of the panel; a single- or multi-layer panel; backlighting on the labels and, if so, what color back lighting; etc. Once we've got most of those questions answered and we've done the layout so we know it's going to fit, then we can start working on pricing. It's pretty much the same for any other type of panel—engine instrument panels, navigational display panels, or whatever. The order in which we ask the questions might change; and there might be some additional questions we ask, or some things we don't need to ask, depending on what the panel is. Of course, we might make some suggestions too, but that's the basic sequence of events.

Custom Electrical Panels and Wiring Harnesses — Mark Rogers

Robin: **With electrical plugs, it makes a big difference whether we're here in the US or in the UK, Israel, or down south in the islands. Do you change how you set these panels up depending on where the boat's going to be traveling?**

Mark: In some cases, particularly with the A/C systems on the boat. Here we can use single pole breakers, whereas in the UK, Europe, and a lot of those countries, they have to switch both sides of the A/C line, what we would call hot/neutral, so sometimes the layout is a little bit different there—we'll just use double-hold breakers instead of singles. In most cases, there's not a lot of difference. The meters we use, for example, are digital meters, most of the A/C ones can read voltage up to 300 volts, so they'll work fine on the 120-volt domestic A/C systems and they'll work on the 230-volt European system with no change or modification whatsoever. We've done a couple of panels where we had a selector switch which selected between different windings on a shore power isolation transformer, what they call an international transformer. By changing the way the transformer is tapped or the way the linings are connected, you can change the input and output voltages on it. We would put in two different inlets on the boat, one for US shore power and one for European. All they would have to do is flip the selector switch to reconfigure the transformer for whichever place they were in. It provided the proper voltage out to the panel; from that point it was all pretty much the same thing. That worked out very well.

Robin: That makes a lot of sense and sounds like it's a lot easier to do it that way than to try to remember. **Let's talk about wiring and lights on a boat for a second. When is the best time to replace these?**

Mark: If the wiring is old, with cracked insulation, for example, or the conductors are turning green, black, or crumbling, it's probably a good time to do it. If the wiring's been exposed to salt water, if the boat probably took on water or sat on the bottom or something, I'd recommend it be replaced. Another place you need to look is wiring to the bilge pump. Usually, down in the bilge, it's damp/wet; sometimes the wiring isn't properly supported up out of the water; it sits in it. You want to keep an eye on that and maybe change the wiring when it starts to look like it might be getting water ingress into the wire itself or wicking up the conductors. If the boat was wired using automotive wire, you might consider replacing the wiring; even worse, if the boat was wired with house type wire—solid conductor stuff like you buy at Home Depot—it's basically not legal to use on boats, but I've seen boats wired with it.

Robin: **Why would they be wired with that? Do boats come that way?**

Mark: No. Usually the owner decides to add some wiring. They run over to Home Depot and they're not aware of the requirements for marine electrical systems. They just go and grab some wire and wire nuts and put the thing together. The problem with using single strand solid wire is that vibration causes the wire to flex and crack after a while, whereas the stuff we use is many very thin strands that can flex a lot and not have a problem.

There's been some discussion about tin wire. We use it all the time—it's not a requirement, just another safety factor. You can use stranded un-tin wire, there's no requirement that says you have to use tin, but we don't use anything but.

Another thing: a lot of people pay ridiculously high prices for name brand marine wire, and they're really paying for the name. A lot of it—the stuff we use—is really very high quality wire; the company that makes it, makes a lot of it for the brand name people, but you can buy it for a lot less—that's something to look at if you're looking at rewiring a boat.

Robin: **Now what about connecting the wires together with wire nuts?**

Mark: You don't do that on a boat—wire nuts are really designed for house stuff. On boats, wiring must be properly terminated with crimped connectors or a proper type of what they call a Eurostyle terminal block, which has not just a screw that screws down into the wire to hold it, but it's got a little plate the screw pushes down against so it doesn't put the screw down through the wires and crush them.

I meant to mention lighting fixtures, especially lighting fixtures for navigational lights that are outside—the sockets on those are prone to corrosion because water can get into them from time to time, then you start having issues there. A lot of times you find your navigation lights are flickering on and off, getting dimmer, or whatever; if that's the case, then the sockets are going. You can clean them, but you really ought to just replace the fixture because it's only going to get worse over time. There's weird stuff we've seen.

Robin: Every time I go on a boat, I never know what I'm going to see either.

Mark: We had a boat here a couple weeks ago that one of the previous owners had added some stuff to. They'd wired it all with #18 or 20 wire, which is way undersized for the loads they wanted to run; they worked, but barely. They'd gotten into an emergency situation—they had a #18 wire feeding the bilge pump, which really should have been a #12—it helps to know some of the marine codes when you're doing this stuff.

Robin: **You mentioned replacing wires if they have been under salt water. Too many times I've seen trailers end up in the water from inexperienced drivers bringing their boats back on land. In this scenario, how often would you recommend changing the wires?**

Mark: It depends on the wires. A lot of trailers are wired with SAE (Society of Automotive Engineers) automotive wire, so probably you'll get a couple of years out of it. The biggest thing with trailers is that a lot of the light fixtures—the brake lights and stuff and the little marker lights—aren't water tight. If you back it in, and you didn't disconnect the lights so they're on when you're backing into the water, salt water hitting the connections, sockets, and stuff, becomes conductive and immediately starts generating green conductive crud and starts eating away at the metal there. First thing to do before you back a trailer into the water is unplug it,

Custom Electrical Panels and Wiring Harnesses

so you at least don't have electricity flowing through. In a lot of cases, you have no choice but to sink the lights while you're launching your boat or recovering it.

As far as replacing the wire, it depends. If they use high quality wire, the stuff can take repeated submersions because it's not sitting in salt water for long periods of time—so it dries fairly quickly. As long as the water doesn't wick up the wires, it's generally not too big a deal. The thing to do, probably, is if you start having some issues with brake lights and what-not, you can usually loosen a screw and pull the wire out of the connection at the tail light and look at it to see if it's corroding. If it is, try cutting it back an inch or two and see if you can get the clean wire to make a new connection at that point. If it's really corroding and wicking up the wire a fairly good distance, it's probably time to cut the wire out and replace it.

Robin: **I noticed when I was doing some research for our interview there were quite a few places they mentioned ABYC and US Coast Guard Standards. What does ABYC stand for?**

Mark: That's the American Boat and Yacht Council. They're the ones that kind of propagate the rules and regulations on small craft. Basically they're a standard setting organization and a lot of their regulations closely follow the national fire codes, electrical codes, and stuff like that; with, obviously, some changes. Things that we talked about—like not using solid wire, or wire nuts, and stuff—they've come out with. They have a very thick book that basically covers all phases of construction of boats up to 65 feet—there's an electrical section, a fuel section, a section on helm visibility, and that kind of stuff—they're the guys that do that. They work with technical committees, the Coast Guard, the national fire code people, and all that. In there, they'll be charts of wire sizing; voltage drop in various currents and distances of run; and all this other stuff—there's a lot of things that enter into it. We follow all of that.

Robin: **Have they ever been known to check out somebody's boat and inspect it to make sure that it's up to code?**

Mark: I don't think the ABYC does, but the Coast Guard would, because they have law enforcement powers. With the ABYC, their stuff is not really law, it's suggestion. But if you have a problem with your boat, a fire or whatever, and the insurance company finds out you weren't following ABYC standards, then you might have an issue. As far as the ABYC stopping a boat and saying, "We want to search your boat," it wouldn't happen. The Coast Guard, on the other hand, they can do a boarding and check; but they're basically checking for safety equipment—whether the boat is in reasonably good shape, that type of thing; safe to go to sea, so to speak.

Robin: **So it's good to follow the ABYC standards, g-d forbid there's an insurance policy that needs to be acted upon.**

Mark: Yeah, it's all based on safety issues, for the most part. They have a thing that's kind of like a regulation, or whatever you want to call it, for line of sight from the helm—whether you can see safely and that type of thing. It's the same thing with electrical stuff, the fuel systems, and all these various "this is how it should be done" types of things.

Robin: **What type of maintenance program should one have for their panels and wiring harnesses?**

Mark: There is not really a lot of maintenance you can do on them other than keeping them clean, making sure the connections stay tight, and that sort of thing. There's nothing that really wears out or that type of thing. As long as the thing is in normal use, and you don't put it under water, there's not a lot to do to it other than keeping it reasonably clean and making sure the connections aren't loose.

Robin: **How should you clean these panels and harnesses?**

Mark: It depends on what gets on them for dirt. Just a damp rag using Windex or something like that'll work perfectly fine on the materials we use. I would suggest you turn the power off to the panel. Even if you're cleaning the front of it, it's probably not a bad idea. As far as behind the panel, about the only thing you really do is look for loose connections and that type of thing. In general, there's not going to be much issue. If dust and dirt get back there, vacuum it out; beyond that, there's not a lot to do.

Robin: **Is it good to clean them at the end of the day when you're done sailing or boating?**

Mark: No. Unless it's getting splashed by seawater or something, which shouldn't happen—an engine panel up at the helm or in the cockpit or something might take a spray every once in a while—but as far as the D/C breaker panel, the A/C breaker panel, that's generally in protected places anyway. Once a year give them a quick clean—open it up and take a look at the connections; disconnect power to the boat and shut the batteries off before you do it—other than that, there's really not much to do.

Robin: **Do they need to coat all the connections with any dielectric material to prevent corrosion?**

Mark: If the connections are in a place where they tend to get some salt moisture, it's probably not a bad idea. Giving them a spray of that type of protectant once a year, when you're commissioning the boat, is probably not a bad idea. If they're in places like up under a fly bridge, underneath the dash panel, and stuff, things probably tend to get damper because it's a bit more open. Up there, you probably would want to spray the terminal blocks with some type of dielectric and keep them clean. Also, it's probably a good idea to get in there every once in a while and vacuum that out, particularly before you're spraying because otherwise you're just capturing all the dust and dirt, holding it in place.

Robin: **When's the best time to replace the wiring on these panels?**

Custom Electrical Panels and Wiring Harnesses — Mark Rogers

Mark: If the wire's showing signs of being cracked or corroded, has been exposed to excessive heat, or has been underwater—you'd want to replace it. What's the best time? When the boat's undergoing a major refit and a lot of the equipment's been removed and you can get at the wiring. Invariably, a lot of wiring is hidden away in tough to get at spots. I know on our boat, when we were rewiring it the first time, it was just a nightmare. A lot of the wiring had actually been glassed in along the hull, so you couldn't get to it. You had to cut the wire where it disappeared under the glass, cut it where it came out again, and run a new wire through a conduit, behind a settee, or something like that. The more accessible it is, the easier it is.

Robin: **How about the boaters replacing these panels themselves, can they do it?**

Mark: Yeah, they can. As long as they have basic marine electrical systems knowledge and a few tools, it shouldn't be all that difficult to take the old panel out and wire a new one in. One thing we highly recommend is a good pair of ratchety crimpers, though. With the $10 ones you get when you buy a package of crimp connectors, after you've done about 10 or 15 crimps you're going to find that your hand doesn't have the strength to crimp them properly. With ratcheting crimpers, once you start to squeeze them, they won't release until you've applied the proper pressure to the crimps, so you know you've always got a good connection. The problem with the cheap ones is that half the time you give a tug on the connector and it comes right off the wire—that's not a good thing.

The customer can replace it themselves as I said with a little bit of electrical knowledge. One of the things we do actually makes it easier for a lot of panel installations, and I don't know of any other panel company that does it, is we'll build a terminal block backplane and harness assembly that goes with the panel. We do that for probably close to 75% of our customers these days. Basically, it's what we discussed a little earlier—a piece of material that's got all the terminal blocks and bus bars and stuff mounted to that, and it's all engraved with everything labeled as to what it is, and a prewired and pretested harness between it and the panel. This whole thing is, essentially, a single unit. You mount the panel and mount the backplane, and you just make your connections, each one where it says to go on the backplane, and you're pretty much done with it. That helps a lot. There's no other wiring that goes to the panel or anything—we've premade that harness; it's all pretested; all the real technical wiring is right there and we've done it all already. If you've got a volt meter with a selector switch to read three batteries, we've got three terminals there labeled 'Battery 1,' 'Battery 2,' 'Battery 3,' and you just connect right to those. You're not doing stuff up on the panel or any place that's the real technical difficult stuff—it's all done; it's all tested and we know it all works. It eliminates an awful lot of headache for the boat owners. And you don't need a schematic or anything or to be an electrical technician to do it—if you can use basic hand tools, cutters, strippers, crimpers, and a screwdriver, you can do the installation yourself.

Robin: **What if they decided they didn't want to do the installation themselves?**

Mark: You can either find somebody who's knowledgeable about marine electrical work or, ideally, find an ABYC-certified marine electrical technician to mount it and wire it up for you.

Robin: **Let's talk for a minute about a boater upgrading their instrument panel—how would they do that?**

Mark: For some customers it's as simple as making a new faceplate. They install their existing gauges, switches, and so on, as long as those things are in good shape; maybe the panel is cracked, or broken, but the gauges and switches all work. We can make them a new faceplate; they just put it together and put it back the way it was electrically; it looks nice and new, and they're all set to go. Maybe they're changing the boat or they want to change the color of the panel, update it or something. We do some double-layer panels—which is essentially the base panel, which is the full size of the panel, with all the holes for breakers, switches, lights, labels, and that stuff; then we can do sort of a bezel overlay just around the outside or setting off different areas of the panel—the overlay could be a different color than the base panel layer is. It makes for some neat, kind of dressy looking panels to do it that way.

Robin: **They can get as fancy as they want or keep it as plain as they want.**

Mark: Yup—we can do anything from a real utilitarian lobster boat looking panel to a megayacht looking panel, and almost anything in between.

Robin: **What type of warranty can they expect with a customized panel?**

Mark: Well, for us, generally, it's 90 or 180 days. If something fails on the panel with normal usage, we'll usually repair it or replace it. If it's been obviously abused, we may decline to do that—if somebody's whacked the panel with a hammer, for example, or sunk it. In most cases, if a breaker or a meter or something in normal use goes bad, we'll supply them with a new one. Because we use high quality parts, generally we don't have too many issues like that.

Robin: **Batteries seem to be a sore point with a lot of boaters. How long do the batteries last and can boaters replace the batteries themselves?**

Mark: They can. Generally, if you're buying a kind of run of the mill generic battery, three or four years would be the average lifespan. If you're buying a good premium type battery—like a Rolls or something like that—and you have a good, well-regulated charging system, your batteries could last…I've seen them last ten years or more. In most cases you can replace a battery yourself, as long as you put the positive wires back on the positive terminal and negative wires on the negative terminal, and you can lift a heavy battery, because some of them aren't light. I've got a large house battery in my boat that weighs 162 pounds—I was wrestling that around this morning, as a matter of fact.

Robin: **What about using aftermarket batteries? Is this a case where straight from the manufacturer batteries work best and you should shy away from aftermarket?**

Mark: We prefer to use a more premium type of battery, although there are some inexpensive aftermarket batteries that are not bad. It's sort of out of our field of what we do.

Robin: **Are there any known cases where an aftermarket battery caused a problem?**

Custom Electrical Panels and Wiring Harnesses — Mark Rogers

Mark: I'm certain there are. I was trying to remember back when we were doing boats. It seems to me we had a case or two where the owner had inexpensive batteries that they grabbed at some discount house or something like that, and they wouldn't hold a charge or that type of thing, but you can get that in anything. We found that, generally, you get what you pay for—if you buy a premium battery, you get premium lifetime out of it.

Robin: **I've seen on some panels that there are different colors. Is there significance to the colors?**

Mark: Not really—it's more of an aesthetic thing. If we were doing an emergency panel, particularly on a commercial boat, we might make that out of red as a function of what the panel is. For the most part, it's a question of what looks good where the panel will be mounted. Does it look better in black, white, carbonate fiber? It's really a customer's choice. We do a number of colors.

Robin: **Can you get these materials engraved?**

Mark: Oh, yeah. Most of the panels we do are either surface engraving—where you're looking at, say, a white panel with a black core, so anything we engrave looks black and the surface is white; or we're doing what we call reverse engraving, where the panel itself is clear—typically an eighth inch acrylic—and then the back side of that has a 10 or 15 thousandths of an inch thick film in whatever color you want to see—typically either matte black, dark gray, or something like that. Then we engrave on the back side, but we engrave everything reversed, so that when you're looking through it from the front of the panel, it looks proper. Then we can paint fill that engraving in virtually any color, or we can backlight it, which is how we do our labels. They're a sixteenth of an inch thick reverse engraved acrylic, and then we backlight it in red, green, blue, white, amber. We had one panel we did with a little rocker switch on it that selected between white and red backlighting—the customer used white in the day time, so it stood out, and at night he went to red.

Robin: **Red's not hard to see at night?**

Mark: Oh no, red's actually real good at night—it preserves your night vision.

Robin: **What's a color that you see a lot?**

Mark: The two colors we use most would be black with white lettering or white with black lettering. Right now we seem to be doing a lot of panels where the base panel layer is the carbon fiber print look and then either a burl wood bezel or black bezel around it. We're doing some where the panel itself is a burl look with black bezel, but black and white are still the most popular colors.

Robin: **Have you done any in what you thought would be bizarre colors that actually turned out to be pretty nice?**

Mark: I can't think of anything that we've done that was bizarre.

Robin: Wait 'til I get my boat.

Mark: Actually, we did a couple of switch panels for a guy in Michigan—nice guy, too; we'd done some work for him before—he wanted a textured blue; he was matching a couple of decorative panels at the helm and he wanted two switch panels that would match that. So we got some blue textured material with a white core, engraved it, made two switch panels out of it, and it actually did look pretty cool.

Robin: **What's the difference between a panel and wiring harness?**

Mark: The panel has all the circuit breakers, switches, meters, and components on it. The harness is the bundle of wires that runs between the panel and the terminal block backplane if there is a terminal block backplane, or from panel out to all the boat devices, if there isn't a backplane. It's like a wiring harness in a car, same idea.

Robin: I never thought of my car as having a wiring harness.

Mark: Oh yeah! Actually, it's a pretty complex one.

Robin: **What's a clever way to repair the rubber sleeve protector on an outboard external wiring harness?**

Mark: What we've done there is taken what is called split loomed tubing—it comes in various diameters and, essentially, looks like a piece of corrugated hose, but it's split length wise—you just open it up, wrap that around the existing wiring harness, and secure the two ends with hose clamps or cable tie wraps or something like that. It does a pretty good job of protecting your wiring harness. We actually use that stuff a lot on the harnesses we make between the panel and the backplane. The other thing we use a lot now is what they call expandable sleeve tubing. It's braided tubing—if you push down on it lengthwise, the diameter on it expands; if you pull it, like pulling on a rope, it gets smaller in diameter and tightens up—it'll fit almost any size wiring harness. It comes in various what they call standard sizes—I think they start at three-eighths of an inch and go up to maybe an inch and a half or bigger. It makes for a really neat-looking installation and keeps everything all bundled together nicely.

Robin: **If someone's having problems with their boat trailer lights, where should they start to diagnose the problem?**

Mark: The first thing to do is check your tow vehicle's fuses. There are fuses for brake lights and all the different circuits. If you're lucky, all you've done is popped a fuse. Generally the fuse block is under the hood or perhaps under the dashboard—it depends on your particular vehicle. That's the first place I would look. Then take a look at the trailer connector where it plugs into the car or pickup, whatever you're towing with. Sometimes they'll get wet and corrode—if they're wet and there's electricity flowing through them, it tends to generate corrosion. Past that, I would check the tail light sockets and the sockets with various bulbs on the trailer. But check the fuses first, because that's the easiest thing to fix.

Robin: **Is there any way to protect these sockets so they last a little longer?**

Mark: If it's not a water tight tail light; and most often they're not, apparently; you can put some dielectric grease on them and insert the bulb into the socket. That'll help, at least for a while.

Robin: **If someone needs a schematic for a wiring harness, can they call you?**

Mark: They can, if it's a harness that we built, then, obviously, we can provide them with a schematic. If it's a harness for a production boat, your best bet probably is to go online, do a search for the make and model of the boat and wiring harness. The other thing is that a lot of times there are user groups for various boat manufacturers, like a Sea Ray users group, a Bayliner® users group, and so on—a lot of times those guys can be a font of information; can tell you where you can find that kind of information. We don't generally have that stuff here, although if somebody wants to give us a call we'd be more than happy to see if we could locate the information for them.

Robin: **What type of information would you need from someone before they call, say they're looking for a schematic?**

Mark: We'd need to know the make, model, and year of the boat; and what particular piece of equipment schematic they're looking for. Are they looking for the whole boat wiring diagram, an engine harness diagram, and so on? The more information they have, the more it helps us get a direction to go in, to give *them* a direction to go in.

Robin: **Any other suggestions on whom else they can call?**

Mark: If you're looking for an engine wiring diagram, try calling the engine manufacturer. You could call a dealer for that type of engine—they have service manuals and they can make a copy of a schematic for you or tell you where you can get one. Again, users groups are a pretty good way to find out that stuff. The other day I was looking for something else and came across a users group for old outboard motors. They had a bunch of old schematics, stuff that wasn't generally available; someone just collected the stuff over the years and had a little library of it.

Robin: That's good to know. I would think, too, that if they belong to any yacht clubs or have access to boat yards or marinas, maybe somebody there would know how to find old schematics.

Mark: Boat yards, usually, if they're a dealer for, say, Yamaha outboards or Johnson motors or something like that, they would usually have a pretty good set of manuals for those things and generally I would expect that you could get schematics and parts lists and that sort of stuff from them.

Robin: **Let's talk for a minute about things changing in the future, as they always do. Are there any new standards that are coming up that boaters need to be aware of as far as electrical?**

Mark: As far as the electrical stuff goes, I know the ABYC is coming out with a new standard for what they call ELCIs (equipment leakage circuit interrupters), which are going to start being required on boats. They were actually supposed to start last year, but because of shortages in the industry, you couldn't get some of the equipment that was going to be required. Some of the bigger ELCIs, like the 50-amp and 100-amp units, just aren't readily available. So they moved that back to, I think it's, July 31st of this year. Basically, what that is, if you're familiar with the GFI outlets in your house—which trip if there's an electrical leakage or grounding problem or something—those protect whatever's plugged into them, that piece of equipment. What they're requiring now is one that will protect the whole boat electrical system, because the regular outlet ones don't protect things like a hardwired water heater, an air conditioner unit, that type of thing. So now they're requiring something that protects all the electrical systems on the boat.

Robin: **Does this have anything to do with a safety precaution for fires on the boats?**

Mark: Not so much fires, that's over-current protection. This is for electrical leakage or people getting shocks or getting electrocuted, that type of thing. It's more of a human safety type of thing than equipment overload. Basically, what they say is, and I'll read this, "ABYC regulation E 13.3.5 states, if installed in a head, galley, machinery space, or on the weather deck, the receptacle shall be protected by a Type A nominal 5 milliampere ground fault circuit interrupter (GFCI)."[1] These are usually the familiar GFCI outlets like you see in your house, which protect against flaws—against devices plugged into them—but don't protect from a failing hardwired device, such as a water heater. "ELCI units are required to be installed within 10 feet of the shore power inlet and offer ground fault protection for the entire A/C shore power system beyond the ELCI unit itself." That's actually off the Blue Sea Systems website. If your listeners want more detailed information, I suggest they go to the Blue Sea Systems website—www.BlueSea.com—there's a wealth of excellent information on electric marine design and equipment there. Anyway, that's the biggest change that I'm aware of at this point that's coming down the road. That probably doesn't affect most boaters in terms of what they're doing, it affects boat builders, because they have to start putting that equipment on. Obviously, if boaters want to upgrade their existing electrical systems to include that is not a bad idea.

Robin: **Is that an expensive proposition?**

Mark: They're not inexpensive devices. I'm trying to remember off the top of my head what the 30 amp one goes for.

Robin: **Nothing on a boat is inexpensive.**

---

[1] http://bluesea.com/files/resources/technical_briefs/Technical_Brief_AC_Ground_Faults.pdf

Custom Electrical Panels and Wiring Harnesses — Mark Rogers

Mark: It is a good piece of safety gear, so I guess in that regard, it's relatively inexpensive compared to saving somebody's life. I don't know what the price is going to be on the 50- and 100-amp ones. The 30-amp ones, if I remember correctly, retail for $175 or something like that (don't quote me because I'm talking off the top of my head). I'm sure the larger ones will cost more. Again, it's a real good investment, because people got electrocuted every year on boats or if there's an electrical leakage on the boat and it's getting to the prop shaft and metal parts underwater and somebody's swimming around the docks, there's been cases where people have been electrocuted because of a faulty electrical system on the boat and they weren't even touching the boat.

Robin: That brings up a good point. When I owned my house, I actually grounded the house in case of an electrical storm. **Is this something similar? I know there have been boaters that have lost their boats because lightning has struck the mast and away the boat goes. Is this going to help protect them for that as well?**

Mark: No—this is protecting against electrical power leakage faults. Basically, what it's doing is it's looking at the hot wire and it's looking at the neutral wire and the A/C shore power system and if the current coming down the hot wire is not exactly the same as the current going back the neutral wire, within 30 milliamps, this thing says, "Wait a minute, that current that's 30 milliamps less coming back the neutral wire than was going down the hot wire, that's going somewhere it shouldn't—I'm shutting the system off." But, as far as lightning hitting the boat, no, it won't help that at all.

Robin: But that's extra current. We're not going to get into this discussion, because I could go for hours with that one.

Mark: It may well trip the unit if it doesn't blow it up from the voltage spike, but lightning is a whole different issue. In that case, you want—and there's a whole argument there about whether you should bond a boat or not bond a boat—well, that's for galvanic corrosion. Our boat was hit by lightning as a matter of fact—three years ago?—lightning hit the top of the mast and pretty much wiped out everything electrical on it.

Robin: I've actually met somebody whose boat caught on fire from being hit by lightning. It's scary.

Mark: A lot of times, if lightning hits the boat, it'll find a place to exit somewhere under water—oft times that place is something like a through-hull transducer or something for the depth sounder—and just blows it right out of the boat and then the boat sinks. We were lucky in that regard—some of it exited through the through-hull, but it didn't blow it out of the boat; but it wiped out an awful lot of electronics.

Robin: **I understand you have clients all over the world. How does that work?**

Mark: It works pretty much the same as if we had a client a state away. Almost everything we do is done via the internet, some phone calls, but most of it's done via the website. We have a ton of pictures on our website and people can see those and see all the various configurations that we've done and get ideas. We email drawings back and forth. Customers send us questions, comments, and suggestions. We send them questions, comments, and suggestions. As we described earlier, the process of how we come up with a design—it doesn't matter if somebody's 50 miles away or 5,000 miles away. In fact, DHL just came about an hour ago and picked up 10 panel faceplates that are going to Australia. We'll never see the boat other than some photographs once they're installed. We never meet the owners. There's lots of emails back and forth.

Robin: **Any other tips you want to give boaters on customizing their electrical or instrument panels?**

Mark: Think about any additions or changes you might want to make in the future and design for those eventualities now. For example, if you are thinking of adding an inverter in the future, you can design for that, so that when you do install it, all you need to do is remove a couple of jumpers, make the connections to the inverter, and you're off and running. We always try to design in 15-20% of the total number of breakers as spares at the time the panel is being built. Somebody's always going to find something to add even if they go, "Nope, I've got everything I want." Next year some new toy will come out and, "I've got to have that," or they want to add another light someplace or something like that. If you're getting a new panel built, try to think of everything, if you think you know everything you're going to want to put on it now, leave space for a couple more items you might add to the boat's electrical system as time goes on.

Robin: **Any last comments on wiring harnesses?**

Mark: We highly recommend if you have a custom panel built, or even if you're buying a production panel from us like one of the Blue Sea's panels, have us build a backplane and harness for it. Unless you're really, really knowledgeable about doing the electrical, or you have somebody doing it for you, if we can make a harness and a backplane, it makes things so much easier. As far as harnessing for the rest of the boat, we can do that as well, as long as we have all the pertinent information, or, even better, if you can tear out the old harness and send it to us, we can copy lengths, connectors, and all that stuff. And send a bunch of notes in terms of stuff you're adding and where it's going to be in the boat, so we can put in the wires for those. We don't travel to work on boats any more—we used to—but if the boat can come to us at our facility we'll be happy to work on it.

Robin: **Where is your facility located?**

Mark: If people want to take a look at what we do, see our website: www.WeWireBoats.com.

Note: Since this interview was conducted, Mark's company name and location have changed. He is now at MMES Custom Panels, 28 School Street, Salem, NH 03079. He can be reached by email at MMESCustomPanels@aol.com, by phone at 603-890-1723, and by fax at 603-890-1728.

Custom Electrical Panels and Wiring Harnesses — Mark Rogers

Closing

Robin: Mark, I want to thank you for being generous with your time today. You've given me, and probably most of us on the call, a lot of insight regarding custom electrical panels, wire harnessing, and lots of other things.

Mark: I hope I haven't introduced more confusion. Thank you so much for giving me the opportunity to discuss what we do. It's been a real pleasure talking with you. We're a niche business, and not a lot of people know about us or what we do. We appreciate the opportunity to make ourselves known.

Key Points

1. Custom panels for a sailboat can have a selector switch for the navigation lights that is fed by a single breaker.
2. To connect a PC to a chart plotter to a VHF radio, use something like the Blue Sea #2408 or similar terminal block with little ring terminals for each connection.
3. To be able to switch between US and European shore power, install two different inlets on your boat and a selector switch to reconfigure the transformer.
4. You know it's time to replace the wiring on your boat when you see cracked insulation; the conductors are turning green, black, or crumbling; or if the wiring has been exposed to salt water and/or the navigation lights aren't working properly. Check the wiring in the bilge pump. Using automotive wire or, worse, housing wire, is illegal.
5. Make sure wires are properly terminated with crimped connectors or a proper type of Eurostyle terminal blocks.
6. Follow ABYC (American Boat and Yacht Council) guidelines. They are a standard-setting organization and many of their regulations closely follow national fire and electrical codes.
7. To prevent corrosion, spray wires with a dielectric protectant once a year when you're commissioning the boat.
8. Generic batteries last an average of three to four years. With premium batteries, like Rolls, plus well-regulated charging systems, the battery could last ten years or more.
9. A clever way to repair the rubber sleeve protector on an outboard external wiring harness is to open up a piece of split-loomed tubing, wrap it around the existing wiring harness, and secure the two ends with hose clamps or cable tie wrap.
10. Think about any add-ons or changes you might want to make in the future and design for those eventualities now.

Notes

Notes

Making a Living as a Professional Sailor
An Interview with Brian Hancock

Introduction

Robin: Hello everyone. This is Robin Coles and it's my pleasure to welcome you to the 2010 Nautical Lifestyle Expert Series brought to you by TheNauticalLifestyle.com. During the next hour you're going to learn about making a living as a professional sailor. With me today, I am honored to have Brian Hancock as my special guest. Hello Brian!

Brian: Good morning Robin.

Robin: Thank you so much for joining me Brian. Arguably, Brian Hancock is one of the most experienced offshore sailors in the United States. He has logged over a quarter million offshore miles racing both fully crewed as well as solo. Brian has competed in three Whitbread Round the World Races (currently known as Volvo Ocean Races). These days he turns his attention to managing and promoting offshore sailing events. He has worked as communications director for a number of high profile international sailing events including the EDS Atlantic Challenge, the Around Alone, and the Oryx Quest, the first non-stop circumnavigation race for maxi-multihulls to start and finish in the Middle East.

In 2007 Brian co-founded his own around-the-world race, the Portimão Global Ocean Race. The event was heralded as an international success by the sailing press.

Brian is the author of seven books and has written for every major sailing publication in North America and Europe. *The Risk of Being Alive* was a best seller. His latest book, *Grabbing the World*, was just released a few months ago. It's a memoir that spans his life growing up in South Africa to the trials and tribulations of starting a global ocean race.

Wow, you've done a lot!

Brian: It has been a lot, but none of it has been work. As you can tell, it's all been play. Sailing and writing don't really qualify as work in my opinion, but someone's paid me to do it. I guess that's one of life's secrets—to find something you like to do and have somebody else pay you for it. So far it's worked out just fine. I'm 35 years into it and, well, I'm 52, but I've been making a living for 35 years and it's all been good.

Robin: Very good. I have to tell you, I read *Grabbing the World* and found it fascinating. It was so emotional, I couldn't put it down. At one point you had me wanting to run right out there and become a professional sailor and get out into the middle of the ocean. At another point, I thought, "No, I really don't want to do that."

Brian: It's like any job, really. Every job has its ups and downs. Fortunately, this job had, for me, more ups than downs. I'm glad you liked the book. Every time you write a book you have to put a piece of your soul down on paper and give a bit of your heart away to the people that read it. Otherwise, it's not really a true and honest reflection of what you're trying to say.

I hadn't even intended to write that book. Books float by on the ether. I was in Maine last summer. I thought about the story and thought, "Well, that's a really good story," and just started to write it. I really had no clue where the book was going. It sort of takes you along and before you know it you've written a whole book. It's really a book that's not for the sailing public—it's more of a human interest story than a sailing story.

I'm not very good at too many things in life. I can sail ok and I can write. I don't know where the writing comes from—it's sort of a gift that I have, I think. I can write well enough that people like what I write, but I can't do much else. I can't sing and I can't dance and I can't paint, I guess I can just write; so I'll stick to what I know. At the end of the day, the books keep coming. As long as people keep picking them up and reading them, it's going to be fine as far as I'm concerned. I just started another book called *Driving the Dream* and we'll see where that one goes. Maybe next summer we can talk about that.

Making a Living as a Professional Sailor

Robin: **Brian, you say that you've made a living as a professional sailor. Are you telling me that you, in fact, have been getting *paid* to go sailing?**

Brian: That's true. Don't tell anybody else, otherwise everyone's going to want to do it. But the secret is really you *can* get paid to go sailing and many of us have been paid to go sailing. But it wasn't always like that. When I started out 30, 32 years ago there really wasn't such a thing as a professional sailor. I had no clue back then that I was going to be able to make a living out of it, because there really wasn't a living to be made. Although professional sailing goes all the way back to the old days when people plied the oceans in clipper ships. They were getting paid, although not much. Then, people would get dragged out of the bars at night and shoved on clipper ships and made to crew, sailing around the world. I guess they were getting a stipend. But, yes, you can get paid to go sailing, both racing and cruising. These days you can expect to get paid really well to go sailing. But it wasn't always like that.

When I left South Africa in 1979, I literally was sailing across the Atlantic in the Cape Town-to-Uruguay Race. I planned to go back and marry my high school sweetheart. I never ever thought I would make a living out of sailing. But once you got going, tasted the freedom on the open ocean…. I got to Uruguay and said, "Well, that was good." The boat I was on was paying my expenses, so I didn't have any out-of-pocket expenses. I carried on with that boat up to the Caribbean and then jumped onto another boat going to England, a boat called *Battlecry*, a British boat. I did the ill-fated Fastnet Race in 1979—survived that one, but only just. Then I did my first long race from England to Australia—a race called the Parmelia Race—in the late summer of 1979. We got paid a little bit of money for that race—maybe $100 a week. Not much, but enough that by the time we got to Australia, with no expenses and no place to spend money at sea, you had a few hundred bucks saved up. All of a sudden, I realized I've got paid to go sailing.

Making a Living as a Professional Sailor — Brian Hancock

When I did my first Whitbread Race in 1981, on an American boat called Alaskan Eagle, that was the first time we really got paid. I think we were the only boat in the fleet where the crew were paid. We got $1,000 a leg. The race was four legs long and it took nine months; so we got $4,000 for nine months of hard work, I guess you can call it, or pleasure, depends on which way you look at it. But, at the end of that, nine months later, I had $4,000 saved up.

Things have just improved from there. I realized that if you had a good work ethic, you worked hard, and you're a good sailor; and if you're companionable (one of the real secrets to being a good professional sailor is being able to get along with people from all different cultures); that someone will pay you for your talent. It might not be a lot, but I got paid. From then on, I never really went sailing unless somebody paid something, and that's sort of how it's worked out.

Yes, I have been paid to go sailing, and I still get paid to go sailing. Just last month I did a wonderful trip from England to Finland sailing a small little catamaran. I made, I think, $12,000 for what was a beautiful summer vacation as far as I was concerned. At the end of it, a guy handed over a check and I went back home having taken a three-week summer vacation and making a pile of cash. Don't tell everyone about it, or everyone's going to want to be doing it.

Robin: Everyone may be thinking about doing it, but I don't think everybody will be doing it. I know I won't be.

Brian: Try it, you never know. Once you actually sit on a boat, which is something you and I love to do anyway, you say, "Man, I'm getting paid for this? It's just incredible." But, along with the money comes some responsibility. To be perfectly honest, in many respects, my getting paid took some of the joy out of it. When you turn your passion, your sport, and your hobby into a career, some of the passion and the love of the sport goes away, because it does become a job, whether you like it or not. You can't change the fact that you're getting paid and there's responsibility that comes with that and a job that needs to be done. So the pure pleasure of sailing is gone. There's an up and a down side, but, I wouldn't change any of it. I've managed to log off 250,000 miles and 240,000 of them have been good. So, there you go.

Robin: **If it was not always a paid job, how did you survive financially?**

Brian: One thing I am is creative. I wasn't going for a paid job when I left on that first boat. I knew I wasn't going to get any money, but I had a little bit of money saved up from working in a sail loft in South Africa. The people on the boat, they'd been around quite a bit before me, and they said, "Look, you've got to trade and barter. What you do is, you buy whiskey in South Africa and you sell it in Brazil." So we stocked up. I bought, I think, a case of whiskey with all the money I had. Whiskey was about $20 a bottle. I stored it on board the boat and when we got to Brazil, you could sell whiskey for about $75 a bottle. We went on the streets, sold our whiskey, and turned our $20 into $75; multiply that by 12 and we had a bit of money there, and then did the same thing. Our expenses were pretty minimal. We were living on board the boat and our food was covered. We didn't have all the expenses you have now like a cell phone and internet connection and all of that. It was really simple living. A lot of food was caught by fishing, so that was all free. We went up to the street markets in Brazil and bought hammocks. Hammocks were really gorgeous and could be sold for a good amount of money. I think we bought a dozen hammocks or so. They were beautiful, intricately woven hammocks. We sailed up to Bermuda and I sold them in Bermuda for three or four times what I paid for them. I remember arriving in the Azores Islands in '79, one of the most beautiful groups of islands in the world. Back in those days, they were still hunting whales. There was a very thriving whaling business, if you can believe it. It seems sort of hard to believe, but there it was, and you could buy scrimshaw—they were selling it right there, very inexpensively, on the docks in the Azores. I remember buying a pile of scrimshaw. Our next stop was England, I remember going into London and selling it in London. That way we sort of made a bit of money. There you go—you turn a bit of this into a bit of that. You just have to be creative. The other thing I was doing was writing for a South African magazine. A friend of mine was the editor of the magazine and he liked what I wrote. He still buys my articles these days, although these days he pays me with cases of wine. He doesn't have a hard American currency, so he sends me a case of wine every now and then. That's it—you have to be creative. Even though the expenses were down because you were living on board the boat, you still needed some run-around money. If you wanted to go out on a date or if you wanted to buy some beer, you needed some money. You have to be creative. I was creative enough to sort of run that fine line between making it and not making it for years. I guess in some respects I still do that. I'm in my 50s and I'm still running a fine line between making it and not making it, except my bills are substantially more than when I was 30 or 20. That's how you do it—you have to be creative.

Robin: **What great training on becoming an entrepreneur.**

Brian: It is a little bit, I suppose. I guess its street smarts as much as anything else. If you talk to the locals, you can figure out how everyone figures out a way to make a living. You just have to be creative about it, if you want to go sailing like I did. I wanted to see the world. You know, I never went back to see my high school sweetheart. By the time I got back, she was married to some other guy. That's a story for another day. But, in the meantime, I wanted to go sailing, see the world, and sail around the world. It had been my dream since I was a young kid, to circumnavigate and, you know, you can't go on somebody else's back. You have to fend for yourself. That's what I did. So, out of adversity comes some sort of creativity. We figured it out. I was not the only one. There were plenty of us doing the same thing. We were all making bits of money and, indeed, we made a nice sum. It is fun; plus it makes for some good stories for a book. Although, I never thought I'd write that book. My first book I wrote back about ten years ago. A lot of those stories show up in that book and it's pretty interesting.

Robin: **What's the title of that book?**

Brian: That book I self published. I didn't have the courage to go to a publisher, though I realize now a publisher would have lapped it up. It's called *Spindrift: True Tales from Scattered Parts of the Planet*. One thing the publishers would have told me back then is 'spindrift'—nobody's ever heard of that word. In fact, most people don't even know what

Making a Living as a Professional Sailor — Brian Hancock

spindrift is, but when a wave breaks and the wind blows, the top that blows off the wave is called a spindrift. It's a word that I love, but not particularly good for the title of a book. But, I sold thousands and thousands of copies. As a self-published author, I was pocketing, I don't know, $15 a book rather than a dollar a book. Once I had a publisher, I was making a dollar a book, so I made a lot less money, but the publisher did fine. It's all about storytelling and sharing the charmed life that I had with people that lived vicariously through what I've done. You've got to tell the stories and put it out there. People buy it. I'm grateful and thankful.

Robin: **What changed over the years to take sailing from an amateur sport to one where those at the top of their game can earn a very decent living?**

Brian: Back in the '70s there was no such thing as professional sailing on any level. There were a couple of around-the-world races, but they were really rag-tag events. You know, the 30 Whitbread races, Whitbread is now the Volvo Ocean Race, those races were sailed by rich owners with a rag tag bunch of adventurers sailing the boats. Even my first Whitbread race, oddly enough, since we're talking today, that boat was owned by an American by the name of Neil Bergt called Alaskan Eagle. He took us down to Washington DC to meet Ronald Reagan and to meet the senator from Alaska, Ted Stevens, who tragically died this week. I was actually living in the US illegally. I was here with an expired visa, and there I was in Washington DC with Ted Stevens, Ted Kennedy, and supposed to be Ronald Reagan. Fortunately, Ronald Reagan was shot a few days before, so he didn't show up. John Hinckley had other plans for the president. That's by way of saying that the owner of the boat was a rich Alaskan businessman, hence his connections to a good Alaskan senator. He fronted the bills and the boat was called Alaskan Eagle and off it went. Four years later when I did my second race, there were a bunch of sponsored entries in the race. I was on a boat called Drum, which was owned and I guess sponsored in some respects by the rock group Duran Duran. They didn't name the boat Duran Duran or anything like that, but the owners of the boat were from the group. There were other boats in the fleet that had sponsorship. Once you start to get money for an around-the-world race from a sponsor, then the sponsor wants something back in return. What they want, really, is not a bunch of rag tag sailors sailing around the world. They want results. They also want their names on the boat—they want the boat and the crew to reflect their brand. That was '85. By '89, the Whitbread Race had become a really big deal and all the entries were sponsored. The budgets were such that one person or two people couldn't put the budget together. You had to get some corporate interest in. Big companies like Steinlager Beer and Fisherman Pico (appliance makers from New Zealand) had big budgets—four, five, or six million dollars for a boat. They didn't want just anybody sailing the boats, they wanted people that could win and produce results. In order to get those people, they were prepared to pay. So they went out and sought the best and the best applied for the job. The money they were offering was good so that there would be some competition amongst the crew to get on the boats. It sort of escalated from there. Back in those days the budget was about $6 million for a big maxi boat. Now, to do a Volvo Ocean Race campaign you're looking at $50 million or even more.

ABN AMRO (a Dutch bank), in the Volvo Ocean Race four years ago, I think their budget was 50 million Euros, so that's a HUGE amount of money. If a company like ABN AMRO is putting that kind of money up, they're not going to look for a bunch of adventurers, they're looking for a bunch of professional sailors. They want the absolute best that are out there to sail the boat, to win the race, to reflect the professionalism of their company and their brand; so they pay money. There was a chap by the name of Lawrie Smith, a British sailor that was sailing in the 1989 Whitbread Race in a boat sponsored by Rothman Cigarettes, back when cigarettes could be advertised. He was the first one that said, "You know I'm good—I've been to the Olympics. I want $1.2 million to skipper this boat," expecting them to fall over and say forget about it. They said, "Fine. You get it. If you're that good, and we think you are, we'll pay you what a professional sailor should be paid." He really raised the bar single-handedly by saying, "Look, we're really good at what we do—we're experts. We're talented and we should be compensated accordingly." Now, that is still nowhere near what a baseball player makes or a golfer makes, and these are probably guys that are at the top of sailing, but it's not a small amount of money. It has changed as money has come into the sport, like it has for most sports. Those that are prepared to mine it and to become the best in the field can get paid quite well for it.

The same thing has happened, Robin, with cruising. When I started out, a big cruising boat was 80 feet. I remember seeing some boats and they were 80 feet long and I thought, "Wow, that's a huge boat." That wouldn't even be considered a big cruising boat these days. A big cruising boat these days is 350 feet or 300 feet or 180 feet or something like that. These are huge boats that cost $20, $30, $40 million to build. You're not going to put an unprofessional crew on; you're not going to put an unprofessional captain on. So, people that have decided not to race, but have pursued the cruising side of things, they're making substantial amounts of money as well. I have a friend who told me the other day that the going rate for a captain on a super yacht is a $1,000 a foot per year. He was running a 150-foot boat, he was making $150,000 a year, and he had absolutely no expenses. Let's forget what he pays in taxes, because I'm pretty sure he doesn't, because it's a roving lifestyle with no sort of fixed base; so he's probably pocketing $150,000 and he's got zero expenses—there's no food expenses, there's no drink expenses, there's no phone expenses—there's nothing. So that's $150,000 net. I wouldn't mind that. How about you?

Robin: I wouldn't mind it either. I have to start at the beginning with my skipper license first. But, now we're talking.

Brian: Not only are you making good money, you're sailing some of these most gorgeous yachts, to some of the most amazing places in the world, and getting paid for it. So, there you go. It's not bad at all.

By the way, I might tell you that I don't have a skipper's license at all. It's really a strange thing, but often I can't get a job sailing because I don't have a license. I don't know why I don't have one, I just haven't put the time in and, obviously, back when I started you didn't need one. So, I guess you and I are the same there.

Making a Living as a Professional Sailor — Brian Hancock

Robin: **If you can make so much more money cruising, why would anyone want to race? It sounds like a very nice life getting paid to sail some of the most beautiful yachts in the world.**

Brian: That's a good question. I think that sailing is like any sport. The only thing that's a common denominator between cruising and racing is that they both happen on a boat. Some people just don't like cruising. I certainly, when I was younger, only wanted to race. I wanted to be very competitive; I wanted to race a boat, not just sit there and watch the world go by. I wanted to get out there in Hamburg Harbor and see if we could win a global race like the Whitbread Race. I had no interest, really, in making any money. I just wanted to be out there competitively on the best and the fastest boats and race. The cruising part sounded fine, and it still sounds fine, but when you're young and ambitious you don't really want to be plodding along on some slow boat—you want to be on a fast boat winning races. That's why I chose that.

What happened was that many of the sailors that started out racing…. I guess it's the same with most sports—you start out racing, you get to the top of your game and race. Then you lose your competitive edge or your interest in pushing hard and you still want to stay in the business. So you get a job as a professional boat captain on a cruising boat. The analogy I'm thinking of is if you're a fighter pilot in the Air Force and at some point you lost your edge or you don't want to be out there as a fighter pilot, you get yourself a nice cushy job with Delta Airlines, or something like that, as a captain on an airplane.

I suppose it's the same thing. Those people that really pushed the edges in the early Whitbread Races, and made a name for themselves, did move on to some of the bigger and better cruising boats. They are living out their comfortable lives on cruising boats, and no longer racing around the world. It gets to the point where you don't really want to be out there risking your life and being cold, wet, and miserable for days on end. You, oddly enough, get older and you get sick of it. So, there you go.

Robin: **Tell us more about your sailing career.**

Brian: I didn't really mean to make a career out of it. I'd read a book when I was 16 called *Dove* by Robin Lee Graham—a lot of people might have read it. He was, of course, a California kid that sailed around the world when he was 16. He came back when he was 21 to become the youngest kid to circumnavigate. They made a movie out of it, also called *Dove.* I saw the movie and that was it for me. The co-star in the movie that played Robin's wife was Deborah Raffin. She was a gorgeous blonde and I was 16 years old and I thought, "Boy, that is the life for me." I went home that night and I wrote on a piece of paper that my dream in life was to sail around the world (and meet a gorgeous girl—I think I added that). I wrapped it up and taped it up and carried that thing with me for years. I don't have it any more, but I had it for years and years. It was my goal and my dream. I had no clue at 16 that it was ever going to happen, but, like anything, if you have a goal and a dream and an idea, your dream can come true, as long as you just keep it as a focus. I went off and did my race to Uruguay and the

Fastnet Race in 1979 and my first long race to Australia, the Parmelia Race, and then my first Whitbread Race. I sort of realized along the way that I could make a living. I'd done one Whitbread. It was such a great experience, I thought I'd go and do another one, then another one. I went back in '85 and did that one on Drum; and back in '89 I sailed part of the race with the Soviet Boat called Fazisi. It's sort of a double-edged sword, to be perfectly candid with you, because once you've been doing it for a certain amount of time, you can get on the good boats and you can get paid well to sail on the good boats and you don't want to give it up.

By the time 1989 rolled around, I'd done enough sailing. I don't know how many miles I'd done, but I'd been at it for 10 or 12 years. I got married and had a small child and I didn't want to be out there sailing. I wanted to home with my kid living on Cape Cod. Life was good. I didn't want to be away all the time. But the problem was, I was in my 30s and the resume was empty. All I had there was years and years of sailing. I wasn't trained or skilled to do anything other than sailing. It really was a problem between wanting to stay around and be on land and be there for a small child and also know that the only place I could quickly make money was at sea. It really didn't work out very well, to be perfectly honest. Marriage was great when we were sailing—my first wife came. I was in the Whitbread Race and it was a big old adventure. But when children are introduced into it, things change for everybody; for the mother, especially, and certainly for me. I ended up going back to sailing as the only way I knew how to make money and live the kind of live that gave me the challenge and the thrill on the open ocean. But then I was away from home and the marriage fell apart.

It's very difficult and, in fact, I'm still balancing that, to be perfectly honest. As you would have read about in *Grabbing the World*, I think on the back cover it says I am, "pushing 50, unemployed, and unemployable." That's sort of how I felt. You know I looked at my resume and it was filled with amazing accomplishments—books, adventures, places I'd been, and things I've done. In terms of a sailing career, it had been wonderful. But if I wanted a real job, one that actually paid and gave me a pension and gave me health insurance, I wouldn't have hired me. I had nothing on there. I had nothing that any sane employer would consider a good resume. There were big chunks in the last thirty years when, if I wasn't sailing, I was hiking through Africa or climbing some mountain somewhere. I was just sort of off the grid somewhere where no one could find me—living life, I guess. But, on the resume it doesn't look good. So, you have to try and forge ahead—make a living out of what I know and what I'm good at.

I realized somewhere in my 40s, that I didn't really want to go back out there and sail anymore. I'd done so much of it and I'd seen so much open ocean that I was sick of it, quite frankly. I didn't want to get up for watch at 2:00 in the morning and get wet. I was lucky enough to get into the race management side of things. I got into doing the writing and PR for these big events—telling the story, essentially, is what it was. I was hired to do the storytelling and the PR for a race called The EDS Atlantic Challenge. What that allowed me to do was be a part of an around-the-world race—actually, that was not around-the-world, it was transatlantic—to be part of a big sailing event and be around the boats and use my expertise but not actually have

Making a Living as a Professional Sailor   Brian Hancock

to go out on the boats. And, that really made me realize, "Hmm, maybe there is another way to make a living using the kind of expertise that I've got."

I was really lucky in 2002, I think it was, to do the communications for the Around Alone. Around Alone is the single-handed around-the-world race—one of the most wonderful events. I was hired to be a part of that event, not actually have to do any of the sailing—in the ports I could sit on any of the boats and it was some of the most amazing boats in the world—but, I had the privileged position of telling the stories of 12 men and one woman sailing single-handedly around the world. I guess my talent as a storyteller gave me that job. So, I slowly transitioned out from the actual, physical sailing—getting out there on a boat and dragging the lines around and sailing across an ocean—to being a part of these big global events that I love being a part of. I was a part of that community, but I didn't actually have to go sailing. I could be a part of it by writing.

But, I'm fairly ambitious—you wouldn't think it looking at my resume of just sailing and writing—but I really wanted my own event. I'd seen races like the Whitbread Race, back in the old days (the old days being the '70s), attract an amazing bunch of people with diverse interests. There was a spirited camaraderie amongst those people. If you could have bottled that kind of energy and spirit, you could have made a lot of money with it. It was just incredible. Professional sailing has changed. You get on board a Volvo Ocean Race boat now and all you get is professional sailors. You don't get that mix of rag tag gypsies. I think a lot of the spirited essence is gone from those early races.

So I started my own race, you know, on the back of an envelope. I was with a friend of mine that thought it would be a really good idea. We would start a more affordable race where the budgets were not $50 million; they were more like $1 million. The boaters were smaller and you didn't need a big crew—you could go single-handed or double-handed. And that was it. Pushing 50, unemployed, and unemployable, that's what we came up with on the back of an envelope one night after a few bottles of red wine. We wrote it down on a piece of paper and, like many things, if you put it down on a piece of paper and you push hard enough, we turned it into a global around-the-world race. So, that's how it is. Unfortunately, if you read *Grabbing the World* to the end, you realized that it didn't have as happy ending as it should. But the point of the matter is we were able to create the event.

I'll probably remain in the sailing industry. I'm doing some other really, really terrific projects. But, I'm having to create them all from scratch. I'm having to come up with the concept, find the money, and push these things through. Nobody's saying to me, "Here's a $100,000 a year salary. Be creative and we'll pay you for it." It doesn't work that way. So, I've transitioned from the actual physical sailing—getting a wet backside, getting up at 2:00 in the morning standing watch—to still being involved in some of these most amazing events with some incredible sailors, flying from stopover to stopover and using my small talent that I have as a writer to make a living out of it. As I've said many, many times, it's been a charmed life. I still believe that wholeheartedly too—to be able to transition out of sailing to writing, which doesn't feel like a real job, is certainly a charmed life. That's been 30, I don't know, 34, 35 years of it, and still going strong, as they say.

Robin: I think the management side that you're doing now is just as important. A lot of people love reading about this stuff, they love hearing about it. My G-d, when the Volvo Ocean Race was going and it was coming into Boston, there were a ton of people around here that were just gravitating to it. Anything that you could write about any of the sail races is well worth it.

Brian: It really is. I was in Boston when the Volvo fleet came in. The Boston stopover was the least attended and the smallest stopover of that whole race. Apparently China and Ireland were amazing. But still, there was an amazing energy and vibe right in downtown Boston and some incredible boats—quite a spectacle. It's great to be part of those events. I feel somewhat detached from them, to be perfectly honest. Although oddly enough, some of my friends that I raced with in 1985, two of them in particular who raced with me on Drum, are still doing it. One of them was skippering one of boats and the other one was navigating one of the boats. I think this is their seventh Volvo Race. They were the old folks amongst the sailors there. I looked at the docks and most of the professional sailors there had never heard of me, probably had never even heard of the boats I raced then, but they're in their 20s. It is a great scene and I wouldn't trade it for anything. I love boats and sailing and that scene.

Robin: What was your most harrowing experience?

Brian: There were plenty of them as you can imagine. With that many miles there's always something that goes wrong. I suppose one of the most harrowing and the most dramatic was a capsize at Cape Horn. And it literally was a capsize at Cape Horn. It was dramatic because it was Cape Horn and because it was a capsize, but it really wasn't, probably, the most life threatening experience we had. It was just a capsize. I'll tell you what happened.

We were on a slow boat, this was in 1981, a boat called Alaskan Eagle, coming into Cape Horn. We were a bunch of baby-faced kids. Back in those days, we had wine with dinner, if you can imagine. An after dinner drink, they're much more professional. But we had—I think I was 21 or 22—we'd been drinking heavily. We were coming in—massive southern ocean rollers knocked around Cape Horn—we brought out some champagne and were really well into it and really thoroughly enjoying the experience. We had a spinnaker up—the owner of the boat was back in Alaska—so we put up this three-ounce storm spinnaker. The wind was blowing about 40 knots. We managed to get knocked down a few times, which was great fun, and finally shredded the spinnaker, sheepishly with a small head fill-up. As we approached Cape Horn the wind really picked up. It sort of funneled between the tip of South America and the northern tip of Antarctica. And, because of the continental shelf, the waves suddenly slow down and they get really, really steep. We were yahooing it up—really just having a great old adventure of young kids on a boat, my first Cape Horn rounding—before we suddenly realized that the seas were huge. At any time in the Southern Ocean, the waves are probably 100 feet from the crest to the trough, but they're a quarter of a mile apart, so they just look like big rolls of water. They're not

Making a Living as a Professional Sailor — Brian Hancock

dangerous at all—you just get these massive things coming up behind you and you surf them. As you get to Cape Horn, the distance between the crests gets foreshortened because of the continental shelf. So, all of a sudden, these waves that had been 100 feet to the length line were now 100 feet, but on a really, really steep incline—the waves were *massive*. We suddenly found ourselves way too close. We were literally about half a mile from Cape Horn itself, in maybe 60 knots of wind. It was an adventure like you just can't imagine—it was great fun.

We had picked up a new crew member in New Zealand. One of our crew from the first part of the race actually went insane; we put him in a mental home in Auckland. That's a story for another day. We put him in a mental home and picked up a friend of mine that was in Auckland who didn't have much experience, but we needed somebody—this was the day before the race started. So, he hadn't had much time to figure out, you know, the boat or helming or anything like that. But at Cape Horn you would like a picture of yourself on the wheel with Cape Horn in the background, so we all took our pictures on the wheel. And he got on the wheel, smiled for the camera, and he turned the wheel the wrong way. All of a sudden we were beamed onto some of these incredibly huge seas facing in towards the Horn itself. We just got picked up by one wave and thrown completely over. We were lucky because we were not that bright. I think I've said before that you need an IQ less than the length of your boat if you're going to sail around the world. So, we were not that bright, but we had been clipped on. We had our life harnesses on, and when the boat when over, the rig went under, and we were all bobbing at the end of our life harnesses. The boat came up, we looked around and we all seemed to be on board. It took another wave and lurched in towards the land itself. We were so close, it was really stupid. We could hear the boom of the water hitting the island of Cape Horn, itself. It was just incredible. Three times the boat went over. Luckily, I guess, on the third time, when it came up, the wind shredded the sails. We were able to jibe and get out of there, sheepishly, with everybody still intact and everybody still on board. We jibed out of there, changed the sails, and got away. But by the time we had got the boat facing in the right direction and under control, I don't know how close we were, but I have a regular photograph taken with a 35mm lens that shows Cape Horn, I don't know, 300 yards away or even closer. It was just right there and we were just being stupid. It should never have happened—the skipper should never have allowed it. But we were all in our early 20s and this was a grand old adventure. If you live to tell the tale, then you have to tell the tale. So, there you go. I guess that was the most harrowing. Certainly, the drama of the fact that it was Cape Horn and the fact that it was blowing 60 knots had added a bit to it. But it wasn't the worse weather I saw.

My sailing through some of the worse weather was in the North Atlantic. I also did the '79 Fastnet Race, where I think 22 people died. I was on a British boat called Battlecry. I knew the wind was blowing hard when I came on deck sometime around midnight. Back in those days there was an old anemometer (device for measuring wind speed) that was just like a dial—it didn't display digitally. Its maximum reading was 60 knots. I came on the companionway and I saw the thing was on 60 and I thought it might be stuck. I tapped it and the guys on deck said, "That thing's been stuck on 60 for hours." It was blowing well in excess of 60 knots. You know, I was 20 or 21, and who cares if it's 60 knots. You feel like you're just living life to its fullest, you're invincible, and life's a big old adventure. I had no idea that that night people were dying and people were sinking and boats were falling apart. We actually were taking on more water than we could pump out. I was on a brand new Swan. It was surprising to us that a boat like that should have been sinking, so we decided to run off to Ireland and retire from the race. Once we got to Ireland we realized what a tragedy had taken place and how many people had died. The funny part of that story, funny in hindsight, I suppose, is I got to Ireland and we obviously couldn't sail the boat, so I decided I would go and see some of Ireland. I stacked around southern Ireland and stepped in fields and went into the pub and what I didn't know was that I'd been reported missing and presumed dead in the local newspaper back home.

My parents had obviously read that and they'd been trying desperately to find out if I was alive. The newspaper had been trying to find out desperately—the local sailor from South Africa was in this race and no one had heard from him. I was just in a pub, chasing after girls and drinking Guinness and I finally bummed a ride back to England on another boat. I got to England, I guess, about two weeks after we retired and thought, "Well, I probably should call home." I had a habit of calling home once every couple of months. I called home just to check in and tell everybody about the great time I had had in Ireland. The paper was desperate—they were sure I was gone. My parents were beside themselves—they were absolutely certain I was dead. And I was just in a pub. So, there you go—plenty of harrowing experiences. Those were the days before email and cell phones, so I excused myself a little bit…these days you can't go anywhere….

Robin: **Was that your most memorable experience?**

Brian: Memorable? I don't know. Sailing is full of memorable experiences and most of them sort of happen magically when the sun goes down on a perfect warm summer night. You can get that sailing off the coast of Boston, you can get it sailing in the Southern Ocean, or you can get it sailing in the Atlantic. It's just the pure pleasure of the open ocean. I guess one of my memorable experiences, by default, was I was sailing my own boat across the Atlantic. I had a 50-foot carbon fiber water-ballasted boat that I was training to do the Around Alone race on. I left the Azores and sailed south. I had been in the habit of sending my wife, my second wife, we were just newly married, just an email every day. The boat had a very primitive email program and I could send an email a day to just let her know how things were going. But, Sunday morning came around and the wind finally swung around from behind and I put up a spinnaker and it was an absolutely perfect summer day—trade winds, I let the autopilot do the driving, and I said, "You know what? I'm off the dial. I'm just going to enjoy this day for everything it has to offer." I didn't bother to turn on any electronics. I didn't care where the course was, I just let the boat blow across the Atlantic. I got a book and a beer and a can of Portuguese olives and I just enjoyed the afternoon on the deck and didn't think anything other than the fact that I was having this most amazing experience all alone out there on this beautiful boat, sailing at great speed in perfect conditions. That was memorable. I guess what happened the next day was even more memorable. When I turned my email on, there was the usual chatty email from my wife saying how things were at home and asking how things were

Making a Living as a Professional Sailor — Brian Hancock

going out on the ocean. And then, of course, I didn't reply. The next email was, "How are things out there?" Of course, I didn't reply to that one. Then I looked down and there were about a dozen emails, all of them seeming more and more desperate. Finally she had said, "If this is some kind of joke, I don't think it's funny, you bastard." She'd been trying to reach me and figured something had gone wrong. And I was just having a glorious, perfect day, off the grid completely, and she was at home thinking the worst had happened.

I'll tell you just one more that occurred to me. Years ago I was sailing up from South Africa to Gibraltar on a small cruising boat with two friends of mine. We'd lost the rudder somewhere between Ascension Island and St. Helena. We'd rigged up a jury rudder across the back and something about the jury rudder attracted dolphin fish—the mahi mahi. We would have a competition. We would get lunch ready and the competition was how long it would take to spear a fish—the mahi mahi, there must have been a hundred of them around the boat so we could pick out one, we could spear fish it—gut it, filet it, fry it, and serve it. The competition was how quick to go from catching a fish to when it's on the table. It was just magic. We would set the table, get the lemon ready, get the rest of the lunch ready, and then look over the side, decide which one we wanted, nail it with the spear gun, we'd have the filet knife ready sharp, and the board ready. Literally minutes after catching the fish, we were eating it. It was incredible.

One day we were sailing along and we had changed time zones. I think it was around noon we decided we would stop the boat—we were actually motoring slowly; there was no wind—and go for a swim. So, at noon we stopped the boat and we swam for an hour. I think there's nothing more amazing and more glorious than a mid-ocean swim. If you go down under the boat you can see these streams of light coming down through the water that seem to go all the way into the depths of the ocean. It was absolutely magical. We swam, we saw fish, and we had an amazing time. Then we got back on the boat. Because of the time change, we were back at 12:00 again. We really had an hour that didn't exist. It was just an hour of pure magic. We turned the engine on again and the ship's time, because of the time change, was 12:00.

So, those are great memorable experiences that you can have anywhere on a sailboat. They're the ones that filter out the bad memories. We sailors are blessed with a short term memory. You forget very quickly how cold, wet, miserable, and scared you were. Very quickly you realize that you remember only the sunrises and sunsets. That's, by the way, why the Volvo Ocean Race and the Whitbread spaced the races four years apart—because it took about three years for you to forget how cold, wet, and miserable you were. You remember the great sunrises, the camaraderie, the sunsets, and you sign on again for another race. Only when you get out there do you remember that the last time you were in the Southern Ocean you said you would never, ever go back down there again. Guess we're best in the short term memory, huh?

Robin: (laughing) Yeah, I can believe that.

Brian: All sailors are like that. Even if you sail in Boston, you can get some incredibly good weather and some incredibly bad weather. When you get bad weather you say, "I don't want to do this again." You get back to land and get into the pub; get back home and have a cup of tea, and you think, "That wasn't so bad." And next time you go out again.

Robin: **What are the drawbacks, if any, of being a professional sailor?**

Brian: I think I alluded to some of them earlier—you can make a good living as a sailor, but the problem is that you have to keep making a living as a sailor because you really are not qualified to do much of anything else. It is a drawback. I had 30 years where my resume, as a sailing resume, was jammed full, but as a regular person resume, it was empty. You have to keep doing it. The problem is, as I found out once I decided I didn't want to sail—I wanted to be with my daughter when she was little—that the only way I could make any money was being away, out on the ocean on a boat. That is a drawback. I wanted to do anything, I didn't care what it was, as long as I could be home with my child who was just tiny at the time. I didn't want to be away. It was agonizing to have to fly to Europe and sail a boat, when all I wanted to be doing was staying on Cape Cod with a small child. I've seen a lot of relationships flourish when there's a focus like an around-the-world race or Whitbread Race and sailing for a living. And I've seen a lot of relationships perish when the reality of the fact that unless you keep going and going and sailing and traveling, your options for an income aren't there anymore. You have to keep earning an income. That's definitely one of the drawbacks. But, some people like it. Some people can continue doing it and they'll keep doing it forever. I was just one of those people that decided I would rather spend time with my child than be out there on the open oceans. So, that's a drawback, but it's really a teeny weenie drawback, I guess.

Robin: **What do you think about all the new rules and regulations being applied to boat captains?**

Brian: I understand why there are rules and regulations, skipper's licenses, and that sort of thing. I understand that a lot of that's driven by insurance and insurance companies. Frankly, I hate it. I think sailing is one of those things we've all turned to because of the freedom it offers and because of the simplicity it offers. Sailing is still one of those things where you can cross an ocean with the wind alone. I understand we live in a bureaucratic world where people have to have rules and regulations, but I just don't like it. I prefer the simplicity of it. I know I'm being unrealistic and I know that I'm being naïve. I had a girlfriend years ago that was pretty as a peach, but she wasn't that bright. With all due respect to her, she got herself a 100-ton license and she couldn't get the boat off the dock, never mind sail it across the Atlantic. But, in the insurance companies' eyes she was more qualified to sail a boat than I was. If she'd applied for the same job I'd applied for, they would've taken her over me, in spite of all my experience. The experience that I had, the miles that I'd had, didn't count for anything if I didn't have quite the right documentation. It's good and bad, but you have to look beyond just the basic bureaucracy of having the ticket. But, I guess I'm a hold-out from the past. I like things more the way they were, but I guess that's unrealistic.

Robin: I actually agree. I think experience definitely outweighs having all these licenses and everything else. I think the licenses are good for some people, because it forces them to learn

Making a Living as a Professional Sailor — Brian Hancock

things. But you can take courses now in learning how to pass these exams; and it's not giving you real world experience.

Brian: Yeah, it doesn't at all. It's driven by the insurance companies. I understand that the insurance companies don't know everybody individually. They put up their policies, those are the policies, and that's that. I applied last year, because I needed some money quickly, for a job delivering one of the boats for the moorings. A friend of mine runs a new boat delivery, if you will, to the charter fleet. He knew of my experience—there are not too many people with a quarter of million miles of offshore ocean racing experience in all kinds of boats. But, he could not get the insurance company to agree. I did not have the ticket, and they said, "Forget about it. We don't care if this guy's been on the moon." By their gauge, I was not qualified to sail a 30-foot boat a thousand miles. So, I didn't get the job. It's ridiculous, but I think when you get to a point in life where insurance companies are running things, the world's gone crazy, in my opinion. I think we need to think things differently. Luckily, this trip I just did last time around the coast from England up to Finland, the boat was not insured. The owner of the boat said, "Fine. If this guy's got plenty of experience, then take the boat." And it worked out just fine. He insured the boat once the boat got there.

Robin: That's a little scary.

Brian: Well, not really. I've sailed my own boat across the Atlantic. I could never get insurance to sail steam ahead across the Atlantic, so I did it alone without any insurance. I guess it just depends on how you view these things. But, of all things, sailing, in its essence, is simplicity. It's why we love it so much. And to bureaucratize it and make it what it's turning into saddens me. When we started talking about the old days of getting around the world and buying whiskey and selling it in Brazil—those days are gone, and it's a shame because they were incredible days of amazing experiences. You just cannot do that anymore. The world has changed so much. C'est la vie. The world's changed and that's that.

Robin: **How does someone get into the business of professional sailing?**

Brian: Well, it's easy and hard. The easy part is what I did and this is something I carry through my life today. Once you set a goal and set a target and decide for yourself that's what you want, inevitably it can happen. If you're young and you want to make a living as a professional sailor, and you decide in your heart that's what you want to do, you put it on a piece of paper, your dreams and goals come true. I read somewhere that goals are dreams with a deadline. You've got to give yourself a bit of a deadline. You can inevitably get into it. How you get into it, I don't know—none of it's easy. Although, let me just tell you something: once you put that down on a piece of paper and you decide it's going to happen, the world magically turns in its own little way to make it happen for you. It's a magical thing, it happens all the time. On a more practical level, you can get on board...if you look around some regattas, and races and stuff, you just show up and get on a boat and crew. If you're a good person and you work hard, you can get on another boat; and another boat might be going somewhere. It might be sailing, say, out of Marblehead, where I live, and then it might be going down to the

Caribbean to do Antigua Race Week. And, if you're on that boat that's going to Antigua, you can go to Antigua Race Week. They might not pay you, but you're down in Antigua Race Week where there are boats that are from all around the world. You might, if you're a good, friendly person, hard working and honest, walk the docks and run into somebody that needs somebody to go to England, just as I did. They might offer to pay you some money to do that. As long as you're there, and you have open mind, and you're honest and you're hard working, you can get into it. You can slowly find your way and your niche—if it's racing or cruising, you'll find that. But it all starts by having the idea and sealing your mind to it. Honestly, this may sound simplistic, but I believe this implicitly because it's worked for me every single time. You put it down, put it on paper, and the world magically turns to make it happen. It's just one of those simple things in life. It's worked for me and I think, as simplistic as that sounds, it can work for anybody. But if you decide you want to be a professional sailor, but you never go sailing, and you never go to the dock, and never talk to anybody, well, it's probably not that easy. Does that sound too simplistic for you? Or do you believe that?

Robin: No, I believe that as well.

Brian: Good. Great, I'm glad you do—all right.

Robin: **What's the future for professional sailing?**

Brian: I think it's only going to get bigger and bigger. It's going to get better and better in some respects, and worse and worse in other respects. I think worse and worse, and I don't really mean this in a bad way, but the real big money is made on big powerboats. The boats that are getting bigger and bigger are the big powerboats. I'm not a powerboat fan, but you can make good money as a skipper or a captain of a big, super powerboat. You can make good money as a skipper on a big super sailboat, but you're so removed from the actual sailing part. You're sitting in, essentially, an office, managing a multimillion dollar business and employees from the deck hands all the way through your chefs. You're removed from the day-to-day pleasure of sailing. So, yeah, I think it's great and it's going places, but it's not really sailing in my opinion—it's just another job. So, that's the downside.

In terms of racing, it's incredibly difficult to get on a Volvo Ocean Race boat now. You really have to be young and athletic and at the right place at the right time. But there are other races opening up. In the race that I started, we got people from all around the world in, and they were able to raise a small amount of money, get a boat, and sail around the world. I think the future is bright. Certainly, if you love boats and you love sailing, and you want to make a living at it, then you can make a living at it. It's very different from what it was 30 years ago. But, with every bit of progress, there's something that I think is not progress. As I said, the captain's job on a yacht really is just like a regular office job except you're on a boat, not in an office. All and all I think the future is good for professional sailing.

Robin: Good. **Do you see yourself playing any part in professional sailing over the next few years?**

Making a Living as a Professional Sailor   Brian Hancock

Brian: Well, as I said before, I'm involved in sailing and I always will be because that's really my first love and my passion, and books and storytelling are there as well. One of the problems is I'm unable to go and, for instance, get a job on a big super yacht. I could—I'm well qualified. If I got my license, I could be making a lot of money on a super yacht somewhere, but I've got children, and I'm married, and I live in Marblehead, and I've got a home. I've got a garden and a lawn. My kids are six and nine and they don't want me out on some super yacht in the Mediterranean, they want me here with them riding bikes. So, that's not the kind of thing that I can get involved in.

But, I want to be involved in sailing, so I've got to create my own projects. That round-the-world race—the Portimão Global Ocean Race—was one of the projects. I'm involved in a project called Speed Dream, which is the quest to build the fastest monohull in the world. We've got a credible design for a 100-foot wave-piercing monohull that will shatter every kind of monohull record that daily run transatlantic around the world. It's a really innovative, ambitious project. It requires about $20 million to build it. But, we're well on our way to raising the money to build a 40-foot prototype. That was just a friend of mine who was the creator and designer behind the Soviet Union Whitbread boat that I raced in in 1989. He's been living in the States. He and I had talked about this concept. We decided to do it; we put it together. He designed this amazing boat called Speed Dream. We're in the process of raising money and I have every expectation that in the next few years we'll build this incredible boat that will set the world on fire, break some records. In the meantime, no one pays me for that. I've got to earn a living doing other things, to keep that dream alive.

The other thing I'm working on now that's really interesting is...as I said, I'm a story teller, but I'm a visual story teller as well. There's nothing I can imagine better than taking somebody and putting them on a Volvo Ocean Race boat, in the Southern Ocean, at full speed, for 20 minutes, just to get the sheer thrill of the experience. A lot of people have said, "Just take me on that boat for one hour, and then I want to go home (not spend the next three weeks out of the city)." Obviously, you can't do that. But the next best thing you can do is create an IMAX movie about it. So I'm working with a friend of mine who's an expert in IMAX movies. We've got a Volvo agreement if we raise the money. We'll work some ways that we can get the cameras on board the boats. We're hoping for the next race, which is 2011-2012, to have not only IMAX cameras on board the boats going around the world, so we can capture the footage on board the boats. We also have a chase boat in the form of a boat called Team Adventure, a 110-foot catamaran that will, in fact, be a filming cat that can chase the Volvo fleet around the world. There are very few boats that can go as fast as a Volvo 70 or even faster. Team Adventure can go significantly faster. So, we'll take a film crew onboard the catamaran and, for the first time ever, get some footage of these boats doing amazing things in amazing parts of the planet, but from off the boat. Then, with the people I'm working with, some very talented film makers and IMAX movie makers and producers, we'll produce a 45-minute IMAX movie about the Volvo Ocean Race. It will capture the experience and the intensity; and you can get it all sitting in your IMAX seat, not even get wet. But you'll know what it's like to be thundering down a Southern Ocean wave at 42 knots, with everything rumbling; raising that thrill and excitement without even getting wet, all for the cost of a ticket. I have these great ideas and big dreams and plans and somehow some of them seem to come true. Oddly enough, if you put it down on a piece of paper, they come true. But if they don't, in the meantime, I've got to earn a living. So I'm writing books and giving talks and sailing and doing some mundane construction work by putting a roof on a friend's house to keep the bills paid while the big dreams are brilliant and being worked on. That's how you have to do it. Nothing is ever handed to anyone, I don't think. You have to work for it all. But if you work for it, you keep being persistent, your dreams come true. I don't have any doubts at this point that Speed Dream will be a reality—next year or it might be the year after, it might be ten years. If you never give up, it'll become a reality at some point. It's the same with the IMAX movie. It would be my absolute thrill to bring an IMAX movie to theaters across the world—theaters that are inland far from the water—and let people that don't know anything about sailing suddenly realize how incredible sailing is and how exciting it is. It's not like watching the grass grow. It's something intense and exhilarating and I think they'll respond to it. For the next ten years I want to write some inspirational books; I want to bring sailing to the big screen in 3D if possible—we'll shoot in 3D anyway; and really get people who have wondered why I'm so thrilled about sailing, why I've made a living out of it, and am so in love with the whole aspect of sailing. They'll get to understand it through the books I'm going to write, and IMAX, hopefully. So, that's what I'm working on. In the meantime I've got to go back to pounding nails into a roof in just a little while and keep the bills paid because those kids, every day, need food. We all know that, don't we Robin?

Robin: Yes, we do.

Brian: It's a tricky balance. You have to balance things out in life. I've managed to run the razor's edge between living an incredibly exhilarating, interesting life, and keeping the bills paid on the home front. My daughter just graduated college, the little one that was two when I was living on Cape Cod and I went off to do another Whitbread Race. She's now a college graduate and I've had to pay for that. That's how it goes. You have to pick your responsibilities. But never ever let the dream go. If you've got the dream, keep it and keep pursuing it and being persistent, and one of these days it will come true.

Closing

Robin: I want to thank you for being so generous with your time today. You've given me a lot of insight that I didn't know and probably most of us on the call regarding the world of professional sailing. I look forward to reading your next book and definitely seeing your IMAX movie.

Brian: Thanks Robin; it's been my pleasure.

Robin: How does somebody get a hold of you if they'd like to get some more information?

Making a Living as a Professional Sailor — Brian Hancock

Brian: Brian@BrianHancock.org is the best way to reach me, because I'm always available on email and not always available on the phone.

You might want to mention my new website, which is CourseforAdventure.com. It's a publishing business, publishing all these great sailing stories—my own and my friends' that have got these books that have come out and been successful as regular print books. We've converted into electronic books and we're making them available electronically, with the addition of video and all that sort of stuff embedded in it for the iPad and Kindle and that sort of thing; bringing out great stories from the past and bringing out new books in the future. You know how that goes. You've got the same thing going with you.

Key Points

1. Once you get money for an around-the-world race from a sponsor, the sponsor will want something back in return. The sponsor wants results and wants their company name on the boat—they want the boat and the crew to reflect their brand.
2. Sailing is full of memorable experiences and most of them happen sort of magically.
3. You can make a good living as a sailor, but then you have to *keep* making a living as a sailor because you really aren't qualified to do much of anything else.
4. To start a career as a sailor, look around for regattas and races. Just show up, get on a boat, and crew. If you're good and you work hard, you can get on another boat. Walk the docks and see who needs somebody.
5. You can make good money as the skipper of a big sailboat, but then you're removed from the day-to-day pleasures of sailing. You're essentially sitting in an office, managing a multimillion dollar business, including managing employees from deck hands to chefs.
6. It's incredibly difficult to get on a Volvo Ocean Race boat now—you have to be young, athletic, and at the right place at the right time. But other races are opening up.
7. If you get your license, you can make a lot of money piloting a super yacht.
8. Professional sailing is a tricky balance between living an incredibly exhilarating, interesting life and keeping the bills paid on the home front.
9. Disadvantages of professional sailing are things like getting up for watch at 2:00 am and often getting wet.
10. Many sailors that start out racing get to the top of their game and then lose their competitive edge or their interest in pushing so hard, but still want to stay in the business. Often, they get jobs as professional boat captains on large cruising boats.

Notes

Notes

Seven Tips for a Successful Sale of Your Used Boat
by Robin G. Coles

The two happiest days in a seasoned boater's life are the day he or she buys their first boat and the day he or she sells that boat. But don't let that expression fool you—there are plenty of great times and memorable experiences in between.

It's a lot easier to buy your boat than to sell it. I guess that's why you see far more articles and books about buying a boat than about selling one. To sell your boat takes time, money, patience, and finding the right buyer. Having to sell your boat first, before upgrading to another boat, can add pressure and be frustrating. But, if you follow the seven tips below, there's a good chance your boat will sell faster than it otherwise would have.

1. **Make your boat more saleable—take these six steps**

    - Declutter your boat and let it shine. A clean boat sells.

    - Don't lose interest. Buyers pick up on this. Staying interested in keeping up with repairs and how the boat looks is extremely important.

    - Fix what's broken. Don't expect buyers to fix things. If something breaks or looks worn, either repair or replace it. This shows the potential buyer that you still care about your boat. That energy rubs off onto the buyer.

    - Clean the engine room. No oil, grease, or paint-chipped parts. Unfortunately, this is the biggest deal breaker. It's like walking into someplace that has mold on the walls, dirty bathrooms, and greasy carpets—a real turnoff!

    - Clean the bilge. Make sure it's not full of dirt, leaves, oil, etc. A smelly bilge is another turnoff, especially for women buyers.

    - Remove personal items. You want the buyers to imagine or envision their own stuff on the boat. Also, any personal stuff you leave on the boat could, and will, be assumed by the potential buyers to be part of the sale.

2. **Determine your boat's best price**

    If you decide to sell your boat yourself, do your homework. Search the internet for boats similar to yours with the same features, model, and year. Look at used boat magazines. What are these boats selling for? What condition are they in? Where are they located? Are they being sold privately or through a yacht broker?

    Yacht brokers can do more research through various websites and books such as *ABOS™ Marine Blue Book*, *BUC® Used Boat Price Guide*, and *PowerBoat Guide*. These books give them an idea of a boat's current value. The websites they use can tell them what a particular boat sold for in the past. If, in your research, you see a comparable boat being sold via a yacht broker in your area, there's a good chance that you should be pricing your boat similarly.

Once you have an idea of how much boats like yours are selling for, you can then make a logical decision on how much to sell yours for. Don't get trapped into thinking that your boat is worth more than it really is; or, if you still owe money for your boat, that you can sell the boat for the loan balance. Timing is everything, and pricing your boat appropriately is what helps it be seen, then sold, promptly.

3. **Take photographs**

Boaters love looking at photographs of boats and their parts—the more, the better. Think about the types of photos you like looking at. Take a walk around your boat and take lots of photographs from different angles of the port, transom, starboard, stern, and bow. On sailboats, take photos of the companion way, mainsail, and mast. If you can get pictures of your boat from the water and/or pictures of your boat in the water away from docks, that will be even better.

Next, take inside photos. Before you do, make sure the inside of your boat is tidy and clean, and that everything you're not selling with the boat is out of the way. In other words, if you are not selling that flat screen TV in your salon, don't have it in your pictures. Take photos of the electronics, forward cabin, engine room, engines, heads, galley, salon, state rooms, v-berth, etc. You'll also need photos of the helm, fly bridge, companion, and mate helm seats. If the boat is on the hard, take photos of the propellers, rudder, and/or keel.

Take overall photos, not just close-ups. Again, look at other boats for sale and notice which of their photos you like to look at—guaranteed, your potential buyers will like them also.

4. **Advertise**

Where you place your ad will determine how much information goes into it. However, the more places you can place your ad, the better are your chances that it will be seen. There are several websites and forums that will let you advertise your boat for free. These include Craigslist.org, BoatBoss.com, and AdPost.com, to name a few. Other sites advertise no fee, but will actually charge you in the vicinity of $350 up front. So, make sure you read the fine print first before placing your boat ad online. Used boat magazines are still a good way to go, but don't limit yourself to just them. They are harder to update with price changes, photographs, etc.

Your ad should include a full description of your boat, the number of hours on the engine and generator, as well as dates and notes on any major rebuilds. Is your boat fresh water or raw cool? You'll want to reveal any weaknesses the boat may have, how long you've owned the boat, and, most importantly, why you're selling it. It's okay to say you're moving up to a bigger boat, stepping down to a smaller one, or retiring from boating. At the end of this chapter you will find a table with a list of specifications you should include in your ad—use this as a worksheet for writing your ad.

Wherever it is, put a "for sale" sign on your boat so others around will know you're selling.

Seven Tips for a Successful Sale of Your Used Boat

Last, but not least, create a sales brochure for your boat and keep copies handy.

5. Time your sale

Most boats sell between March and September, with a lull in late August and early September. During April through June, people are looking, especially, for purchase by the July 4th holiday. November quiets down again. If at all possible, have your boat in its natural environment (the water) for the best show. On average, it takes a good three to six months to sell a boat. However, some boats have been known to sit for years. It depends on how well you priced your boat to sell, how clean it is, and how well it's advertised.

6. Decide whether to use a broker

If you don't have time to do the research to write and place ads, create and put up signs, take calls and make appointments, show your boat, or sell your boat, a broker is the best way to go. A broker can do all the running around for you, i.e., place the ads, qualify the buyer, show your boat, etc. A broker has access to other brokers; better websites on which to place ads than non-brokers have, such as YachtWorld.com; and the used boat books mentioned in Tip 2 above.

Most boat brokers charge a 10 percent commission, though some charge less. Most brokers truly earn their commissions.

7. Be careful about upkeep and use during the selling process

Maintain your boat insurance until you close the deal.

Keep the area around the portholes clean, the batteries acid free, and no mold or mildew showing anywhere. If you're demonstrating the boat, take off the plastic. Let the potential new owners feel the wind in their faces.

Don't use your boat after you've signed a purchase and sale agreement (P&S) and/or have a deposit from the buyer.

If your boat is old and/or hasn't had been surveyed recently, contact an accredited marine surveyor and have it done. Either way, have a copy of the latest marine survey for your boat available for review by potential buyers.

Have receipts on hand for big-ticket items you've bought and repairs you've done, or the name and contact information of the service center that did your repairs, in case your potential buyer or the marine surveyor asks to see them.

As mentioned in Tip 4, here is a table that you can use as a worksheet for developing effective text for advertisements and brochures about your boat.

My Boat

Basics	
Boat name	
Type of boat	
Year built/year first used	
Current price	
Brand/manufacturer	
Model	
Location used/stored	
Hull material	
Engine/fuel type	

Additional Specifications and Information	
Specs:	
Builder	
Designer	
Dimensions	
LOA	
Beam	
Maximum draft	
Displacement	
Bridge clearance	
Engines:	
Engine brand/manufacturer	
Engine HP	
Engine model	
Cruising speed	
Maximum speed	
Engine hours	
Tanks:	
Fresh water tanks	
Fuel tanks	
Water heater	
Galley	
Accommodations	
Fly bridge	
Other:	

Appendix I: Glossary
from The Nautical Lifestyle 2010 Expert Series

A/C – alternating current

ABOS™ Marine Blue Book – since 1949; current values and product specifications on more than 300,000 boats, motors, and trailers

ABYC – American Boat and Yacht Council

ACV – actual cash value; as compared to agreed value when insuring boats

Aileron – French for "little wing;" a hinged flight control surface attached to the trailing edge of the wing of a fixed-wing aircraft; used to control the aircraft in roll; two ailerons are typically interconnected so that one goes down when the other goes up: the down-going aileron increases the lift on its wing, while the upgoing aileron reduces the lift on its wing, producing a rolling moment about the aircraft's longitudinal axis (en.wikipedia.org/wiki/Aileron)

AIMU – American Institute of Marine Underwriters

AIS – the **Automatic Identification System**

Alinghi – a professional sports team; twice winner of the America's Cup (2003 and 2007); Swiss (www.alinghi.com/en/alinghi/story/index.php)

Anemometer – a common weather station instrument for measuring wind speed; derived from the Greek word *anemos*, meaning wind

ARC – automated radio check

Around Alone – a round-the-world single-handed yacht race, sailed in stages; first done in 1982; originally known as the BOC Challenge; currently known as the VELUX 5 OCEANS Race (en.wikipedia.org/wiki/Around_Alone)

Bayliner® – a boat manufacturing company/brand of boat

BoatWizard – a private website for YachtWorld.com member brokers to enter listings and access the Multiple Listing Service (MLS)

Bradfield, Sam of Melbourne, Florida, has spent his career developing foil-born sailing craft; he co-founded Hydrosail Inc; designs include the Windrider Rave, a hydrofoil trimaran designed for recreational sailing (www.multihull-maven.com/Designers/HydroSail_Inc._(Sam_Bradfield))

Brown, Jim – multihull sailor, designer, and builder (see chapter entitled "Multihulls")

BUC® Used Boat Price Guide – aka "The BUC Book;" used boat pricing guide since 1961; lists current market values of many types and sizes of used pleasure boats, motors, and trailers; pricing derived by correlating multiple dealer, broker, surveyor, and manufacturer reports

CAD – computer-aided design; the software to do it

Close-hauled – sails trimmed flat for sailing as close to the wind as possible (Answers.com); sails braced sideways to the wind (256.com/gray/docs/nautical.html); sailing as close to the wind direction as possible (no boat can sail directly into the wind), also called beating (en.mimi.hu/boating/close_hauled.html)

Constant camber method – Technique, pioneered by Jim Brown with Dick Newick and John Marples, to achieve the advantages of a cold molded boat with less labor...specifically developed for narrow multihull hulls (www.smalltridesign.com/Trimaran-Articles/Construction-Methods/Constant-Camber.html)

COSPAS – Cosmitscheskaja Sistema Poiska Awarinitsch Sudow: the first Russian search and rescue satellite system, established 1979; cooperating member countries are Canada, France, Russia, and the United States

Credit scores – see FICO credit scores; credit bureaus may each have a unique method for determining a credit score

Cuddy cabin – A small cabin or cook's galley on a ship not tall enough to stand in. "Cuddy cabin," while redundant (cuddy means cabin), is a common term among small boaters. A *cuddy boat* has a small cabin with a small galley and small head—it may also have a small berth—is popular with people who want a little shelter and storage space, but not a full cabin boat. (answers.yahoo.com/question/index?qid=20070419185903AARvYHX)

D/C – direct current

DSC – digital selective calling: in emergencies, single button on VHF radio sends distress call with boat's description, current location, and radio call name to surrounding boats and US Coast Guard

EDS Atlantic Challenge – a sailing race for single-handed yachts with a crew that appears to have been run only once—by seven yachts, in 2001

ELCI – equipment leakage circuit interrupter

EPIRB – emergency position-indicating radio beacon, used on boats and airplanes

Fastnet Race – a biannual, classic offshore yachting race, held since 1925, covering 608 nautical miles; starts off Cowers on the Isle of Wight in England, rounds Fastnet Rock, passes south of the Isles of Sicily, and finishes at Plymouth in southern England; sponsored by Rolex since 2001 (en.wikipedia.org/wiki/Fastnet race)

FCC – Federal Communications Commission (United States)

FICO credit scores range from 300 to 850; developed in the US in 1958 by Fair Isaac Corporation (now FICO); use statistical analysis to determine the probability that an individual will pay his or her debts; used by lenders when determining whether, and at what interest rate, to extend credit or make a loan to an individual

Appendix I: Glossary — 2010 Nautical Lifestyle Expert Series

GFCI – ground fault circuit interrupter

GPIRB – global position-indicating radio beacon

GPS – global positioning system

Heave-to – way of slowing a sail boat's forward progress, as well as fixing the helm and sail positions so the boat need not be actively steered

Heeling – leaning or tipping to one side, caused by the wind's force on the sails of a sailing vessel (websters-online-dictionary.org)

HIN – hull identification number

HTTPS – hypertext transfer protocol secure, at the end of an internet address line; indicates safer, probably encrypted, communication with that website

Hydrofoil – any liquid-based structure that provides lift because of its attack or camber (en.wikipedia.org/wiki/Hydrofoil)

Ian Farrier pioneered the modern trailerable trimaran with the patented Farrier Folding System (www.f-boat.com)

Jones Act – also known as the Merchant Seaman Protection and Relief 46 USCS Appx § 688 (2002) Title 46. Appendix. Shipping Chapter 18; protects the rights of persons who may be injured or die while working at sea in the US

Lee shore – stretch of shoreline to the lee side of a vessel, the wind blowing toward it; if you stand on a beach looking out to sea with the wind blowing at you, you are on a lee shore

LifeSling – the **LifeSling Overboard Rescue System** is an approved throw-able life saving device to have onboard boats

LNG - liquified natural gas tanker

LUT – local user terminal; ground receiving station for satellite signals, such as VHF radio distress calls; signals forwarded to MCCs

Marples, John – multihull designer and sailor; frequently collaborates with Jim Brown (www.multihull-maven.com/Designers/John_R._Marples)

May Day – distress call, repeat three times

MCC – Mission Control Center; receives and disseminates distress calls downloaded from satellite to LUTs

MIASF – Marine Industries Association of South Florida

MMSI – Maritime Mobile Service Identity numbering system

NADA – National Automobile Dealers Association; also lists boats; nadaguides.com is an online guide for selling and pricing boats, etc.

NAIS – the **Nationwide Automatic Identification System** is a VHF and satellite-based identification, tracking, and communication system being set up by the U.S. Coast Guard

NAMS® – National Association of Marine Surveyors®

Newick, Dick – multihull sailor and designer; Sebastopol, CA (www.wingo.com/newick)

NFPA – National Fire Protection Association

NMBA – National Marine Bankers Association

NMMA – National Marine Manufacturers Association

NOAA – National Oceanic and Atmospheric Administration: a US Department of Commerce agency that maps the oceans; conserves their living resources; predicts changes to the earth's environment; provides weather reports; and forecasts floods, hurricanes, and other weather-related natural disasters

Oryx Quest – the first round-the-world yacht race to start and finish in the Middle East (en.wikipedia.org/wiki/Oryx_Quest)

P&I – a **protection and indemnity** insurance policy provides a form of liability coverage specifically designed for maritime exposures and maritime law

PDF – portable document format file type

PFD – personal flotation device

Phenolic hammer – a plastic deldrin-head hammer used to percussion-sound fiberglass boat hulls without damaging the gelcoat finish during marine surveys

PLB – personal locator beacon; small and portable, used by/on a person during an activity, such as boating, skiing, or climbing; signal enables exact locating in water or on land

Parmelia Race – a yacht race held in 1979 to commemorate the 150th anniversary of the arrival of the first British settlers at the Swan River Colony, 38 yachts in the 11,350-mile race left from Plymouth, England, in October 1979, and finished at Fremantle, Western Australia; included boats from Australia, South Africa, France, the UK, Holland, Poland, Italy, and Spain; the longest-ever staged yacht race at the time (en.wikipedia.org/wiki/Parmelia_Yacht_Race)

Portimão Global Ocean Race – a yachting race for single- and double-handed yachts and small budgets; held first in 2008-2009; initiated by two former professional yachtsmen, Josh Hall and Brian Hancock; there were six yachts (two solo, four crews) in the first edition of the race, which started in October 2008 in Portimão, Portugal, and finished back in Portugal in June 2009 (en.wikipedia.org/wiki/Portim%C3%A3o_Global_Ocean_Race)

Appendix I: Glossary

PowerBoat Guide – **annual price and value guide** used by yacht brokers and dealers

Proa – (pronounced **proh**-*uh*) aka prau, perahu, or prahu: **a type of multihulled sailing vessel**; in Western languages, a vessel consisting of two (usually) unequal length parallel hulls; sailed so one hull is kept to windward and the other to leeward, so it must "shunt" to reverse direction when tacking

Raymarine® – **develops and manufactures electronic equipment** for the recreational boating and light commercial marine markets

RCC – **rescue coordination center;** receives distress call information radioed in via satellite

Rescue 21 – the United States Coast Guard's advanced **command, control, and communications system**, created to improve its ability to assist mariners in distress and save lives and property at sea; being installed in stages across the U.S.

RBIEF – **Recreational Boating Industries Educational Foundation,** a Michigan scholarship foundation

Rotomolded polyethylene – Rotational molding, also known as rotomolding, is a process for creating many kinds of mostly hollow items, typically of plastic; products include kayak hulls (en.wikipedia.org/wiki/Rotational_molding)

RTCM SC 101 – **Radio Technical Commission for Maritime Services Special Committee 101**: an international non-profit scientific, professional, and educational organization; special committees chartered to address in-depth radio-communication and radio-navigation areas of concern to membership; SC 101 addresses digital selective calling (DSC)

SAE International – the **Society of Automotive Engineers** is a global body of scientists, engineers, and practitioners that advances self-propelled vehicle and system knowledge in a neutral forum for the benefit of society; among other things, they set wiring standards

SAMS® – **Society of Accredited Marine Surveyors®**

SAR – **search and rescue** mission

SARs – **US Coast Guard search and rescue coordinators**

SARSAT – **Search and Rescue Satellite System** (United States)

Scrimshaw – **engraved pictures** and lettering, highlighted with a pigment, by whalers, most commonly **on the surfaces of the bones and teeth of sperm whales**, the baleen of other whales, and the tusks of walruses (en.wikipedia.org/wiki/Scrimshaw)

Sea Ray – a boat manufacturing company/brand of boat

Sea Tow® – private marine assistance provider for recreational boaters

Shine Micro – automatic identification system (AIS) technology developer

Shotgunning – the process of **submitting loan application information to several potential lenders simultaneously**; this lowers an individual's credit score because of "multiple or excessive inquiries"

Simrad – **fish finding and fishery research equipment manufacturer**; based in Norway; part of Konsberg Maritime's Subsea Division

Smith, Lawrie – born February 19, 1956; **British sailor**; won a bronze medal in the soling class at the 1992 Summer Olympics with Robert Cruikshank and Ossie Stewart; **skippered various yachts at the Whitbread Round the World Race** in 1989–90, 1993–94, and 1997–98 (en.wikipedia.org/wiki/Lawrie_Smith)

SOLAS – **the International Convention for the Safety of Life at Sea** is a maritime safety treaty; divides international waters into regions

Spindrift usually refers to the spray blown from cresting waves during a gale; this spray, which "drifts" in the direction of the gale, is one of the characteristics of a wind speed of 8 Beaufort and higher at sea (en.wikipedia.org/wiki/Spindrift)

SSB radios – **single side band radios**

Strake – a strip of planking (in a wooden vessel) or of plating (in a metal one) that forms **part of the shell of the hull of a boat** which, in conjunction with the other strakes, keeps the water out and the vessel afloat; runs longitudinally along the vessel's side, bottom, or turn of the bilge, usually from one end of the vessel to the other

Stringer – **a longitudinal internal member, in a boat, that adds stiffness** and may facilitate the mounting of further internal structures

Under-wing – in a multihull vessel, the underside of the bridge structure or arm that holds the hulls together

USCG – **United States Coast Guard**

U.S. Coast Guard Title 46 pertains to shipping; see also Jones Act (ecfr.gpoaccess.gov/cgi/t/text/text-idx?sid=b5bb8938f3017710e4359600df690da1&c=ectr&tpl=/ecfrbrowse/Title46/46tab_02.tpl)

USL&H – **United States Long Shore and Harbor Workers Compensation;** a federal act designed to provide compensation to an employee if an injury or death occurs upon navigable waters of the US

USPS – **United States Power Squadrons®** is the largest US non-profit boating organization. Set up in 1914, USPS is now a 45,000-member (450-squadron) educational group dedicated to

Appendix I: Glossary

making boating safer and more enjoyable by teaching classes in seamanship and navigation. They also help boaters obtain MMSI numbers and provide free vessel safety checks.

USSA – NAVTECH US Surveyors Association provides marine surveyor education at all levels

VHF – very high frequency radio waves; radios that tune to same

Volvo Ocean Race, formerly known as the Whitbread Round the World Race, is a **yacht race around the world, held every three years** (en.wikipedia.org/wiki/Volvo_Ocean_Race)

VTS – vessel tracking service

Whitbread Round the World Race – see Volvo Ocean Race

Windjammer Barefoot Cruises – based in Miami Beach, FL, operated cruises in the Caribbean and Central America on old-style sailing ships from 1947 until 2007 (en.wikipedia.org/wiki/Windjammer_Barefoot_Cruises)

YachtWorld.com – a **website and brokerage firm for yacht brokers**

YBAA – Yacht Brokers Association of America (formerly YABA – Yacht Architects and Brokers Association), founded in 1920, promotes high standards and cooperation among North American yacht brokers

Appendix II: Gelosarel
from The Nautical Lifestyle 2010 Expert Series

Coles, Robin G.   TheNauticalLifestyle.com

Books

Among the Multihulls: Volume One by Jim Wesley Brown. BookSpecs Publishing, 2010.

The Case for the Cruising Trimaran by Jim Brown. International Marine Publishing Company, 1983.

Piloting, Seamanship, and Small Boat Handling by Charles F. Chapman, with revisions by Elbert S. Maloney. Sterling Publishing Co., New York, earliest publication 1922, most recent edition (64th) 2003.

Dove by Robert Lee Graham. Bantam Books, 1972.

Grabbing the World: A Memoir of Inspiration, Perspiration, and Betrayal by Brian Hancock. Great Circle Press, 2010.

Maximum Sail Power: The Complete Guide to Sails, Sail Technology, and Performance by Brian Hancock and Sir Robin Knox-Johnson. Nomad Press, 2003.

The Risk in Being Alive: One Man's Adventures Across the Planet by Brian Hancock and Skip Novak. Nomad Press, 2003; revised and rereleased as *Grabbing Life: High Adventures on Land and Sea – a Memoir*, by Brian Hancock. Great Circle Publishing Company, Kindle edition, 2011.

Spindrift: True Tales from Scattered Parts of the Planet by Brian Hancock. Great Circle Press, 2000.

ABOS™ Marine Blue Book (see below for website or go to amazon.com)

BUC® Used Boat Price Guide (see below for website or go to amazon.com)

PowerBoat Guide (see below for website or go to amazon.com)

Websites

406Link – satellite-based system to check functioning of a PLB or EPIRB	www.406Link.com
ABOS™ Marine Blue Book	ABOS.com
ABYC – American Boat and Yacht Council	www.ABYCInc.org
ACR Electronics – manufactures and sells EPIRBs	www.ACRElectronics.com
Ad Post – free online classified advertisements	AdPost.com
AIMU – American Institute of Marine Underwriters	www.AIMU.org

Blue Sea Systems	www.BlueSea.com
Boat Boss – free, online, local boat and marine classified advertisements	www.BoatBoss.com
BoatUS	www.BoatUS.com
BUC® Used Boat Price Guide	www.BUC.com
Coles, Robin G.	www.TheNauticalLifestyle.com www.RGColesandCo.com
Course for Adventure (see also Brian Hancock)	www.CourseforAdventure.com
Craig's List – free, online, classified advertising; sites by city; check for US or international city	www.craigslist.org/about/sites for example, boston.craigslist.org
Cruising World magazine	www.cruisingworld.com
Discover Boating – information on boater safety, boat maintenance, boating destinations, and tips on buying a boat	www.DiscoverBoating.com
DSC – digital selective calling information	www.VHF-DSC.info
Farrier Marine, Inc.	www.f-boat.com
Garmin®	www.Garmin.com/Garmin/cms/site/us
Global Marine Insurance Agency	www.GlobalMarineInsurance.com
Hagerty Insurance – known for insuring wooden boats	www.Hagerty.com
Hancock, Brian	www.BrianHancock.org www.CourseforAdventure.com/journal
H_2O Limos	www.H2OLimos.com
Johnson outboard motors	www.Johnson.com
Kourtakis, Chris	www.H2OLimos.com
LegalZoom.com – quick, inexpensive personal and business legal advice and information	www.LegalZoom.com
McMurdo – manufactures and sells emergency location beacons	www.McMurdo.co.uk
MMES Custom Panels	www.WeWireBoats.com
MMSI – Maritime Mobile Service Identity number	www.BoatUS.com/MMSI www.USPS.org/php/MMSI/home.php
Modern Multihull History Project, The (see also OutRig!)	OutRig.org

Appendix II: Glossary — 2010 Nautical Industry & Expert Sources

	OutRigMedia.com
Mystic Seaport (museum)	www.mysticseaport.org
NADA – National Automobile Dealers Association (guide books)	www.NADAGuides.com
NAIS – Nationwide Automatic Identification System (of USCG)	www.USCG.mil/acquisition/NAIS
NAMS® – National Association of Marine Surveyors®	www.NAMSGlobal.org
New England Multihull Association	www.nemasail.org
Newick, Dick	www.wingo.com/newick
NFPA – National Fire Protection Association	www.NFPA.org
NOAA – National Oceanic and Atmospheric Administration	www.NOAA.gov
NMBA – National Marine Bankers Association	www.MarineBankers.org
NMMA – National Marine Manufacturers Association (trade association)	www.NMMA.org
NSBC – National Safe Boating Council (educational; made up of over 330 boating organizations)	www.SafeBoatingCouncil.org
OutRig!: The Modern Multihull History Project	OutRig.org/OutRig.org/OutRig.html OutRigMedia.com
PowerBoat Guide – annual price and value guide used by yacht brokers and dealers, available in hard copy and on CD	www.PowerBoatGuide.com
Raymarine®	www.Raymarine.com
Rescue 21	www.USCG.mil/acquisition/Rescue21
Rent by Boater	www.RentbyBoater.com
SAE – Society of Automotive Engineers	www.SAE.org
Sail magazine	www.sailmagazine.com
Sail America – industry association promotes sail boat shows and other sailing-related events	www.SailAmerica.com
SAMS® – Society of Accredited Marine Surveyors®	www.MarineSurvey.org/index2.html
Scanlan, Rob – master marine surveyor; Nahant, MA	www.MasterMarineSurveyor.com
Sea Tow®	www.SeaTow.com
Searunner multihulls	www.searunner.com/about.html www.ehow.com/list_7668356_searunner-trimaran-specs.html

Boating Secrets: 127 Top Tips To Help You Buy and Enjoy Your Boat

Shine Micro	www.ShineMicro.com
Simrad	www.Simrad.com
Suite 101 (online magazine)	www.Suite101.com
TowBoatUS – see BoatUS	www.BoatUS.com
USCG – United State Coast Guard	www.USCG.mil
U.S. Coast Guard Title 46	ecfr.gpoaccess.gov/cgi/t/text/text-idx?sid=b5bb8938f3917718e4359600df690da1&c=ecfr&tpl=/ecfrbrowse/Title46/46tab_02.tpl
USCGA – United States Coast Guard Auxiliary	www.CGAux.org
US Coast Guard's Boating Safety Division	www.USCGBoating.org
US Department of Homeland Security	www.DHS.gov/index.shtm
USPS – United States Power Squadrons®	www.USPS.org
USSA – NAVTECH US Surveyors Association	www.NAVSurvey.com
Yamaha outboard motors	www.Yamaha-motor.com/outboard/products/lifestylehome/home.aspx
Weather	www.Weather.com
Weather Underground	www.WUnderground.com
West Marine – boating supplies	www.WestMarine.com
Wikipedia	en.Wikipedia.org
WoodenBoat magazine	www.woodenboat.com/wbmag/index.html
WoodenBoat School	www.thewoodenboatschool.com
Wyand, Timothy	www.Examiner.com/x-15246/Richmond-boating-Examiner
Yacht World	YachtWorld.com
YBAA – Yacht Brokers Association of America	www.YachtCouncil.com/default.aspx?did=14
YouTube	www.YouTube.com

Appendix III: Contacts
from The Nautical Lifestyle 2010 Expert Series

Coles, Robin G. – Interviewer, producer, author   TheNauticalLifestyle.com

Brown, Jim – *Multihulls*
email: OutRig.org@gmail.com
websites: OutRig.org and OutRigMedia.com

Coburn, Jim – *Financing a Boat Purchase*
email: CoburnAssociates@SBCGlobal.net
phone: 586-530-3935

Hancock, Brian – *Making a Living as a Professional Sailor*
email: Brian@BrianHancock.org
websites: www.BrianHancock.org and www.CourseforAdventure.com/journal

Kourtakis, Chris – *Buying a Boat* and *Digital Selective Calling, the Automatic Identification System, and Automated Radio Checks*
email: Chris@H2OLimos.com
website: www.H2OLimos.com
phone: 248-890-1116

Rogers, Mark – *Custom Electrical Panels and Wiring Harnesses*
email: MMESCustomPanels@aol.com
website: www.WeWireBoats.com
phone: 603-890-1723

Scanlan, Rob – *Marine Surveys*
email: Rob@MasterMarineSurveyor.com
website: www.MasterMarineSurveyor.com
phone: 781-595-6225

Smith, Mike – *Insuring a Boat*
website: www.GlobalMarineInsurance.com
phone: 800-748-0224

Sorum, Alan – *Search and Rescue*
website: www.suite101.com/profile.cfm/ASorum

Stefka, Brian – *Rent Your Boat*
website: www.RentbyBoater.com

Wyand, Timothy – *Bad Storms/Heavy Weather*
website: www.Examiner.com/x-15246/Richmond-boating-Examiner

Acknowledgements

Life is full of challenges. Believe me when I say I've had more than my share. But I truly believe that everything happens for a reason—good or bad. Not that one necessarily asks for the bad things to happen.

Only after having my life turned upside down—starting in June 2000, when I was misdiagnosed with MS, and then learning, a year later, that I had cancer and wasn't likely to live ten more years—did I decide it was time to live life and not sweat the small stuff so much like I used to. So here I am writing this acknowledgement and the first two people I'd like to thank are my doctors, Dr. Michael Britt and Dr. Kenneth Miller, for keeping me healthy. It wasn't easy.

This decision took me to learn to sail, travel Europe more, and visit over 300 marinas in the US and abroad. It was an assignment gone wrong that turned out TheNauticalLifestyle.com and this book. But I'm glad I was given that opportunity. Thank you to everyone I've met and spoken with in the marine industry, you have all widened my horizons in one way or another.

To my speakers: Captain Chris Kourtakis, Jim Coburn, Mike Smith, Rob Scanlan, Brian Stefka, Timothy Wyand, Alan Sorum, Jim Brown, Mark Rogers, and Brian Hancock, it seems like only yesterday we were juggling our schedules to do these interviews. Your willingness to give of your time and knowledge for this project is truly appreciated and I thank you from the bottom of my heart. I wish you all much success.

Others I'd like to thank are Fifi Ball and Marjory Thomas, my writing buddies for five years. Their encouragement and tweaking of my articles really helped. Especially Fifi for taking the recording transcripts and turning them into a readable work. And Mark Hendricks, his ISS Group, Dave Peterson, and Jim Reynolds for their countless hours of phone support as this project took on a life of its own.

I would be remiss if I didn't mention my aunt, Dorie Shoer, and my boys Joshua and Lincoln Sziranko, who would throw my words, "Go for it" back at me when I talked about this project. Last but not least, thanks to my best friend George Ryder for encouraging me to follow my dreams and opening up my world. I love you guys!

About the Interviewer:
Robin G. Coles and TheNauticalLifestyle.com

Robin G. Coles is a passionate marine enthusiast and sailor who has interviewed countless industry experts as well as visited, interviewed personnel at, written about, and photographed hundreds of marine ports in the US and abroad.

The ocean both scares and exhilarates her, as it should any boater—one minute it is as calm and smooth as glass; the next a stark raving maniac, as crazy as life itself.

Though Robin has had many challenges in her life, she has always managed to bounce back. Her time on the ocean has been her most rewarding.

Robin has authored a newspaper column and a variety of articles, newsletters, case studies, reports, and technical documents about boating and non-boating topics.

Robin has been a shutterbug from as far back as she can remember. Her photographs have been featured on the cover of the *2008 Winthrop Phonebook*, at the 2009 IPEVO show in Las Vegas, and on a local real estate website. To see/read her boating related media, go to TheNauticalLifestyle.com/TransientTalk. Her non-boating related media can be found at RGColesandCo.com.

In Robin's spare time she loves to walk the beach, photograph a variety of subjects, read good detective stories, travel, cook, crochet hats for preemie babies and shawls for four-to-six-year olds in cancer wards, write, and sail Boston Harbor.

Robin lives on a peninsula near Boston Harbor and Logan Airport, where she sails and works with business owners around the world via satellite phone and internet.

Index

A

ABOS™ Marine Blue Book, 194
ABYC, 31, 161, 164, 168, 171
acknowledgement. *See* rental:agreements
aileron, 160
AIS, 121, 126, 127, 128, 129, 133, 134, 135
Alinghi, 144
anemometer, 184
ARC, 130
automated radio checks. *See* ARC
automatic identification system. *See* AIS

B

back plane, 156
bad storms, 87, 104, 107
bankruptcy, 58
battery
    aftermarket, 165
Blue Seas, 155, 158
boat loans
    15 years, 56
    30 years, 54, 56
    balloon-type, 59
    bill of sale, 57
    contract, 56, 57, 63, 65, 69
    convertible-rate, 59
    delivery receipt, 57, 69
    documents, 56, 57, 61, 64, 68
    down payment, 57, 59, 66
    excessive inquiries, 61
    financial statement, 56, 68
    fixed-rate, 59, 69
    hidden fees, 63, 69
    identification, 57
    interest-only, 59
    no-down-payment, 66, 67
    Proof of insurance, 56
    simple interest, 59, 69
    title, 57
    Typical, 55, 56, 68
    zero-down-payment, 66, 67
Boat Wizard, 31

BoatUS, 131
Bradfield, Sam, 160
broker, 9, 16, 17, 19
Brown, Jim, 136
Brown, Woody, 139
BUC® Used Boat Price Guide, 36, 41, 194
buy your boat, 194
buying a boat, 5, 6, 9, 10, 11, 12, 13
    120-point inspection, 10
    boat show, 6, 17, 18, 20, 21
    boating education, 5, 7, 20
    cruiser, 6, 7, 8, 9, 19
    dealership, 10, 12, 14, 15, 17
    documentation, 12, 16
    family dynamics, 6
    fees, 12
    finances, 5, 20
    mistakes, 11, 12
    north, 13, 21
    Repossessed, 21
    runabout, 6, 7, 8, 19
    steps someone should take, 5
    wooden boat, 12

C

catamarans, 136, 137, 138, 139, 140, 143, 144, 145, 146, 148, 149, 150, 151, 152, 153, 154, 155, 156, 157, 159, 162
    Swiss Alinghi, 157
channel 70, 121, 122, 123
Choy, Rudy, 139
climb the mast, 29
close hauled, 96
clouds, 97, 100, 101, 102
    cumulonimbus, 100, 101
    cumulus, 100
    mackerel scales, 101
    mares' tails, 101
    thunderstorm, 88, 96, 97, 98, 100, 101, 102, 103, 104, 107
Coburn, Jim, 54
constant camber, 136, 137

COSPAS, 115
credit application. *See* financing:application
credit score, 44, 45, 57, 58, 61, 62, 66, 67, 69
cuddy cabin, 141
custom panel, 155, 156, 157, 170, 171
    Battery, 163
    European system, 159
    fuse block, 157, 167
    marine standards, 157
    night vision, 165
    warranty, 164

D

dielectric protectant, 171
Digital selective calling. *See* DSC
dry rot, 27
DSC, 121, 122, 123, 124, 125, 126, 127, 129, 131, 132, 133, 134, 135
    channel 70, 121
    VHF radio, 121, 122, 123, 126, 127, 128, 129, 133, 134

E

ELCI, 168
EPIRB, 110, 114, 115, 116, 117, 118, 120
    battery, 117
    buying, 117

F

Farrier, Ian, 156
fetch, 94, 95, 107
financing, 54, 55, 57, 58, 59, 60, 61, 62, 63, 64, 65, 66, 68, 69
    application, 56, 57, 60, 61, 62, 63, 64, 66, 67, 68, 69
    boat loans, 55, 56, 57, 59, 60, 61, 62, 63, 64, 69
    boat show, 61, 62, 67
    budget, 55, 59
    chartering, 59
    commercial, 54, 59, 60, 69
    commitment time, 67, 68
    first step, 55, 68
    fishing, 59
    live-aboard, 59, 60, 69
    rate lock, 67
    recreational, 54, 59, 60, 69
    recreational boat, 59
    refinancing, 66
    rent a boat, 60
    service company, 57, 61, 62, 63, 64, 65, 66, 67, 69
    shotgunning, 61, 69
float plan, 109, 112, 119

H

hammer
    modified ball-peen, 26
    phenolic, 26, 27, 36
Hancock, Brian, 174
heaving-to, 99, 100
heavy weather, 87, 88, 107
HIN, 16

I

inspection, 22, 23, 26, 29, 33, 36
instrument panel, 164
insurance, 22, 23, 24, 25, 29, 30, 31, 32, 36
    actual cash value, 36, 37
    agreed value, 36, 37, 40, 41, 51
    boat policy, 36, 37, 42
    exclusions, 38, 39, 40, 51
    fuel spill, 38
    hull, 37, 42, 43, 47, 51
    intentional acts, 40
    latent defect, 39
    lay-up, 38
    liability, 51, 74, 76, 77, 78, 79
    Lloyds of London, 37
    loss payee, 56, 65
    marina, 37, 40, 42, 46, 47, 49, 52
    pollution, 37, 38
    pollution coverage, 37, 38
    protection and indemnity, 37
    rider, 23
    wooden boat, 47

wreck removal, 37
yacht policy, 36, 37, 39, 40, 43, 45, 49, 50

J

Jane, Doug, 155
Jones Act, 40, 45

K

Kourtakis, Chris, 5, 121

L

lay-up, 27, 28, 34
life jacket, 109, 110, 114, 116, 117, 119
   federal law, 110, 120
   float coats, 110
lightning, 88, 101, 102

M

Mackerel scales, 101
maintenance, 5, 12, 14, 17, 20, 21
mares' tails. *See* clouds
marine survey, 15
marine VHF radio. *See* VHF radio
Maritime Mobile Service Identity. *See* MMSI number
Marples, 155
May Day. *See* search and rescue
McKenzie, Fred, 139
MMSI number, 124, 125, 128, 129, 133, 134, 135
monohull, 136, 137, 141, 142, 143, 144, 145, 146, 147, 148, 149, 151, 154, 155, 156, 158, 162
multihulls, 136, 137, 138, 139, 142, 143, 144, 145, 146, 147, 148, 152, 153, 155, 156, 157, 158, 159, 160, 161, 162
   Achilles heel, 144
   advantages, 136, 144, 146, 147, 148, 162
   capsize, 146, 147, 152, 163
   disadvantages, 136, 142, 143, 144, 147, 148, 149
   displacement, 150, 156, 157
   Hydrofoils, 159, 163
   J foils, 159, 160
   ladder foils, 159, 163
   T foils, 159, 160

N

NADA, 31
NAMS, 15, 29, 36
National Marine Bankers Association, 30, 37, 54, 61, 63
New England Multihull Association, 137
Newick, Dick, 139, 142, 153
NMBA. *See* National Marine Bankers Association
NOAA, 112, 115, 116, 117, 118, 119, 120

O

oil testing, 26
OutRig, 137, 161, 162

P

P&I. *See* insurance - protection and indemnity
percussion-sounding, 22, 26, 27, 32, 36
Piver, Arthur, 139, 140, 141, 154
PLB, 119
policies, 72, 77
pontoon, 6, 8, 19
Powerboat Guide, 31
PowerBoat Guide, 195
proa, 137, 153, 154, 162, 163

R

reef, 91, 96
rent your boat, 71, 75, 76, 84
rental
   agreements, 73, 74, 75, 77, 79, 84
   bareboat, 71, 72, 73, 74, 82, 84
   breakeven price, 82, 83
   calculator, 82
   charter, 72
   dockside, 71, 72, 73, 82, 84
   expenses, 77, 80, 82, 83, 85
   insurance, 74, 75, 76, 77, 78, 79, 80, 83
   live-aboard, 82
   non-passive risk, 75, 77
   occupational license, 81

passive risk, 74
policies, 75
rental agreement, 73, 75, 84
systematic risk, 75, 77
umbrella policy, 78
waiver, 85
waiver and release, 74, 75
Rogers, Mark, 155
rotary switch, 157
running aground, 104, 105

S

safety check, 110
   fire extinguishers, 110, 119
   LifeSling, 111
   vessel, 110
sailing in a blow, 95
SAMS, 15, 29, 36
Scanlan, Rob, 22
schematic, 167
Sea Tow, 131
sea trial, 23, 24, 26, 28, 32, 34, 35, 37
search and rescue, 90, 93, 109, 111, 112, 113, 114, 115, 116, 119
   hailing and distress, 112
   man overboard, 111
   May Day, 112, 113, 120, 122, 131
   On land, 109
   on the water, 109
   PLB, 114, 115, 116, 117
   Rescue 21, 111
   SARs, 109
selector switch, 156, 159, 163, 171
self-bailing cockpit, 88
sell your boat, 194
   advertise, 195
   photographs, 195
   yacht broker, 194
   yourself, 194
short-hauling, 23
shrink wrapping, 28
shunting, 153
Smith, Lawrie, 179

Smith, Mike, 37
Sorum, Alan, 109
standard. *See* rental:agreements
static, 102
Stefka, Brian, 70
strakes, 26
stringer, 26
surveyor, 22, 24, 25, 29, 30, 33, 35, 36, 37
surveys, 22, 23, 24, 25, 26, 27, 29, 30, 35, 36
   condition and valuation, 22, 23, 24, 28, 32, 36
   engine, 23
   financial, 22
   insurance, 24
   pre-purchase, 22, 23, 24, 31, 32, 36
   wooden boats, 26
Swiss Alinghi. *See* catamarans

T

terminal block, 156, 158, 160, 162, 163, 166, 171
   Eurostyle, 160, 171
testing, 22, 24, 25, 26
   compression, 23, 24, 25
   oil, 26
   pressure, 22, 23, 34, 36, 37
trimarans, 136, 137, 138, 140, 141, 143, 144, 146, 147, 148, 149, 150, 151, 152, 153, 156, 159, 163

U

US Surveyors Association, 29

V

VHF radio, 109, 111, 112, 113, 114, 117, 119
   channel 16, 122
   RTCM SC101, 123
von Schwarzenfeld, Wolfgang Kraker. *See* Wolfgang

W

warranty, 9, 11, 15, 17, 20, 25
wave

breaking, 93, 95, 99
size, 88, 90, 94, 95, 106, 107
waves, 88, 90, 91, 92, 93, 94, 95, 97, 99, 105, 106, 107
rogue, 93, 94
weather
cold front, 101
extra-tropical cyclones, 89
hurricane, 89, 90, 95, 103, 107
national weather service, 112
nor'easter, 89, 92, 93, 95, 101, 107
rain squall, 104, 105
thunderstorms, 96, 100, 101, 102, 103, 104
tropical storms, 90
warm front, 101
winds, 88, 89, 90, 92, 96, 97, 101, 102, 105, 106, 107

Wharram, James, 139
wiring, 155, 156, 157, 159, 160, 162, 163, 166, 167, 170, 171
wiring harness, 162, 172
Wolfgang, 139, 140, 141
wooden boat, 26, 27, 36, 47
Wyand, Timothy, 87

Y

Yacht World, 31

TheNauticalLifestyle Order Form

Telephone Orders   Call 339-532-8334
                         and have your credit card ready

Postal Orders
   TheNauticalLifestyle
   C/o Robin G. Coles
   P O Box 520461 ~ Winthrop, MA 02152
   orders@TheNauticalLifestyle.com

Please send the following:

☐ Boating Secrets: 127 Top Tips To Help You Buy and Enjoy Your Boat,
by Robin G. Coles $29.97

☐ TheNauticalLifestyle Expert Speaker Series Complete live interview series of 11 Marine Industry experts on CDs,
by Robin G. Coles $97.00

Please send more FREE information on:

☐ Other books   ☐ Other Audios   ☐ Speaking/Seminars
                   Or visit www.TheNauticalLifestyle.com

Name_____
Address_____
City_____ State_____ Zip_____
Telephone_____ Email_____

Payment:
☐ Check   ☐ Mastercard   ☐ American Express   ☐ Visa   ☐ Discover

Account Number_____ Expiration Date_____
Cardholder's Name_____ Cardholder's Signature_____

www.ingramcontent.com/pod-product-compliance
Lightning Source LLC
Chambersburg PA
CBHW080027180426
43195CB00052B/2608